THE MAGIC OF

Friendships, Soul Mates,
and
Twin Flames

By
Robert Wilkinson

Cover Art: "Libra"
By Mary Katherine Kracht
astrallogicconsulting.com

KDP Independent Publishing Platform,
North Charleston, SC

ISBN: 978-1-940751-08-5   2022

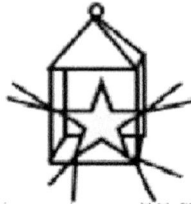

CONTENTS

Acknowledgements

I would like to thank everyone I have ever known for helping this book come to pass. Without my knowledge of the many shades, levels, and nuances in relationships I could not have offered you the wisdom in this work. I also want to thank every person who ever ordered my Love Reports and gave me feedback, as they too contributed to the depth and breadth of this book.

I also want to acknowledge my appreciation for those who offered to read this at various points of its construction, since each offered valuable insights that the contents would be helpful for all who want to move into healthy relationships. You have my sincere gratitude for your willingness to take the time to read the drafts and offer me your feedback.

As with all my publications, I want to offer my highest gratitude to the generous donor who made the Fifth Ray Publishing operation a reality, enabling me to create this work freed of the usual publishing and editorial politics. And finally, utmost appreciation goes out to Bernadette, my Associate Editor who brought her educator's eye to the work. Her patience and brilliant Mercury retrograde insights contributed to make this the extraordinary work I believe it to be.

So here's to Venus, the beautiful part of us which honors harmony, fairness, and the dances between all of us, the One who leads us to our friends, Soul Mates, and our Twin Flame.

PREFACE

ASTROLOGY AND LOVE – KARMIC DANCES WHICH FREE THE SOUL

Life is about relationships. The longer you live, the more you have. We have happy ones, sad ones, great ones, lousy ones, those we're happy to be done with and those we wish would never end. It is the intention of this work to help you know the qualities of your perfect mate, who will show up as a Soul Mate who could turn out to be your eternal Twin Flame.

Finding our perfect mate is a challenge like no other, and worth everything we put into it. What better way to live life than with one's perfect partner, a friend and Soul Mate you can live with, love with, and feel deeply connected to for your entire life? This journey begins with us, knowing ourselves as a result of the countless relationships forged over the years so we understand what is truly best for us and who we can truly love with all our hearts.

This work comes from a lifetime of experience. It is a work forged from life, love, romance, sorrow, headaches and heartbreak, but also indescribable joy and knowing the heights the depths of love. Through my many relationships, as well as those of my friends and clients, I've come to know the universals in great partnerships and marriages. Along the way I've learned all there is to know about Soul mates and the Twin Flame through direct experience.

All that said, this is also an astrological resource, using the tools available through that sacred science to know the qualities of our perfect mate, our Twin Flame. Using the lens of astrology, this work will take you on an amazing journey as we explore being a human, falling in love, falling out of love, and becoming strong and clear so the Light of our Love attracts our Twin Flame.

Astrology and Love have been linked since the beginning of time. Astrology shows us what we love and need, who and what we are attracted to and why, as well as when we might find our true love. Astrology is the best tool I've found to help us understand our loving wisdom which allows us to grow into our greater Self. As we grow, our love grows, and we find all kinds of people who we might love, and who might love us as we both change, grow, and become a perfect image of our heart's desire.

As eternals having human experiences, we are loving, wise intelligences learning how to find what will bring us happiness and a more fulfilled life. We begin by learning from our parents and immediate family, and as we grow our ability to love also grows. Along the way we learn about love by who we say yes to, and who we say no to. Even though we didn't have much control over our childhood and the family and friends we wound up with, as we grew older and had other relationships we had the blessing of being able to choose who we wanted as our friends and who we didn't.

The immature learned forms of love we experienced as children over time gave way to the greater love we feel as adults. As our love grew, we learned how to open to different things and people to know what we truly love and what we found was just the appearance of love. The beauty of astrology is that it shows us how our living love has grown over the years. Love is eternal; astrology measures the timing of eternity, and shows us the unique qualities in each moment, as well as our unique qualities which attract us to various Soul mates, one of whom is our Twin Flame.

Love in a greater sense is both mystical and magical, as is astrology. Love shows us our "brokenness" and our wholeness, as does astrology. There are infinite ways to explore both, and in both we must "romance the Beloved" if we would see the object of our search come forth. The beloved is within us, as an image close to our heart. If we want the Beloved to show up, we must get clear about our heart's desire, which happens through time and experience which yield self-knowledge. Along the way we learn the difference between conditional love and unconditional love, since the first changes as we grow and the second is who we truly are behind what we show to the world.

As we learn to turn conditional love to unconditional Love, we become our Higher Self, and who we attract changes. As our ability to give and receive love grows, we find ourselves attracting more loving beings. Absolute and ideal Love is an eternal and infinite uniting force. As our love grows, we find ourselves knowing a feeling beyond our changing emotions, a greater love which is our comfort in times of trouble and ecstatic joy in moments of triumph. As we grow in our love, we find more ways to recognize true love in the dances we do with others.

We all have an innate "Urge to Merge" which keeps us searching for "the one" who might bring us happiness and fulfillment, who might love us for who we are without drama, resistance, or control issues getting in the way. In our search for someone who might be our perfect mate, we try on many relationships. Some are strong, some are quiet, some are passionate, some are fun, and some are gentle. They all teach us about who we are, what we like, and what we used to like but no longer care about.

Astrology shows us the timing on what we agree to and who we dance with. The timing of our relationships sets a swirl of multi-level karmas into motion, creating consequences that reverberate across space and time. In this work we'll speak of all these things and more, and explore ways to know ourselves as well as others so we understand the traits of our perfect mate, the value of friendship, the qualities of a Soul Mate, and how to prepare to welcome our Beloved across time, our Twin Flame.

INTRODUCTION

I originally wrote major parts of this book with the title "PROFESSOR ROBERT'S MOJO LOVE REPORTS" because they were the most thorough analysis of mate signs ever done. While the reports were very well received over the years, after contemplating how I could help the greatest number of people learn how to recognize their perfect mate, a book seemed to be the way to go. And so our adventure begins!

All of us who have had a compatibility report done to find "our perfect mate" were told they have the qualities of the sign opposing our Sun sign. We've been told that because we are a Libra then the opposite sign (Aries) is our natural mate, or that because we have a Gemini Sun sign, then we're supposed to get along with Sagittarius. Then we meet someone who has their Sun in the sign opposite ours, and find that we are not compatible in the slightest. Why is that?

While our mate will have many of the qualities of the sign opposite our Sun, it's not the only sign that matters, which is more often not the Sun sign opposite ours. Our Sun sign shows us who we are as a shining light in our world. It is our love, light, integrity and autonomy to be who we really are. This inner Light force is a constant throughout our life, but also not entirely the whole of who we are. We are definitely the traits of our Sun sign, but because we are not perfect Beings, there are many constructive as well as destructive ways we exhibit those qualities. It's the same for everyone; we are much more than just our

Sun sign, and different people have different ways of "being their Sun."

For instance, it's never a good match for a constructive Taurus to try to be with a destructive Scorpio, or vice versa, even if they are supposed to be natural "mate signs." If we're trying to find someone who is good and kind, we won't have a good relationship with those who lie or are negative and hurtful. To find our perfect mate, we must have the courage to be our Inner Light, our Sun, since our integrity always leads us to people we could love and trust, and who would love and trust us, for the rest of our days.

While our Sun sign is very important in showing us some traits of our perfect mate, there are other astrological factors which shape our quest for the Beloved. One is our Venus sign position, which shows us what we value and what we like: What kinds of art, what kinds of food, what types of pleasures, what types of interactions, and other things we appreciate. That's why Venus contacts will be very strong in our perfect mate!

Whenever your Sun is in the same sign as someone else's Venus, they will naturally and instinctively like you. Conversely, if your Venus is in the same sign as someone else's Sun, you will naturally and instinctively like them. As you can see, knowing your Venus sign is also very valuable in finding out who you could really like.

Of course, it comes with the same caution I suggested for Sun sign contacts. If your Venus is operating constructively, and someone else's Sun or Venus is operating negatively, though you may have affection for them or they for you, you definitely cannot afford to tolerate destructive or abusive behavior. Just because we like someone doesn't mean we're supposed to be pleasant and agreeable while our life is wrecked!

This is where we have to be clear about the source of the problem. Sometimes it does involve our behavior, sometimes it involves another's behavior, and sometimes it's just life circumstances intruding on our comfort zone. In these situations astrology helps us sort out what's ours and what's not.

Another extremely important factor in our relationships is our Moon sign. Our Moon symbolizes our comfort zone, our personal feeling-space. Our Moon sign shows us who and what fits in well with our everyday life and habits, our needs and feelings, our insecurities and how we would like to be nurtured. Since the Moon also shows us how we package our personality, harmonious contacts between our own and another's Sun and Moon, or the Moon and Venus, indicate the possibility of a greater love and affection from those who share these contacts with us.

Other planets also help us in our quest for our ideal mate. At their best, our Jupiter sign shows us who will bless us and expand our imagination and opportunities, just as our Saturn sign shows us who will teach us the most important lessons of our life and help us mature, even if it involves tough choices. Our Mercury sign shows us how we perceive and understand our world. Mercury contacts between people encourage us to think and share information, and different points of view. People with planets contacting our Mercury will stimulate us to think about all kinds of things, and you'll always have something to talk about. Mercury influenced couples talk with each other all the time about all kinds of things!

Mars shows us the types of people and experiences who quicken the pace of our life. They are the ones who sometimes annoy or aggravate us, and spur us to action and always get us moving, for better or worse. Venus in one person's chart contacting the Mars in another's chart can lead to very intense physical passion. Though it can be tempting "to throw fate to the wind," if one's Mars contacts another's Venus, a degree of caution is in order, or you could be dealing with unintended consequences which quickly get out of hand. Venus-Mars contacts are passionate and volatile, but also very exciting!

Uranus, Neptune, and Pluto are generational planets, and symbolize invisible transpersonal and global forces operating on a meta level. If one or more of these contact personal planets between two people, you can bet there's a karmic connection, where both of you will be transformed in unexpected ways. It shows a cosmic influence or an "invisible hand" at work in your relationship.

If these planets in someone else's chart contact a planet in your chart, they represent something beyond what you could see or imagine or understand before you met them. They will revolutionize your life in unpredictable ways related to your larger spiritual quest for truth. How our planets impact others and how theirs impact us is discussed further in Chapter 6 on Synastry, Composites, and Compatibility analysis.

Even though our Sun sign and the other planetary signs are important in knowing what our ideal mate would look and act like, our Ascendant, or Rising sign, is also of paramount importance. The Ascendant is how we view ourselves, our world, and the people in it. It symbolizes our self-image relative to the different departments of our life, such as money, family, health, partners, profession, friends, and so forth. Our Ascendant sign and the sign opposite that are often found in the chart of people we're naturally attracted to. My Leo rising has always found its way to people with Sun, Moon, or Ascendant in Leo and Aquarius my entire life!

Most people believe their perfect mate is based on the Sun sign because they have no idea how important the rising sign is, or may not know their rising sign, which is based on what time of day we are born. However, if you do know your Ascendant, I definitely recommend looking at that sign as well when you get to Chapter 7, which offers the qualities of the mate for each sign. That chapter will give you a more complete picture of your ideal mate. The sign opposite our Sun is how our Sun naturally expresses itself; the sign opposite our Ascendant is how we naturally view "the other," whether mate, partner, "balance wheel," or just an equal. Looking at the traits of the signs opposite both our Sun and Ascendant gives us major clues in how we can express our Light and self-image to attract someone who might be our Beloved.

This book offers your personal formula for relational happiness. What you are about to read will show you the traits of the person who is most natural for you, as well as practical advice to hold near your heart as you embrace the adventure of finding your Beloved, your Twin Flame. This work explores what your Beloved is like, and what you'll need to be aware of so your quest for your perfect love stays on track.

The journey you're about to begin will reveal you to YOU. By the time this journey is done, you will know more about you than you did when you began this adventure of self-discovery. I guarantee it will be worth every minute of your time. This book will help you remember the love you are, and the love you're here to live. While this Earth isn't about getting what we think we want, it is about us becoming better people and receiving our heart's desire as we have dared to dream it and live that dream the best we can, given the limits we all inherit until we break free.

It is possible to live a greater life, but we have to imagine it and wait for the door to open and then walk through that door. Daring to put our heart on the line is a bold thing; daring to do it as long as it takes to find the Beloved is truly a timeless task worth undertaking.

This is where being alert to the magic of "time windows" makes it clear that what is possible in one moment may not be possible in another. That is unique to each of us. But within those time windows, all kinds of things can happen, depending on our individual circumstances. And those who serve Spirit often find miracles happening within certain time windows.

If life is about learning to love, to give love and receive love, then what better thing to do than enjoy life the best we can? And because we learn so much about what love is and what love isn't through our dances down the road of Life, we can reveal the greater love we are by accepting each challenge with as much goodwill as we can, since everything else just clouds our mind and obscures the love we ARE every second of our existence. So as you take this journey, remember to smile at your memories, thanking the lords of karmas for thinking so highly of you that they gave you so many relationship karmas to work through so you'll be ready to greet your

16

Beloved with a smiling face, a shining heart, and a clean karma.

We've all had countless memories, good and bad, of loves lost long ago, as well as slight delights which we'll remember for the rest of our days. All our difficulties made us who we are today. Thank your good heart for making it to where you are, and thank you for being right here, right now, reading these words, thinking your thoughts, feeling your feelings, and being the loving Spirit/Soul you are.

What you read here will be helpful whether you are searching for the first time, or trying again after the difficulty of a breakup. After all, it's based on who YOU are, and offers you a vision of the traits of those you could attract as your ideal mate and partner, regardless of what that person might look like. What you read here will give you the power to shape your attractions so you find your Beloved in a form most agreeable to you.

Enjoy, imagine the many possibilities, and attract your ideal mate!

CHAPTER ONE

THE JOURNEY OF DISCOVERY

We dance with many people throughout our lives. Along the way we find that we're all flawed in some way in our "perfectly imperfect" human condition. That includes you and me and everyone else. From childhood we all experience parts of ourselves we don't understand and don't know what they're about or how to change what we feel needs to be different.

Even when we know we need to look at something and deal with it, we often aren't comfortable with the process of feeling so exposed or flawed. Because all of us go through this at times, and because none of us are perfect, there will be misunderstandings. But we can learn to be clear about who we are and what we need in each moment.

We live in a mysterious and confused world, where a lot of things don't make sense. Because life is a never ending journey where almost everything eventually passes away, we all know the disappointment when things end, or take a direction we didn't anticipate and may not like. So while we all want to feel confident as we move through our challenges and triumphs, it's also perfectly natural to feel a lot of uncertainty and confusion as we navigate life's changes.

Because we don't have perfect knowledge there is much we don't understand as we move through life on our journey of self-discovery. With each new thing we find out about ourselves our self-image changes. Then we have to reevaluate many things about who we think we are, what we believe, and what we do and don't like since each new thing we learn affects who we are.

Along the way we meet all kinds of people who play out roles in our lives. Some we feel we've known before, while others feel like it's a brand new opportunity to get close to someone we hope we can be friends with. Sometimes we are naturally harmonious, while other times we have to learn how to get along or say goodbye so we can open the door to a better life. Each of us makes our choices, and every person we part from opens the door to a new person who might become a friend.

We all have problems expressing ourselves from time to time. Sometimes people have a conscious motive in what they say or do, but it's just as true many things occur without any conscious intention. Often problems or misunderstandings happen because we or they express something which could be taken more than one way. A lack of clarity about priorities and how deeply each has been affected by past experiences are also factors in our relationships, sometimes revealing hidden agendas, including those no one knew they had!

Many difficulties happen because of a misunderstanding about ourselves or another. I've learned to be cautious in attributing blame to some interactions, as often the friction between people is simply a case of one human being crashing against another human being without meaning to. Because it's difficult to know ourselves, it's equally difficult to know who someone else is at the core of their being. That's why it's best to take time to get to know someone before discussing a lifetime commitment!

As we grow in awareness, we all learn some problems are preventable while others are not so preventable. These are times when either we can do something to change what's happening or we can't, and even when we can, we're still limited by our skills and what created that problem to begin with.

The Value of Discernment

All relationship challenges force us to trust our wisdom distilled from prior experiences. Life is about learning to discern what is in our best interests. In the process we learn about our values which inform our judgments. We all judge. What to eat, what to wear, who we want to be friends with, what tasks we'll do today, and many other choices throughout our lives. Everyone judges all the time. There's nothing wrong with judging since it's how the mind works, doing its "compare and contrast," "sequence and selection" process. However, not all judgments are accurate, true, good, or useful. A good judgment call can save our lives, while a bad one can create unnecessary problems.

Our ability to know what works for us and what doesn't helps us sense who might be good friends and companions on the road of life, as well as spot the predators and bad people we need to avoid as much as we can. Our discernment helps us navigate the twists and turns of life, avoiding unpleasant people and experiences while finding good people and opportunities to grow into better relationships. Of course, some encounters cannot be prevented if we need to learn how to deal with those problems for our greatest growth and sense of well-being.

In our constantly changing and evolving interactions, some people will be honest, while others are dishonest; some people will be hard working, while others will be lazy; some people will be careful, while others will be careless; some people will gladly share and be shared with, while others will be selfish and egocentric. These are all judgments, but we ignore them at our peril. While sometimes our judgments may not be perfect, they're all valuable to show us how we've grown in discernment. Knowing what's healthy and what is unhealthy is how we survive and do well in the future!

Learning to Dance

We learn a lot about who we are and what we're willing to tolerate by how we respond to the challenging people in our lives. While we all like pleasant interactions, we take major evolutionary leaps when we decide to be strong in turning away from relationships which have become hurtful or are undermining our self-esteem. If this life is a journey of ever-greater self-awareness and our ability to claim the happiness which is our divine right, then even difficult relationships help us stick up for what we believe in, finding heart strength and courage in choosing the way which is right for us.

Sometimes we find ourselves in a mutual attraction which would work perfectly if only we were in different circumstances. Though we may be extraordinarily attracted to another, and they to us, sometimes the world's demands and pressures force us to make decisions we may not want to make. Regardless of what we want or intend, the river of life has its own flow, taking us where we must go rather than where we think we want to go. When life puts us at a transformational junction, we find out a lot about our weaknesses and our strengths.

Because we don't have perfect perception, sometimes we or another don't have enough knowledge to make clear decisions because we are not aware of the best options for each of us and both of us. Generally people do whatever they need to in the moment to relieve the pressure and aren't thinking about ultimate causes and best responses to those pressures. These are times when ego defenses cause problems which compound the tension.

Even in the worst of situations, the best we can do is take the high road while refusing to get thrown off our center by the choices another is making. Sometimes we didn't cause what's going on and there's little to nothing we can do about it. Then we have to figure out what is in our best interests and do that.

After enough experience dancing with others, we learn how to be fluid at the hard edges of our interactions, and by knowing how to deflect blame or guilt we should not take on, we can lighten our load while not aggravating the tension already there. As we learn not to take on fear, blame, guilt, or shame, then we will not accept it from another nor project it on another. This frees us from falling prey to a lot of problems.

When we're young and on the make, we're all chasing beauty, and are attracted to the people we think are beautiful. Of course they're never as incredible as we imagine, but we still hope they will be. Over time we understand they are not who we believed they were, just as they find we are not who they believed we were. Then the awkward moments happen when we're trying to figure out how we can relate harmoniously with the person in front of us. Still, even when things are at their worst, the only good response is to be as compassionate and forgiving as possible, of ourselves, others, and the whole generic human condition.

Sometimes relationships change or end because of estrangement or a misunderstanding. These help us get clear about our motives and what is driving us apart. This reflection strengthens our integrity. While we all want to do our best to reconcile with someone we like or love, it's equally important to recognize when something's done it's done. There is no blame in realizing when something doesn't work for us.

If we're not communicating, no longer have shared hopes and core values in common, and have tried every avenue to move forward, then we must be realistic. It takes two to create and maintain a relationship, and if it's not a good fit, then the most compassionate thing to do is turn to the new life chapter that already awaits our consideration. From there we walk on, usually toward something better than what has been.

Love Naturally Grows Over Time

I've had many relationships this life. Obviously, some worked out better than others. I've had good ones, bad ones, joyous ones, sad ones, heavy ones, deep ones, shallow ones, and everything in between. Some began good and ended badly, while others began in difficulty and became blessings beyond description. The best were all friendships. The worst were when those friendships ended for whatever reason.

Some love is easy, while some love is tough. Our hearts grow both ways, as we learn through fundamental differences as well as through the joys of intimacy. We learn through our commitments to others and their commitments to us. We learn through short term passions as well as through the comforting warmth of a long and totally committed love. In every loving relationship in our lives, if the root of love is deep enough, it will outlast and outlive any external storm. The root of love is the root of life.

Life is about growing and evolving in our ability to love and be loved in healthy ways. All our worldly interactions teach us about what we love, and through a lot of hit and miss guessing and hoping we often wind up wondering why they happened. I believe many times our interactions help us work through karma so we can become more conscious why certain people showed up, what we were to learn from them, and why we either want more experiences like that or never want to have those experiences again. Ultimately all our relationships teach us to value good people and experiences and avoid those which undermine our sense of power to move forward to a better life.

All genuinely deep loving relationships take time to develop. That's why it's always best to look at it as developing friendships. If we're friends, there's nothing to fear as we learn about each other, and how we each came to be as we are. Over time, as we share the good and bad in our backgrounds, we come to see everyone's on a journey to find happiness, love, abundance, and an agreeable self-expression, even though our sense of these changes with time and experience.

That's also why relying on our initial impressions won't give us the whole picture. Obviously when we meet we each want to look our best, even when we're struggling inside. That's why no matter how exciting and inviting someone may be, it's always best to let the relationship develop naturally and organically without too many initial expectations and assumptions about how permanent it will be. If we have patience with the process, eventually we'll know all we need to know about another.

We all have baggage. The baggage changes throughout life, with one set of issues before the age of 27 and a different set of issues after 29. Who we are, what we want, and who we attract is far different at 25 than when we're 35, 45, or 55. This is due to a number of evolutionary cycles we all go through which test our ability at key points to grow in our positive self-expression. As we learn to express the best of our inner planetary qualities, transmuting the problematic qualities, we naturally change who we attract.

We all have things to work on in our personality. So does our perfect mate. In fact, the instant we begin our relationship dance with another, we both begin to re-shape our expression in ways we never imagined before that moment! That's why even in the times which most challenge one or both of us, we'll be growing individually and together, becoming more aware of what we want and what we don't.

Because we are individuals on our own unique path to fulfillment, we have to be true to ourselves, regardless of what others think. Our free will is our strength and means to claim our power to choose what will fulfill us, and because of our emotional changes at key points, we find we no longer need certain things nor do we care for them any longer. Later in this work I'll give you something about the dance of the Progressed Moon with transiting Saturn, and how these indicate where we're at in terms of our progressed personality, needs, habits, and what we care about during different chapters of life. These two factors show us what we need, what we don't need, what we can live with and what we cannot live with.

Ultimately, every relationship of our own choosing is about friendship. If we are true friends with another, we allow them space to grow and unfold in their unique way, and they allow us to grow and unfold in our unique way. As we dance down the road of life together, at some point either we're dancing in the same "sphere of love" or we're not. All of us need time and space to change what we need to, and our friends are always a source of support. We'll discuss the importance of making friendship the foundation of our relationships in Chapter 4.

CHAPTER TWO

HISTORY AND THE KARMIC FACTORS IN RELATIONSHIPS

We are attracted to many people throughout our lives, but because we don't know them before we have been with them a while, we need a degree of caution as we figure out who's right for us. While we often work off of first impressions, if we want healthy long term relationships, we need to consider other important factors which affect where we're coming from and whether we have a good chance of making it as a couple.

A Historical Perspective.

The modern era has brought a new dawn to how relationships are formed and sanctioned by society, and many things we currently believe about partnerships and marriage are of relatively recent vintage. For thousands of years, marriages were arranged by parents, usually based in tribal or class divisions.

The middle of the 20th century brought the first widespread "marriages for love" rather than being arranged by elders. This broke the centuries' old social order of women being chattel to be shopped around to whomever Dad thought made the best prospect. Love had nothing to do with it. Marriage was entirely about preserving the family line and fortunes. Things were so class-driven that it was almost unthinkable for someone from a rich family to marry someone who was poor. In many societies, having a lover while married was okay as long as it didn't challenge the family assets or lineage.

The post-World War II world left a lot of that behind, though of course there are still "rules of engagement" for those who want to court and be courted by another. While each generation has its own rules and standards in the 21st century, there are certain universals each generation has to face as they make their way through the snares and pitfalls of relationships. One of those universals is that all our rules and assumptions about relationships are challenged at major points of emotional shifts associated with the progressed Moon and key Saturn transits, which we'll discuss later.

While a person's family and cultural heritage is not as all-important as it used to be, most of us are still finding ways to transcend certain rules and expectations we learned growing up. We're still products of our background, and as we dance with others, we learn which of our cultural assumptions are valid for us, and which need transcending. Our background shapes our opinions more than we suspect, and this conditions our initial approach to our relationships. Our history in relationships shapes our desires, our expectations, our impressions, and our judgments. And yet, each new person we meet provides potentials we might not imagine, since there is more we don't know about others than we do know in the initial stages of exploring the possibility of a long term relationship.

Most are attracted to another by a combination of physical, emotional, and mental energetics. However, there are many other considerations which are very important in determining if someone is suited for us and we for them. Among various factors to look at, is one liberal and the other conservative? Is one open-minded and the other rule-bound? Are they fixed or flexible? Stubborn or reasonable? Educated or uneducated? What are their aspirations? Is their vision compatible with ours? Of course, these can and will change as we dance down the road of romance or friendship, but initially these sorts of questions let us know their priorities and if we fit with them.

The birth order of two individuals can be an important factor in a relationship, since an eldest child has a different approach to life than the youngest in a family system, and people without siblings have a much different attitude than those who were raised with brothers and sisters. The expectations our families had for us shaped our personality and responses, which is why it's crucial to explore cultural assumptions and potentially different ways we have of responding to similar situations. Knowing these influences can help us shape how we envision our relationship developing so we can know where we have mutual interests and an ability to work and play together cooperatively in building a relationship which is satisfying to each of us.

That said, I've seen countless types of "mixed marriages" work, where the couple has different values and even different lifestyles but are able to make the relationship work over the long haul by mutual respect, affection, and the ability to allow each to do their own thing in their own way.

The Family and Cultural Matrix

Our family and cultural programming is a major factor in who we're attracted to until we step outside of those expectations. Throughout our childhood and early adult life, we had to respond the best we could to the unfamiliar experiences of life. While our preferences are shown by the planets in our birth chart, who our parents and authority figures approved of and who they didn't were major factors in shaping our likes and dislikes, and therefore how our planets manifested. The mix of our chart tendencies with the rules we lived within were powerful forces in shaping our personality, and set up cause and effect cycles which played out long after those initial events and our responses to those events.

Because as children we desire to please, we identify with our family elders. Our parents' fears and expectations became our fears and expectations. Their harsh judgments became our harsh judgments, and we learned to play for their approval, as well as the approval of our peers. While we were "free" to express ourselves, we still had to operate within the rules of our family system, since to step outside of those boundaries brought us criticism or punishment for defying the system.

When we are young children, we take it for granted we must model the behavior and protocols of the adults around us. This is a function of the Moon, the means by which we adapt and mirror the authorities in life. When we become teens and young adults, we still are heavily under the influence of cultural norms, and try to define who we are within those norms, even as we seek experiences outside of those known values.

Unless we consciously change them, these behavior patterns reside in our subconscious mind, and are awakened by all kinds of events and interactions. That's why if we are not aware of our subconscious desires, or what arouses them, we are attracted to all kinds of relationships, some healthier than others. We can learn a lot from how we respond to each and every one, since who we attract is a combination of our projections as well as our deep unfulfilled desire for "the One." These projections and unfulfilled desires naturally attract people who we believe are our ideal mate who will fulfill theses desires and projections.

Childhood is where we begin exploring how to create an ego able to hold its own in the world so we can interact with others as equals. We all want to feel safe expressing ourselves in the world. That's why we choose to emulate certain values which permit us to grow within the relative safety of our family and cultural matrix. This develops our ego, but that's not really who we are; it is a manufactured entity and a temporary place holder until we find ways to enhance its power, or transcend it entirely. Our ego is constructed to deal with the pressures of the social environment we confront when we are young, but over time we realize our ego isn't able to deal with that which is outside its preconceptions.

Crises of Growth Show Us Our Truth

In our evolution, we find ourselves in situations which force us to reaffirm the responses we know, or set them aside because they are inadequate to resolve the crises we confront. In these moments of crisis we are given the opportunity to choose better responses. The key to our happiness, in life and in relationships, is to learn to be conscious in the choices we make and why we are making them. Are we trying to conform to a set of inadequate or unfulfilling behaviors? Are we trying to fit the unknown into the known? Are we trying to use the skills of a child to deal with the crises of adult life?

Our lives challenge us to become more mature in our expectations and how we deal with crises of growth. As we become more mature, we can know when and how to change our response to what life brings us. Each time we realize we have to change our assumptions, we take a natural evolutionary leap. As we go through our changes, we leave old ways of life behind, and come to new awareness and new views.

Everything we go through strengthens our ability to express our essential nature and not our manufactured ego traits. This allows us to leave a lot of assumptions behind as we grow into a greater spiritual maturity. We can see this happening in our interactions, since they give us opportunities to express the positive traits in each of our planets, helping us develop healthy ways of relating to ourselves and others. As we open to learning what we have to learn to resolve crises and come to a greater sense of our freedom to act as we need to, we find that the universe is working as one power to bring us to our best and highest self.

When we choose different ways of responding outside of the "group think" or "consensus reality" of those we're raised with, we are moving through a crisis of growth. As we become more at ease claiming our power to be as we need to be, it strengthens our ability to be clear during those times when we confront our need to follow what we know is right regardless of whether others approve of it or not.

When we hit a life crisis, we have to accept our need to go through a personal transformation. A crisis usually occurs when we are trying to live an old way that we no longer believe in, or which no longer fulfills us. This often requires breaking with traditional beliefs and responses which those around us may take for granted. The clash between old and new assumptions, beliefs, and inertias gives us great opportunities for self-discovery as we grow to a greater awareness. From one point of view, all crises come from our "true Self" hitting a limit and revealing something requiring our ego's attention and skill in dealing with it.

Our Planets Show Us Our Path to Freedom

The planets in our natal chart represent various parts of our personality. We are how our planets express their energies both personally and with others in the physical, emotional, mental, and spiritual levels of our life. Our planets show us how our likes and dislikes, our healthy and unhealthy responses are evolving through our interactions with other people.

Each planet represents a part of us which evolves throughout our life. Briefly, our Sun sign shows how we are enlightened and enlighten others, and our Moon shows us our personality and ways we like to live life on a day to day basis. Venus is what we like, Mars is what spurs us to action, and Mercury is how we coordinate all the parts of us. Jupiter and Saturn are the parts of us which are more social, cultural, and spiritual, as Jupiter expands our vision while Saturn teaches us the limits we need and the limits we no longer need, particularly the limits of our religion and belief systems. While the values and responses of our childhood conditioning and early adult assumptions are necessary up to a point, because of our eternal nature, our own evolution inevitably leads us to crises of individualization. These challenge us to learn skills helping us transcend conscious and unconscious patterns which create trouble, problematic emotional responses, and ineffective ways of dealing with crises. We'll discuss more about our planetary lights in the next chapter.

All of life makes us more aware of self-perpetuating negative influences we must transcend. As we become more aware, and choose to transmute negative and ineffectual responses into positive and more effective responses, we strengthen our ability as Soul/Spirits to cultivate and maintain good human relationships as well as healthy attitudes about who we are, who we're not, and what we're here to do and be. Then we've effectively transcended any sense of helplessness when confronted with a crisis, since we've claimed our power to be as we need to be, unhindered by family, religious, or cultural limitations.

Transforming Our Wounds Into Strengths

One key to knowing we are as we need to be is when we recognize that we are not at the mercy of our woundedness, and can respond with strength rather than weakness. We are all wounded in countless ways as children which we don't understand. This leads to a sense of helplessness or inability to act in effective and satisfying ways. We must confront and heal these if we are to be functioning adults in healthy relationships, since none of us needs to have our childhood baggage messing up perfectly good adult relationships. In our search for better relationships, we have to overcome our learned tendencies to fear, or clutch, or yield to impatience, confusion, or doubt, since none of these will bring us our ideal.

As we grow in self-awareness, we realize we can reflect on our deficiencies and transcend them through changing our reaction to those perceived deficiencies. As we learn coping skills, we can look with compassion at things which we once feared, as well as our former reactions, and feel a greater compassion for ourselves as humans learning how to love. Then we see we are autonomous, conscious Soul/Spirits, unafraid of whatever we might confront, because we have left ineffective responses behind and claimed our power to become healthy individuals.

As we grow, we meet others who were wounded when they were younger. Some of these are the same wounds as we have, just in a different context. These are important relationships because in sharing our experience, we see how our coping skills can help them, and their coping skills can help us. As we learn how many pleasurable and painful experiences we share with people we meet, we understand how connected we are with others. While exploring our wounds can be difficult and lead to misunderstandings, as we open to learning from others and sharing ourselves with them in appropriate settings, we find strength and connectedness.

When we heal our wounds and turn those experiences into strengths, we transmute any sense of victimhood into courage, compassion, and understanding. Then we become a source of healing and validation of the power of Love to redeem the promise of a better life for those we meet who share those wounds. Through healing our wounds and learning to live well despite them, we bring meaning and purpose out of these larger events. As we learn to cope with our debilities and find ways to live so they don't hinder us, we find fellowship, compassion, and connectedness with other wounded beings. Over time this offers us the ability to set aside harsh judgments, eliminate any sense of shame or blame, and overcome any sense of isolation and separateness.

In healing our wounds, we become a living symbol of the power of love to redeem all things, bringing forth the Light that shines through us as a result of becoming our Higher Self. As we heal our wounds, we transform the experience of those wounds, both large and small, into the power to realize and demonstrate a higher purpose and service in the world. Our wounds are the gateway to freedom. Our debilities show us the way to healing and power.

The Value of Friction

While we all like pleasant interactions, we also encounter friction, often arising from circumstances without us doing or saying anything. Why do certain encounters generate more friction than others?

While relative harmony and friction can be seen in the placements of our planets in another's chart, and theirs in ours, there is a powerful spiritual factor which determines how much friction there is. Because we all need to grow sometimes we are challenged by people and circumstances so we can come to a more spiritually harmonized view.

Many of us have struggled with the fact that throughout our lives, though we may try to harmonize with others, some people just aren't able to harmonize with us. These are situations where we came together with hope and optimism, but then because of whatever, the relationship just never did come together. While some of this can be seen in the planetary positions, other times it seems like a mystery why we didn't click.

We see this in every family. Even though we share genetics and a similar family and cultural matrix, each family produces unique personalities making their choices. Certainly we don't have the same charts, the same spiritual awareness, or the same reactions to events which shape our personalities.

This is true for everyone we meet; we each have our own level of personality integration, we each have our own desires, healthy or unhealthy, and our limitations due to our subconscious mind's programming from the family and cultural matrix. Obviously we all want harmonious relationships with others, but we each have our limitations, which is why we will never be accepted by some people. If their path is contrary to ours, it is difficult to find common ground.

It is normal to expect reasonably harmonious relations with others. That's why we search for them. However, from a spiritual angle, we grow through the Cosmic force of Fire by Friction. In any dynamic relationship, there will always be some small level of friction to spur the relationship forward. It doesn't have to be a difficult friction, which we have more control over than we think. Even the grind between us and another could polish the gemstone of the Soul in each of us.

As we move through both harmonious and difficult relationships, Fire by Friction will always move us to a greater integrated awareness of how every important relationship helped us grow. The friction which lights up life's truths for us is how we evolve into wisdom. Of course, as we grow we come to know that some things and people must change or be left behind, since there's no way to continue what has been. That's when the friction can become so intense we have to part. The more intensely we loved another, the greater the heartbreak. Still, even our broken heart can mend if we remember the love which is all around us.

It's easier to risk our hearts when younger because of the sense that there's always someone else right around the corner, but as we get older, we find we have to be discerning in our relationships since our hearts don't heal as easily as when we were younger. That's why we cannot lightly surrender our heart to another until we know they will not treat cheaply what we value.

While many struggle with issues of love and trust after heartbreaking experiences, they help us become stronger and clearer about our love, who to love, and how to spot signs and signals showing us a potential problem. This helps us learn to trust the signals we're getting about someone or a situation. When you're concerned, pay attention. We all have to learn to trust the warning signals which come our way. All warning signals let us know that one or both of us must change certain patterns in the relationship. Here's where we confront the questions of "can they/we change?" and "will they/we change?"

Spiritual Friction

Over the years, I've observed that people with powerful spiritual planets activate that energy in others, which we'll discuss in detail in Chapter 6. It works without intention, and creates an energy others respond to according to their level of awareness. So it is possible our Uranus could awaken something in others without either of us knowing what was going on. It's easy to see that an invisible force activating an awakening in another might be misunderstood and become a source of conflict if the one who is awakening doesn't have a spiritual practice.

Neptune dissolves and expands the sensitivity to the collective field. Pluto brings purification and experiences of "the underworld of existence," whether past or present. An unintegrated personality often fears these things. If our energy is activating a transformation in another, things could get frictional in all kinds of unsuspected ways if they choose to respond from the lower ego rather than their Higher Self.

If our Saturn activates another and they haven't dealt with fear or taking responsibility for their actions, they might become afraid of us or evasive, since that's their lesson. We may not be doing anything except breathing, but if our presence precipitates a spiritual crisis in another, a) we cannot take it personally, and b) we must become the positive expression of the negative planetary energy they're demonstrating.

If they are afraid, we must be clear, loving, and unafraid. If they are impatient, we must be patient and thoughtful. If they are touchy and defensive, we must be detached and positive. Our responses may or may not be received as we would like, but our behavior is not dependent on anyone else's attitude or mood.

You can also apply this to many frictional encounters with people in your past. If the lessons stuck and activated a growth pattern in you, it was friction activating your spiritual potential by the person who rejected you, or attacked you, or refused you. All conflict serves a spiritual purpose in helping us choose wise responses despite the friction.

Because we ARE Love, we naturally radiate care to others we meet, hoping to find resonance. As we become a living Light in our world, some will respond with love and others will feel fear. How another perceives our love and care and responds to it is entirely up to them.

While we always have to own our part in any interaction, because of who we are and what we are to learn from and teach others, whether we want to or not, it's really less about us and more about the energy we bring to each encounter. We are radiant loving wise Beings, each in our own way. As we express these qualities and remember we are all as surrounded by love and community as a fish by water, we will find our friends, as well as our Beloved, through both the friction and harmony of life.

Karma, Relationships, Conflict, and Growth

Often we meet people due to past karmas, while other times it's a choice made in the moment. While some relationships are "destined," many others happen because "It seemed like a good idea at the time." While we can always find understanding despite problems, we can avoid a lot of headache and heartbreak by knowing when a relationship has run its course and it's time to leave.

How long a relationship lasts is entirely up to how we treat each other, since even apparently good ones can turn sour due to all kinds of reasons. Some relationships are tested through circumstances that aren't the fault of either person. The trials of life help us understand our strengths and weaknesses and what we are and are not responsible for.

All relationships evolve as a result of how people behave toward each other. As we get to know someone, we see them more clearly. While we all have idiosyncrasies, we have to learn which behaviors are harmless and which are deal breakers. Regardless of personal style, we are never supposed to put up with non-loving, abusive, manipulative, or one-sided relationships.

When certain people come into our life, karma is set into motion by our choices. We begin many relationships in a burst of hopeful potential, and have pleasing experiences. However, as both of us are still learning about ourselves and each other, there are bound to be points of misunderstanding. These are the times when we hope we've found the love of our life, only to find they were a Soul mate who stretched us to our limit.

Conflict is not necessarily bad if it helps us know who we are and who another person is. But if we are to grow closer rather than apart the differences which divide us must never be greater than the love we share. We learn from both pleasurable and painful experiences which offer us ways to create better karmic relationships and experiences in the future. Everything depends on our attitude and the view we take of what we're going through, since by our willingness to have a positive attitude we naturally attract people we might love and who might love us.

Our internal imagery constantly attracts people and experiences we believe we want. Often we are attracted to someone without really knowing them

43

which leaves a door open to us being seduced by an image of who we hope they will be rather than who they really are. (We'll explore the nature of seductions, why they are to be avoided, and how they're different than courtship in Chapter 5.) The problem with being seduced is that seductions usually lead to unhappy experiences. That's why we have to take a new look at what we think we want from time to time, since we may not want to attract certain types of people we used to.

Our subconscious mind believes it wants certain things. We learned a lot of desires as children, and these created images of what we believed we wanted. Some of these are still in our mind even as adults. We've all chased a lot of desires which only led us to difficult experiences. It's why we have to become more aware of what is good for us, here and now.

As we become more self-aware of what feeds our love, we naturally don't want certain things we used to, and people who once fascinated us no longer attract our attention. This also happens when our subconscious mind fixes its attention on a new desire. We always have to monitor our instincts to make sure they are leading us to our heart's desire, or if they've brought someone else who will eventually move on once we both have learned what we needed to learn.

Our subconscious mind projects its images out into the world. They lead us to what we feel will fulfill us, whether it will or not. We all have attractions which will be fulfilled in some way unless we "unlearn" them. As we learn to question whether certain desires and attachments are good, or true, or useful, we quickly know which desires we must leave behind.

Sooner or later, we always attract our heart's desire. Finding our true love requires learning how to image our heart's desire without allowing the seductions of our subconscious mind to distort who our loving heart might attract. There is a certain magic and mystery to our journey from lesser loves to the Beloved. Timing is everything on shifting directions in who we attract and who is attracted to us.

Because of our karmas, there are many people we must dance with throughout life. We dance because we are attracted to each other. Because people each have their own road to walk, sometimes we find we are not in harmony in various ways. Those are the relationships where we learn to be true to ourselves and listen to our hearts. In overcoming the tendencies to desire things which lead us into pain, we learn to examine what we want and why we want it. This eventually leads us to much better relationships over time.

The heart is a muscle which becomes stronger through use. Even when our heart is hurting, by going ever-deeper into the secret it holds for you, eventually you will become the greater Love you seek. Regardless of whatever has been, our quest to find our true love begins with us learning to love ourselves no matter what we're going through.

If we are to recognize the Beloved, we must heal ourselves and not be seduced by unconscious desires. This means feeling all we need to feel so we can heal our emotional wounds which obstruct our ability to BE the Love we are. We know we're healing when we feel ourselves being happier, and are feeling "an attitude of gratitude" for our friends and lovers along the way, since they all taught us about a facet of Love which helped us grow.

45

We're here to learn what Love is and is not, and in our moments of headache and heartbreak, find ways to turn conditional love into unconditional Love. This is why we have friends, help mates, and Soul Mates. While these relationships may at times be difficult and even break our heart, ultimately all our friends and Soul Mates we meet on the Path of Life show us the way to become better people and more in touch with our heart. As we live the Love we are, eventually we'll recognize a transcendent Love in the eyes of a Friend. Then we are approaching the threshold of being able to recognize our Twin Flame.

* * * * * * * * *

Our perfect and ideal mate is shown in our astrological birth chart. It is our blueprint and roadmap showing us what we need to learn about our Beloved. Our chart holds the secret of who we are, and in knowing that we are able to recognize and accept an ever-greater love. The rest of this book offers ways to get beyond the guesswork involved in wondering who you should be with, and will give you a clear picture of the character traits of the "perfect mate" who already resides in your own consciousness.

By understanding our Moon and Venus traits, we can know our family tendencies and what we find beautiful, as well as how to be at ease with others, caring and concerned without giving up our strength, values, or ability to take care of ourselves. Learning to recognize and know our likes and needs leads us to healthy ways to express the best of our Moon and Venus energies, and leads us to pleasurable life experiences. Through knowing these parts of our inner nature we know how to care and be cared for, and how to be open to others without attracting hurtful experiences.

Each of our inner planetary energies can help us recognize the Beloved. The Sun will illuminate the Beloved and help us to see their shining qualities. Jupiter will helps us open to the greater adventure the Beloved will bring. Saturn will help us hang in there, "for better or for worse," as we and our Beloved walk the Path of Life together. That's what we all long for, and that's what we can all find if we're willing to do whatever it takes for a greater Love to come forth in our life.

48

CHAPTER THREE

WHO WE ARE DETERMINES WHO IS RIGHT FOR US

When searching for our true love, it's important to remember some sign energies are more compatible, while others are less compatible. Each sign has a special relationship with every other sign, and while some are harmonious, others are not. This is due to the harmonics of the holistic energy field. While we all have all the signs in our chart somewhere, each of us have more of some signs, and less of others.

This is beyond Sun sign astrology; it's why there are parts of us which seem to be at cross-purposes with other parts of us. However, even the signs at cross purposes to each other show the grounding, the balance, and the fulfillment of every other one. Each sign has its "useful relationship" with all the other signs, which is why we are able to adjust to circumstances and bring forth the best energy we can in the moment with the person we're with. Just because we have Sun or Moon or Venus signs which are said to be incompatible, we can always find points of harmony and understanding which can help us to move past points of friction, both within ourselves as well as with others.

Our birth chart shows when we were born into this "12 fold reality." Our birth planets in the houses show us what we came in with, and what we're here to master across the 12 Evolutionary Fields of human existence. Each part of us is learning how to manifest our best on the material, emotional, mental, and spiritual planes of the personal, interpersonal, and transpersonal dimensions of life.

How we cultivate the strengths of each of our planets and all of our signs leads us to apparent successes in some relationships, and apparent failures in others. Through our experiences, we find that signs which are supposed to be harmonious may not result in harmonious experiences, and signs which are supposed to be frictional to each other actually help us learn when to say no or set a boundary. We need "checks and balances" as we learn what's true for us and what is not.

Knowing our limits, what we will and won't put up with, allows us the freedom to be ourselves in our relationships. This is one way to overcome difficulty through re-focusing on what is positive and good for us. When we can move through challenging times and events and change negatives to positives, we claim our power to be our most joyous Self with others. As we embrace expressing the good, true, and beautiful in our lives, we find ourselves in harmony with ourselves, even in frictional conditions. That allows us to express our best Self, regardless of outer circumstances.

Because we have all 12 signs somewhere in our charts, we all have Aries somewhere in our inner landscape, even if we don't have a planet in that sign. We all have Cancer somewhere, even if it's "intercepted" or we have no planets there. As we are always learning about several sorts of sign experiences simultaneously, over time we can recognize and deal with all the energies regardless of the situation. Sometimes the energies are flowing;

other times they're stuck or jammed. Again, each sign has other signs which give harmony and understanding, while other signs challenge us to act or not act to resolve the conflict.

Because all the planets in our chart describe various people throughout our lives, over time we attract people with strong sign contacts between our charts and learn what we are in harmony with, as well as others who reveal what we don't like. We'll discuss "planets as people" later in this chapter.

The signs we have a problem with show us parts of our inner self we need to correct, or make peace with, or transform so the positive traits of those signs can come forth. An "affliction" in no way condemns us to misery or malfunction, but it serves as a guide so we can eliminate or change frictional energies to come to peace with who we are and the life we choose to live. Friction often helps us listen to our inner voice so we can follow our heart rather than get distracted by people who may not know what they're doing or saying. So let's take a look at the planets, the signs, and the relationship between the signs so we can understand how various parts of us relate to other parts of us and others.

The Planets

Each of our planets represents a "Light" within us, and each is important in showing us our inner makeup and how we naturally respond to circumstances and people. Each planet has its own "department of labor," or area of influence. Each has its constructive and destructive modes of operation. That's why two people with planets in the same sign might have some traits in common, but express them in totally different ways.

When operating in a healthy manner, our planets lead us to positive experiences, or at the very least, allow us to navigate difficulty in ways which are perfect for us. When our planets express in dysfunctional ways, they bring maladjusted conditions, difficulties, and problems. Because each interaction brings out certain qualities, when we find ourselves in difficult relationships, those are the times we're challenged to change how we express ourselves, turning toward our highest and best interests.

Our ability to choose how we deal with difficulty is the one power we have to change course if we need to, or defend what we hold dear if needed, without guilt, shame, or fear undermining our strength. We have the power to decide how our planets will manifest for good or ill. Our task is to turn our negatives into positives so we may have happy and fulfilling lives. Ultimately we are responsible for our lives and happiness, and have the ability to turn to better things any time we choose.

Astrology provides us a structure to understand the various energies of our personality. Each planet has its unique function in our makeup, and each can bring us into a greater conscious awareness of our special qualities, showing us who is and is not a good fit for who we are at our heart's core. The planets show our personal inclinations, our social instincts, and our path to higher realizations about who we are in the larger life and love around us. Though I touched on this briefly in the last chapter, let's take a closer look at what each planet represents in our internal landscape.

We'll begin with the Sun, symbolizing the Light/Life we ARE. It is our power plant where we shine out our integrity, the core radiance of our Star Self. It is the center of our personal solar system and the giver of life, how we are illuminated, and how we illuminate others.

The Moon symbolizes our "package of personality" as we feel our way through life's experiences. It is the sum of our habits and immediate feeling responses in the here and now. Our Lunar expression is continually shaped through imitation, reflection, and emotional receptivity as we move through life interactions. Our Moon sign reveals our primal needs, feelings, and emotional instincts. The Sun is our light and the Moon is our reflected light. The Sun is who we are, and the Moon is how we experience that in an "up close and personal" way.

Mercury represents how we process and coordinate the various areas of our life and mind, as well as perceptions, ideas, and the myriad details of things we have to do. It is the part of us which integrates Spirit, Soul, and matter using "receptive mind." Mercury, also known as Hermes, is "the Guide of Souls" and coordinates our receptivity to Spirit as we learn how to master things, feelings, and our mind.

Venus represents those things we like and find beautiful, attractive, and valuable, whether people, art, food, or anything else there is to like. It is associated with what we idealize, and shows our cooperative, creative, and romantic inclinations. Venus symbolizes social emotions, and as its symbol is a hand mirror, it represents our vanities, charm, and aesthetic inclinations. As this is a book about the powerful part Venus plays in our relationships on our quest to find our perfect partner, I'll give you more about Venus later in this chapter. We'll discuss what Venus in each sign means in Chapter 8.

Mars represents how we mobilize, activate, and rise to immediate challenges. It is said to be the "fight or flight" principle and how we "attack the problems of life." Mars spurs us to action, and the way we mobilize right here and now. Our Mars' sign shows how we advance and retreat as we move through our desires and interactions with people and circumstances.

While the Sun, Moon, Mercury, Venus and Mars are all primary parts of our personal life, Mars also plays a big role in our social life. Mars is really a "personal-social" planet, and represents our socialized desires as well as how we initiate action in our social world. A healthy Mars expresses as healthy personal and social desires.

Jupiter expands the personal and social functions of our Sun, Moon, Mercury, Venus, and Mars into the social-cultural and philosophic realm. Our Jupiter sign shows how we view an expanded universe, life adventure, and Truth, and represents imagination, "optimistic mind," and how we see greater vistas of opportunity. This part of personality teaches us to understand the eternal abundance of the Universe by giving us those things we need when we need them. It shows us our ability to bless and be blessed, as well as how we are protected even in difficult times.

Saturn teaches us how to mature gracefully despite limiting conditions, and brings us into our power to shape our destiny through the conscious choices we make. Our Saturn sign shows both what oppresses us as well as how we can take command of our life direction at key points of choice and change, throwing off the chains which hold us back from fulfilling our purpose for being alive.

Jupiter and Saturn work together to show us how we expand our vision and sense of what's possible within the boundaries of our imagination and experience symbolized by Saturn. Jupiter wants to believe all things are possible while keeping the freedom to run away from those things we believe are too much trouble. Saturn shows us our "bottom line," and how we are limited by necessity as well as fear. Saturn is the part of us which can eliminate fear, revealing our path to mastering our responses and showing us the way to become fearless, mature, and disciplined as we embrace a greater understanding leading us to wisdom. Those who are interested in finding out about the power Saturn offers us to live a highly fulfilling life should consult my book Saturn: Spiritual Master, Spiritual Friend.

Uranus, Neptune, Pluto, and TransPluto are generational and subgenerational influences, representing the larger spiritual field in which we live and awaken, and transform the limitations of our personality. We'll discuss the influence these spiritual planets exert in our relationships in Chapter 6.

The Signs

As noted earlier, there are 12 signs, and every planet in our chart is in one of them. Because of our unique makeup, some of these planets are harmonious with each other, and some are not. The complexity of human nature and our need to learn through both harmony and friction is why some parts of us get along with other parts of us, while other parts require self-awareness and consciously chosen

55

changes so we get all parts of our personality working together for our greatest good.

The uniqueness of our internal makeup is why we're illuminated by certain people and situations, and not by others. It's why we really like some people more than others. Some signs seem to uplift us, while others seem to bog us down in major ways. How we dance with the energies in our world reveals how integrated we are or aren't, and what we're learning about our willingness to have happy and fulfilling relationships. As we learn and grow from life experiences, we have the ability to become healthy integrated personalities.

While there are 12 signs, because all signs have an opposing sign, as we grow through our relationships, we learn to deal with 6 polarized energies as they offer opportunities to move into greater awareness. Any two signs that oppose each other are two faces of one coin, a polarity of the expression of each other. Thus they are natural mate signs, and why many Astrology texts say that opposing signs make for good partnerships.

The 6 polarities are Aries & Libra, Taurus & Scorpio, Gemini & Sagittarius, Cancer & Capricorn, Leo & Aquarius, and Virgo & Pisces. Each of these sign pairs represents an archetype, which we'll explore briefly in Chapter 5. These signs always oppose each other, whether we have a planet in one and not the other. While often opposite signs are a natural match, this is not an absolute by any means, even though there is a definite attraction between signs that oppose each other. Of course, an opposition may be productive of great give-and-take, or great battles, depending on a host of things. As all signs externalize through the opposite sign, by knowing the traits of opposing signs, we can see if someone or something is out of balance.

Signs that "square" (approximately 90 degrees from each other) are said to produce friction, but they can also generate great energy to act productively when the tension is used wisely. The signs which square are Aries/Libra with Cancer/Capricorn, Taurus/Scorpio with Leo/Aquarius, and Gemini/Sagittarius with Virgo/Pisces. When it comes to conflict between the signs, the solution to the conflict is in the positive expression of the signs opposing those in square, since those are balancing forces to the energy of the square.

For example, if we encounter a conflict involving Aries square Cancer energy, then we must wisely apply positive Libra and Capricorn traits to resolve the tension. If we're dealing with Taurus square Leo energy, then we must apply positive Aquarius and Scorpio traits to achieve healthy balanced functioning.

Fire signs (Aries, Leo, Sagittarius) are generally harmonious with Air signs (Gemini, Libra, Aquarius). Water signs (Cancer, Scorpio, Pisces) are generally harmonious with Earth signs (Taurus, Virgo, Capricorn). There are exceptions to this when a planet is at the beginning or end of a sign, since then planets in signs usually disharmonious with each other can find harmony or vice versa. As we evolve from our lower self to our Higher Self our sign expressions get better and better, and we bring the positive traits of those signs to the relationships in our lives. That's when we begin to attract friends rather than those who are a struggle. It's also why as we evolve we quickly know whether we want to deal with someone or not, and we've raised the level of our planetary expression, attracting people who are best suited to us.

The magic of all of this is we get to learn a lot from various experiences about who we are along the way, and how well we are handling how we express our planets. As our planets progress through our lives, they show our changing tastes and values, and why we are no longer attracted to the things and people we used to be. It doesn't mean our youthful attractions were bad, or our current ones good. Our progressions just show us our internal evolutionary track, and why we move through various types of experiences with all kinds of people when we do.

Each Planet Symbolizes Many People Throughout Our Life

So why do people appear and disappear from our lives? Besides the obvious "real world" factors, as well as psychological changes, each planet in our chart represents one or more people in a given life chapter. That's why as we evolve we find some people disappear while others appear. Astrological progressions and transits are very important in marking who goes and who comes, and when. Each planet represents an important person in our life, as well as many people in our past, present and future.

The way it works is simple. If each of the planets represents part of our inner makeup, then as we shape our character by our interactions with people and the world, we make choices which change the quality of our responses. For example, when we were young our Sun sign was represented by our father and our Moon sign our mother. Our brothers and sisters were represented by other planets, maybe even an entire configuration in our chart. As we get older, the planets no longer are exclusively represented by our family, and increasingly reflect our friends and colleagues.

That's why some people disappear in our lives. They served to represent a planet in the "solar system" of our life up to a point, and then for whatever reason, or for no reason, the person symbolizing the planet no longer represented that quality within us. When that happens, the magnetic attraction holding us together no longer has resonance and the bond is severed. As an aside, "severing" is a quality of Mars. Due to Mars' duality, all relationship endings challenge us to find grace in action, rather than fall into error through anger, angst, attacks, impulsiveness, or irritability.

Changing Our Expression Changes Who We Attract and Are Attracted To

When a relationship ends, it's time for us to re-image our inner planetary function that person represented. All relationships fulfill some potential, and when the potential is used up and there's no more potential in that relationship, it must end. The good news is that because Nature abhors a vacuum, that planetary quality will soon be filled anew by another we've attracted based in who we have become. By taking a look at our past relationships, we can see who we were and who we've become, and how some qualities we used to be attracted to no longer work for us.

Looking deeper, we can see how when one person left, another person embodying that planetary energy showed up at some point, and we danced with them for as long as they represented that quality. Of course, just as others are represented by our planets, we also are a planet in their lives. Often it won't be the same planet, since each learns different lessons depending on the season of life we're in. We become different planets to many people, mirroring the dance we're doing with them.

If we are important to them, we often assume the role of an important planet, whichever one in their chart fits our qualities. Those doing transformational work often act as Uranus, Neptune, Pluto, or TransPluto in another person's life. Since these planets symbolize invisible spiritual factors beyond individual control, their transformational energies usually show through the quality of one of the visible planets as well as the invisible planet. Yes, we can be two planets for another, just as others who affect us spiritually are to us.

Since planets symbolize forces both inside us and outside us, it is easy to see how our planets resonate with some people and not others. That's the basis for compatibility charts. But they also represent energy fields we carry with us which manifest through people and interactions in our world.

Our Jupiter shifts may or may not mean a Sagittarius or Pisces person in our lives will appear or disappear, since besides its association with those signs, Jupiter could very well just be a person with Jupiter prominent in their charts. However, you can bet that when an Aries or Scorpio enters or leaves our life, it does have something to do with Mars, regardless of any other planetary energy they may represent.

Throughout our life, Jupiter represents people who open our imagination, or give us a long journey, or show us how to be more generous or humorous. Jupiter symbolizes all our teachers who opened a broader or wider view or understanding. It also symbolizes all who protected us, or blessed us, or who gave us something we needed which gave us hope. Of course, it also symbolizes those who taught us through extravagance, waste, or extreme events.

When we were younger, our Saturn was no doubt represented by the elders who taught us to be afraid, or made us believe we were bound by some inflexible rule or expectation, whether personal or societal. As we get older, Saturn can be our boss, or any authority figure who shows us our limits, duties, and responsibilities. Saturn can also represent those we meet in power situations, or circumstances where we're in a position of power or responsibility. These will be people of experience, understanding, and wisdom who will be reliable in discharging their duties.

Mars was always present during the endless succession of people who aggravated us, irritated us, or sharpened us up. While some Mars people in our lives triggered our need to fight or flee from hassles, others taught us to be good warriors, defending what needed to be defended. When we learn how to mobilize our energies in a focused and determined way, Mars is always somewhere in the mix.

As I offered earlier, some of the most important people in our lives were represented by more than one planet. They may even have symbolized an entire configuration in our charts, where we learned how to balance the opposites, triangulate into a broader understanding or effectiveness, or integrate a focus in a polarized situation. They also could represent any chain of events which transformed our lives for better or worse if they embody a planet precipitating dynamic activity.

By exploring how we came to have certain character traits we can understand how certain people gave us patterns to imitate or follow which created those traits. When we learn all we can from acting out traits we adopted in the past, we end them and find new personality traits to express. Seeing how some of our old traits were associated with certain people, we can understand why those people left, often for no apparent reason.

We learn what we are here to understand through our interactions with the world. Once we learn our lesson on any level, then we move to a new way of framing that lesson, ultimately so we can serve ourselves and our world from a place of conscious wisdom and compassion. While we may regret the passing of certain people, even those partnerships we loved, the passages show us our larger path to ever-broader realizations of who we are, here and now.

So next time you wonder why someone is in your life, remember that it may be to learn to say yes, say no, say maybe, perhaps glimpse a greater reality, or dance a more enjoyable dance on this beautiful Earth. In any case, no matter how close or distant, appreciate all those who brought you to the dance, since God loves gratitude.

Desire, Magnetic Attraction, and Finding Your Perfect Mate

If our inner nature conditions who we dance with, then improving our planetary expressions are the key to attracting someone who could be our ideal partner. There is a Divine Law called "Magnetic Attraction" which guarantees we will find people who resemble the pictures in our desire-mind who we believe we want and need for fulfillment. And just as we will find those who we think we desire, others are also attracting and being attracted to who they believe will fulfill their dream.

Our subconscious mind holds different images of the Beloved and we spend our life searching for people who resemble those inner pictures. It's why someone "feels right," or doesn't. Your ability to attract your perfect mate, or ideal partner, starts with getting clear about what could be true for you. This involves examining your wants, needs, desires, and values, since these are involved in who you attract, and why.

When we aren't clear about who would be our best partner and life mate, it's easy to mistake desire and neediness for love. An ideal and timeless Love is a transcendent uniting force, and through astrology we learn the timing on how Love expresses itself in our lives. Through our responses to those we're attracted to and those who are attracted to us, a swirl of multi-level karmas go into motion which create consequences in the future. Sometimes our responses create pleasurable experiences and relationships, while other times we are forced to grow through painful and unwise choices in partnerships. We learn from both, and they all offer us ways to create new future karmic connections and experiences. Everything depends on our attitude and how we greet opportunities to grow beyond old desires into a greater love.

Using the Moon and Venus Wisely To Make Our Relationships Better

By understanding the qualities of our Moon sign and our Venus sign, we get clear about our needs, likes, dislikes, and what nurtures our sense of emotional security. When young we all learn some unhealthy emotional responses, but as we mature we can release attitudes and behaviors which only bring us pain and suffering. As we let go of unfulfilling inner pictures, we change who we attract, and eventually understand the qualities we want in our ideal mate. Venus, taken with the Moon, gives us a huge amount of information about the emotional elements of our personality. By elevating our Moon and Venus functions, raising their expression to a higher level, we attract more perfect forms of our ideal in both physical and psychological realms through setting aside old insecurities (Moon) and vanities (Venus).

A healthy Moon allows us to care for ourselves and others in ways which are perfect for the need of the moment. We are no longer troubled by insecurities or feel unable to take care of ourselves, or behave in immature ways hoping to find someone who will fulfill our childish needs. As we change our Lunar expression, we change who we feel close to and want to be around, and through a process of selection and reflection, we eventually start attracting people who are able to care for us in ways which are healthy and perfect for who we are.

On our path to find our perfect mate, we must unlearn some things we learned from our family and cultural matrix. As we learn to let go of patterns of attraction which cause us pain, we can embrace ways to live which strengthen and fulfill us.

Our Moon goes through ten thousand changes in the ways it expresses itself in our lives. By knowing some qualities about our ideal mate, we can avoid inappropriate relationships and many unnecessary wounds. Though our ideal may change as the years go by, if we get clear about what a healthy relationship would feel like, we can navigate the changes in our relationships knowing we're on the right track.

The Moon, being naturally reflective, adaptive, and insecure, can be strengthened and nurtured by the qualities of our Sun and its abundant Solar force. The Sun shows how we pour out infinite light and warmth to our world and our heart's desire. By using the Sun to strengthen our Moon's expression, we are able to capture reflected forms of our heart's desire rather than reflected illusions that leave us feeling insecure and needy.

The Sun illuminates the integrity of our healthy loving friendships, which are the only solid basis of lasting relationships. When we attract our heart's desire, it will always manifest as a loving friendship, regardless of whether the element of romance is present. Our Moon will give form to our Sun's Light through the healthy Lunar quality of tenderness, nurture, and genuine caring with safe environments. When these are present in a relationship, then the Lunar contact is healthy.

Venus, on the other hand, symbolizes the principle of romance and what we like. It is our ideal of grace, charm, and beauty. Venus shows us our self-reflection of all we believe is agreeable in ourselves and therefore is agreeable in others and to others. As you can see, this creates misunderstandings when what is agreeable to us is not necessarily agreeable

65

to others, and why often when we believe we are being charming others may not respond as we hoped.

Venus does not feel as deeply as the Moon. Venus symbolizes the social feeling-function in us which is more outwardly oriented and eager to please and be pleased. While the Moon represents our internal feelings, Venus represents our external feelings. Venus is the part of us that wants to be beautiful, be surrounded by beauty, and see beautiful things and people in our world. When our Venus isn't healthy, we can be seduced by superficial forms, images, and manifestations of what is agreeable rather than recognize the deeper truths and realities in self and others. When our Venus is healthy, we are living our love of beauty and the beauty of love.

We all need the affectionate and pleasing experiences that Venus symbolizes. In our search for Beauty, however, we need to make sure that we are also searching for Truth and Goodness. These are all the higher traits of Venus, and so if we aren't seeing Truth or Goodness in another, then that form of Beauty is probably not appropriate for us. As we learn to recognize these higher qualities of Venus within ourselves, we are offered opportunities to show these to others. As we refine our Venus and allow it to become the embodiment of Truth, Goodness, and Beauty, we naturally attract others who fulfill our higher aspirations. Through our willingness to refine and elevate our Moon and Venus functions, we bring an entirely different quality to our relationships, and attract those who are beautiful, elegant, charming, and nurturing.

This is where the power of our Sun can radiate an intense positivity that lets our light shine so the beloved can see where our heart is at. We have the power to radiate our heart's strengths in our world, and only have to choose to shine our light when we can. The quality and strength of our personal positivity is a combination of technique, inner connectedness, and heart-centeredness. It is our true spiritual path to power, love, and wisdom. The Sun and the Moon are core principles in our direct experience of life and profoundly shape how we express who we are, who we think we need, and who we attract.

We can find our heart's desire. We just have to get clearer and clearer in our imaging of the ideal traits we desire in our partner. Think back on all the people in your life who loved you and accepted you for who you are. Remember those who encouraged you and recognized your good qualities. Remember the friends who you liked to be around and liked to be around you. Each one of them loved you for who you are. If you were loved then, you are loved now, and could attract others who will love you in the future.

Take a new look at the qualities you believe your perfect mate would possess. All your best relationships gave you clues and signals about what lit up your life and opened your heart. Be willing to visualize your heart's desire, and imagine attracting someone with the best qualities you've experienced. Eventually you'll see a form of your ideal made manifest, since we have the power to generate that which is pleasing to us by using our Moon and Venus energies wisely.

Receptivity to the Beloved

It takes practice to make a habit. That's the Moon. We polish the picture of our perfect mate and our own sense of beauty using our Venus. Be clear

67

and positive about what you want, letting go of any negative attitudes and expectations, including agreeing with others' pessimism. Just because we had difficult relationships in the past doesn't mean we won't attract our heart's desire in the future. If we stay positive and centered in all our relationships, eventually we'll attract someone who could be our Beloved. The best part of this practice is we feel so much better in the long run, and our happiness is not dependent on anyone else.

We can prevent many misunderstandings by getting clear about our inner ideals and living those ideals as consistently as we can. Life and relationships are a never-ending series of choices, and sometimes we settle for less than we need to. That usually happens when we're insecure or bored. Just remember that as you begin to attract the Beloved, you don't want to take a mate who is less than the best who will love you, be good to you, and with whom you could create a happy and fulfilling life together.

Rather than limit ourselves through pessimism because of past difficult relationships, we can always change our expectations and allow our imagination to dream of better ways to be with others which will be more fulfilling than the ones we've had in the past. As we open to being the most courageous, strong, and loving person we can be and trust we can attract someone who could love us in an ideal way, eventually we'll see the manifestation of our heart's desire.

A Closer Look at Venus

As I offered earlier, Venus is what we like. It represents our social emotions, our values, our aesthetic sense, and how we enjoy life. It is how we capture the desires of Mars. It is the planet associated with romance, equal relationships of all sorts, and all of life's pleasurable experiences.

The sign it is in shows how we express appreciation, as well as the types of art, people, and beauty we are instinctively attracted to. Therefore, it is an important planet when examining interpersonal harmony between us and others, since Venus links us emotionally with others in our world. It symbolizes our personal way of interacting with all we like, and our way of securing our ideals as well as the desires we assume will make us comfortable. Venus, taken together with the Moon, gives us a huge amount of information about the emotional elements of our personality.

Venus is said to "rule" Taurus and Libra, and is "exalted" in Pisces. This means Venus is naturally the traits of the signs it rules, and grows as it adopts and demonstrates positive Pisces traits. Venus is strong, sweet, stubborn and pleasant like Taurus, and desires fairness, balance and harmony like Libra. It is truly the planet of "right relations." The sign a planet is exalted in shows its "grounds of greatest growth," meaning that Venus grows toward its best expression through the compassion, restraint, empathy, and forgiveness of Pisces. That's why Venus, when pleasant, firm, just, balanced, empathic, and compassionate, operates to attract others with these traits.

Venus is never very far from the Sun. It is always either in the same sign as our Sun, or in one of the two signs just before or just after the Sun. The ancients believed Venus as a morning star has a different nature than when Venus is an evening star. A morning star is one you see on the Eastern horizon before the Sun rises; an evening star is one you see on the Western horizon just after sunset. So when Venus is in a sign behind the Sun, it's a morning star and when Venus is in a sign in front of the Sun it's an evening star.

As Venus was associated with Ishtar, She was both a Goddess of Love and a Goddess of War. The ancients believed Venus as a morning star was a Goddess of War, and as an evening star was a Goddess of Love. I would say the dual qualities of Venus are explained by Venus ruling both Taurus and Libra, as Taurus is in the axis of the Warrior/Guardian archetype and Libra is in the axis of the Lover/Relator archetype. We'll briefly discuss the archetypes at the beginning of Chapter 5.

Apart from mythological attributes, when your Venus is in one of the two signs before the Sun sign, you lead with your feelings and hunches and follow up with decisions and actions later on. When your Venus is in one of the two signs after the Sun sign, you decide and act first, and feel things and check it out with others later on. Everyone fits one of these two descriptions, and one is not better or worse than the other. Each has its place in the grand scheme of things. Either your light leads you to what you like, or what you like leads you to your light.

When your Venus is in the same sign as the Sun, then depending on whether it is earlier or later in that sign, one of the above is true, but with an added important component of Venus blending with your basic character, shown by the Sun. With Venus conjunct (near) your Sun, you act and decide with a constant awareness of how your Light and Likes are received by others, and how your relationships are illuminated in your Life. Sun conjunct Venus is illumination through Venus, with added value in the ability to expressing pleasing forms of illumination.

When someone has a Sun conjunct Venus, then feelings, values, and aesthetics infuse every act to a greater or lesser degree, and every act is taken with sensitivity to social conditions. These are people who are usually well-liked by one and all. These two planets together often accompany an artistic gift, physical beauty, and an ultra-social nature, usually expressing charm, elegance, and reasonableness, unless other planetary influences indicate the contrary.

All that said, remember that we are constantly learning about ourselves through the reflected forms of beauty that we capture. At various times in the life, our Venus will be impacted by and express other sign characteristics, such as the signs it progresses through as we grow older. There are other astrological factors that also shift our Venus expression that are too numerous to explain here. Still, enjoy this journey of learning about your relationships, yourself, and your beloved, and open to attracting your ideal of beauty, culture, and style!

CHAPTER FOUR

FRIENDSHIP AND THE SQUARE OF RIGHT RELATIONS

Life can be a funny thing. Throughout our lives we continuously interact with others. We meet people socially, through work, and sometimes the connection just appears, like when we meet someone in a grocery store. Some of these meetings result from past life karma, while others are part of the karma we're creating now. Both show us key elements in our "Hero's Journey" through this life.

We meet a lot of people, and while most are cordial or neutral, many others test us to stay in our own power rather than give it to them. These are usually not our friends, even if they do help us get clear about boundaries. The interactions which could become friendships are the ones which bring forth mutual respect, genuine affection, and a desire to continue the interaction. By finding what you share and enjoy in common, you'll know quickly where another's head and/or heart is at.

While it's a given that we all bring baggage to each interaction, that baggage does not have to be a hindrance to cultivating a friendship. A friendship is mutual. How another values our friendship, and how much we value theirs, eventually makes it clear how close we can be. That's why your Beloved will always be a true friend, since you will each value the friendship above other considerations.

So what is friendship? Think of your true friends. They may have disagreed with you, but never made you feel slimy or used. They may have busted you on some part of your personality, but they never did it to hurt you or make you feel humiliated. Your true friends were always straight with you, since true friendship involves heart, integrity, honesty, respect, and willingness to be creative in how you each contribute to and share your common joy.

A friend never undermines you. A friend never makes you feel like you are unworthy. A friend never bullies you. A friend is always kind to you, even when they're challenging something you're doing, feeling, or thinking which would damage the relationship (or you!) over the long haul.

Our Beloved Will Be Our Best Friend

Any close relationship, whether casual or serious, whether long or short term, must be founded on friendship. It doesn't mean you will necessarily agree on everything, or even have the same approach to problems and solutions for stressful situations. But apart from your differences, there will be mutual beneficial interests, and ideally you'll both be at ease with the other regardless of the differences. The best friendships are those where both take the initiative to maintain and improve the friendship. In a true friendship you each willingly find shared ways to be where both are happy with what is in the moment. It may not be perfect but you can build it together. In any friendship, each gladly shows care for each and both. Again, a true friend would never take advantage of you.

This holds especially true for anyone we might marry. All the long term marriages I've known were based in a strong friendship, where there was both attraction and cooperation as well as mutual respect and genuine affection. While we always want to feel "chemistry" with those we hope are the Beloved, it's not really a very reliable barometer for knowing how suited you are for each other. Even a very strong attraction may not work out well over time, especially if you have different values or life goals, or if one of you is going higher and deeper into a spiritual life and practice while the other is more focused on materialism and worldly things. Then even fantastic combinations of planets and signs cannot prevent problems arising from a lack of spiritual compatibility.

It's always a joy when we find another with complementary skills and interests, This can make for a very fulfilling friendship. Over time it can lead to a strong attraction, but never forget it's easier to find a lover than a friend. If physical intimacy would mess up the friendship, then it's probably best not to go there while maintaining what the friendship was originally based on, and what it has come to be.

Each of us must feel welcome to express our own voice. All of us need the space to grow in our interactions with others in our world. Each of us must be able to respect our truths as well as another's truths. Loving another for life is a divine dance, and as we and others change, we see how free we are to be as we truly are, even as our hearts and lives are totally committed to our Beloved. A contented and happy heart cannot be divided.

As we embrace greater loving relationships, eventually we'll catch glimpses of what our ideal love and perfect partner might be like. As we grow into an ever greater ability to know what love is and become easier at giving and receiving love, we begin to see that we have actually become the greater Love we've longed for, and find our ability to love and be loved has expanded beyond our wildest imagination.

Love is an aspect of our essential nature. Knowing we are eternal Soul-Spirits who are forever growing into a greater loving wisdom through learning how to give and receive Love helps us remember what's important through all our life changes. Through our absolute freedom to choose our course in every moment of our existence, over time we can grow in our natural ability to give and receive love, attracting friends, help mates, Soul Mates, and eventually our Twin Flame.

Love and friendship are of the heart, as well as the mind. And a true friend is worth more than all the gold ever mined.

The Square of Right Relations

Over the years, I've seen there are four basic requirements for establishing a healthy permanent relationship. If these 4 are an active part of our dance together, then we could be friends, lovers, or partners across years and even lifetimes. I've seen these four factors determine the health of every single relationship I've ever known, and it seems to be universally true. I have termed it "The Square of Right Relations."

If we want to know if a relationship will last, whether romantic, business, "just friends," or any other that we want to have longevity, there are 4 things that must be cultivated and remain a constant. These go for both old and new relationships. Any and all relationships which have these four factors present have been winners.

These four requirements are:

1) If you're good to him/her;
2) If you're good for him/her;
3) If s/he is good to you;
4) If s/he is good for you.

When the answer to these four are a constant "yes," then a relationship will be healthy. However, because how we define these four qualities changes over time, we cannot assume what was true in the past is necessarily true here and now. By taking a new look at these questions from time to time, we can keep our relationships fresh. A benefit of reviewing these questions is that often we don't really get whether these are true in in the interaction until some weeks, months and even years down the road. Taking a fresh look at how good we are to and for each other keeps our journey with each other honest and fresh as we each grow separately and together. Then we can make changes as we need to and won't get stuck in attitudes which no longer fit what's happening.

However, if any of the four questions lapse into a "no" or "I don't know," then it's a signal of potential problems. When we realize that we or they are not good to each other or for each other, then we both must take the initiative to restore the good that could be, or be willing to walk on so as not to damage them or be damaged by them. Restoring the good involves exploring what we each actually care about, as well as our mutual willingness to find a way forward which is agreeable to both of us.

The Square of Right Relations applies to all our human relationships. It can also be said that some relationships are only good for us as long as we need to learn certain things, and then they dissolve after a time once we've fulfilled the purpose of that interaction. These worked, but only as long as they needed to.

We've all had romantic relationships that ended for whatever reason. It is fairly safe to say if a romantic relationship ends, that person could not be our Twin Flame, even if they were a Soul Mate for that chapter of our life. (I discuss the Twin Flame, and how they are different from a Soul Mate, in Chapter 10.) Some romances only last until one or both participants use up the potential, after which one or both begin to repolarize toward someone else, or perhaps just go their own way.

When a romance ends, many search for someone new, often immediately after the old relationship ends. This usually is not a good idea because every ending leaves many things unfulfilled. The unfulfilled expectations of a relationship which has ended creates a void which we want to fill, and here's where our power to take charge of who we attract is most needed.

After a breakup it's crucial to remember that we are now free to be ourselves on our own terms. We can foster our current healthy relationships, and after stilling the old instinctive yearnings, can continue to improve ourselves and our awareness and grow into healthier relationships. As we grow, our attractions improve.

I believe we need to reclaim the power we gave away to others before we begin dating again. While there's no set timeline, it's always better to be feeling strong and complete before doing a dance with others. Because of the projections we had and received, we need time to remember the love and wisdom we are, realizing what we need to realize. That way we don't bring the unhappy baggage we confronted at the end of previous relationships into new relationships.

No one should welcome the Beloved with a hurt attitude. Be happy within yourself for making it this far, knowing what you do, and affirming that all the good traits of previous attractions could happen again, without the bad qualities you overlooked in your quest for relationship. We want to attract someone in the right way and time, but not through neediness or thoughtlessness. By stepping back from our insecurities and hurt feelings, remembering we can attract and be attracted to the love of our life in the right way and time, we give ourselves the space to take a look at what is driving our desire.

Usually, because of all that was not fulfilled within us in a previous relationship, we are attracted to others who seem to offer us a contrast that feels better than what we left behind. I've seen this to be true whether we're youths, adults, or in the season of the grey hair! If there are still unfulfilled urges that drive us to want to jump out of one difficult relationship into another which seems to promise a better experience, we often wind up in what are called "rebound" relationships. Here I'll offer that not all rebound relationships are necessarily short term or unhealthy.

Modern psychology warns us against rebounding. However, I've seen that when a person falls into a "rebounder," sometimes it's not a bad thing. Even if it doesn't last all that long, sometimes we "rebound" right into the arms of the one we're supposed to be with for however long and for whatever reason.

Again, rebounds may or may not be temporary, especially if we find ourselves in an intimate relationship with someone who is really good to us and for us, and inspires our heart to be good to them and for them. Then we may have "rebounded" out of a relationship which outlived its time right into the arms of a Soul Mate.

Because the Square Of Right Relations applies to both genders across all types of relationships, whether romantic, business, friendships, or even just casual acquaintances, if you ever wonder whether a relationship is truly healthy, ask yourself the 4 questions: Are they good for me? Are they good to me? Am I good for them? Am I good to them? (Of course, sometimes we may have to view it from the angle of "us," in asking: Are they good for us? Are they good to us? Am I good for us? Am I good to us?

If the answer to all 4 of these are "yes," then you can bet you're in a good relationship. And yes, these questions need to be asked from time to time from different perspectives. As we dance through life's experiences, there are many ways to be good to and for each other. That allows us the pleasure of discovering new ways to be and things to do, and keeps our relationships fresh!

Trust and Respect

An essential in any long term relationships involves trust and respect, which are core ingredients in any true friendship. Trust can only be cultivated through honorable actions over time. This is why it's always good to allow any relationship to take its natural course, developing organically, and not try to rush things. As we have shared experiences over time, we get a sense of who they are, their strengths as well as what triggers spontaneous responses, both good and questionable. Then we know how much respect they have for us, themselves, as well as more evolved human qualities.

Without mutual respect, there can be no trust in the best sense of the word, since mutual respect allows each to be authentic without fear of ridicule or attack. When we respect each other, then we can be who we truly are, and we can trust them to be who they really are, and neither of us has to fear corrosive judgments or manipulation.

Unfortunately, it's easy to slip into error, take things for granted, and wind up in a misunderstanding. This is where we have to step back from snap judgments and kneejerk reactions. Sometimes bad motives or intentions are attributed to a simple misunderstanding. These sorts of impulsive reactions damage the relationship even when the relationship is otherwise healthy.

All of us have had one or more untrue accusations aimed at us in our lives. These teach us to be careful who to trust and how quickly we can trust them. It also teaches us to trust our inner voice when it tells us to be circumspect. When we learn to trust ourselves, then we know who to trust and why.

Trust in our relationships takes months and even years to develop, and can be shattered in an instant. Whether a simple misunderstanding or a deliberate attack, mistrust can kill a previously good relationship so it should be avoided. To know the truth about another, even for an instant, must accompany a trust in our own wisdom to know what to do or not do.

While it may take a while to come, we must trust our wisdom to show us our Way.

As it has been said since antiquity, patience is a virtue. I have found many misunderstandings can be cleared up by showing patience toward others. If we don't overreact too quickly, sometimes potential problems are easily resolved. The ones which aren't are still best addressed with patience and the wisdom which comes with patient reflection.

Patience and reflection lead us to trust our take on things, or modify our view. Patience and maturity lead us to respect ourselves and trust ourselves and our wisdom which are the first steps to a greater respect for others. When we honor our wisdom born of our direct experience, then our appreciation for the wisdom of others grows. Over time, a shared respect and trust leads us to excellent friendships.

By what another says to us, and how they say it, we can know where their hearts are at. As mutual respect is built through shared experiences, we come to a greater trust in the bond we share. As we learn to embrace our greater wisdom which grows as we share it with others, we leave behind the need to look "out there" for answers that we can only find within. Finding wisdom, we find love, trust, and respect, and will forever know it in the presence of others.

CHAPTER FIVE

Courtship and Seduction - We Dance in Many Relationships throughout our Lives

As we embrace the adventure of our "Hero's Journey," we find there are 6 great archetypal roles, or Grand Masques, which we wear as "faces of personality" in our world. In Astrology these are found in the 6 sign polarities. As mentioned in a previous chapter, there are 12 signs, with six opposing the other six. Each sign expresses its qualities through the sign opposing it. These six polarities represent archetypal energies which work both together and separately while dancing as a duo.

The six primary internal archetypes which we externalize in countless ways throughout our lives are the Lover/Relator (Aries/Libra) with its focus on the "I-Thou;" the Warrior/Guardian (Taurus/Scorpio) with its focus on stability; the Questor/Magi (Gemini/Sagittarius) with its focus on experimentation; the Innocent/Primal (Cancer/Capricorn) with its focus on self-interest; the Ruler/Orphan (Leo/Aquarius) with its quality of nobility; and the Healer/Shaman (Virgo/Pisces) with its focus on finding a new quality of life. We all have each of these in our charts, and throughout our life we are given opportunities to perfect how we express each of these.

While a comprehensive exploration of these astrological archetypes is beyond the scope of this work, we can see from these sign pairings that there's a planetary dance going on between Venus and Mars, Mercury and Jupiter, and the Sun and Moon with Saturn. It's easy to see that a healthy planet will express the best of its archetypes. Just as Venus has a lover side and a warrior side, a healthy warrior is a healthy lover, and vice versa; a healthy healer is a healthy magician; a healthy ruler is an innocent who instinctively does their best.

The dance between our archetypes leads us through experiences teaching us how to express each of these energies in balanced ways. By learning and demonstrating each of these in the right way and time, we achieve fluidity as we do our Being. While all of these are important factors in our ability to recognize the Beloved, for now let's take a look at the Lover archetype, since that's how we'll become the love we seek!

The Lover

We dance with our inner Lover archetype as we move through the entrances and exits on the stage of life. If we are to be healthy Lovers, and attract healthy Lovers who will appear as friends, helpmates, Soul Mates and our Beloved, we have to learn to recognize true love and affection, as well as healthy boundaries and loyalties, and the difference between seduction and courtship. By knowing the difference between what love is and isn't, and learning to spot unloving behavior, we move into ever better relationships and become our healthy Lover archetype. So let's explore the Lover!

The Lover, or "Relator," is the part of us which seeks relationship with others, our Higher Self, and Spirit. Both Aries and Libra show us the axis of the "I-Thou" relational dance in our charts. We discover our inner and outer Lover archetype and how we wear that Grand Masque (and the Grand Masques of our

84

other archetypes) through our relationships. As we grow from infancy to adolescence into adulthood we learn to imitate these archetypes through what we've learned from others and things which capture our imagination.

As we learn to imitate various archetypes they become fixed as images in our emotional body. We do some of these consciously, but others lurk in the subconscious mind. It's why sometimes we don't know we're being a certain way or acting out a certain unconscious role, until a) someone points out what we're doing, or b) we have an electric breakthrough moment when our Higher Self holds up the invisible mirror to our mind and we awaken to what we never saw before that moment.

The Dance

Every relationship mirrors who we are. Every dance we do with others teaches us about the love we want by showing us who we are. As we dance with others we are shown our attachment to certain perceptions, as well as ways of relating to others which (for better or worse) show us what we attracted. Successful interactions show us our heart's expression in our dances with others. The unfortunate and/or difficult relationships teach us what we need to learn about boundaries, expectations, and/or unhealthy desires.

In our interactions with people and things we gain understanding through both pleasurable and painful experiences. While some interactions make us want to retreat into our private world forever, never leaving our private echo chamber and house of mirrors created by our memories, life will forever call

85

us to new relationships because of our "urge to merge." The trick is not to let old difficult relationships cloud our view of what our new relationships could be.

All relationships show us what we do and do not like or admire, or perhaps what we need to learn to like or admire. In learning what to embrace and what to refuse, we learn what matters a lot, what matters a little, and what doesn't or shouldn't matter at all. Sometimes it's as simple as learning to tolerate relatively harmless dislikes so we can allow other people space to be themselves.

Others also go through this in their relationship to us. We usually don't have problems with what we both like; the rub is found in what one or both don't like, which is when small frictions become the grist for the mill of Soul. These are situations where we both learn the art of give and take. Our inner Lover must learn give and take in relationships and treat others as equals in the dance while maintaining autonomy and fair exchange.

This leads us to balanced loving friendships with those who share our deeper feelings and thoughts regardless of our disagreement about the minor details of everyday living. Small frictions should never lead to a violation of boundaries, free will, or our sense of loving God, Spirit, and each other. If we feel these are violated, then a coercion is attempting a seduction.

We owe it to ourselves to be treated with respect, love, affection, and friendliness. As we learn to embrace and demonstrate these qualities in our personality, we simultaneously learn to recognize these in others.

Navigating the Pleasure-Pain Duality

Because we choose to dance with others, we have all kinds of experiences. Of course, some are easy and some are difficult. While often these are determined by the fact that we don't control how others will act, each one can teach us something about our patterns of attraction. As we see what we don't want, we can choose to change the ones which aren't good for us.

We all like pleasurable experiences with others. However, there is no one we will ever be totally compatible with. All of us have a mix of similarities and differences with others. This is why knowing what attracted us to another helps us see why things develop as they do, and what parts we're playing in the dance. How we navigate the differences generates dynamic harmony or friction.

All of us bring attitudes and preexisting beliefs to every relationship. Every interaction shapes our attitude in countless ways, which then shapes our future interactions. However, like many other things in life, these change over time. Sometimes, for any reason or no reason, what was once pleasurable between two people becomes painful. It may or may not be personal, avoidable, or even the "fault" of one or the other. Life goes on, and we all grow in ways we may not have expected. Just because we've danced with a Being for a while, even years, doesn't mean we're necessarily supposed to dance with them indefinitely. Different seasons of life require different ways of living, different skills and realizations, and different people bring out different parts of us.

If we want good relationships, we must become aware of our preconceptions, since they determine if we're seeing things clearly. We must also become aware of our expectations and projections, which we'll talk about later. For now, know that many preconceptions and insecurities fall away like shadows at high noon when we realize we're with a spiritual Sister or Brother and know we can allow our true Self to come out. Our Beloved will always share a spiritual harmony with us. They may or may not express their spirituality as we do, but they will honor our way of communing with whatever "Higher Power" we believe in. These are the relationships where we find we have things in common we both enjoy, since they help us build emotional capital for the future.

The dance is endless since we'll always meet other people. As we grow, we'll learn everyone helps us to a deeper well-rounded understanding of who we are and what's right for us. Everyone we meet shows us who our ego thinks we are, and also what is yet to be found.

An Introduction to Seduction

When we first meet someone, unless we are at ease and operating from our higher awareness, we greet them with a manufactured image of who we want them to see. We want to look our best, offer them what we think they'll like, and hope that we find pleasing ways to be. While there's nothing wrong with trying to appear at our best to another, and it's always good to look and sound good when we first meet another, we always have to remember there's more to this person than we know. If we want happy and healthy relationships, we have to learn to spot certain behaviors so we aren't stuck in situations which drain us rather than empower us.

Here I'll offer that it's usually better not to adopt a mindset that normal interactions could be seductions. Relationships are pretty natural when no one's playing games or overthinking whether there's a seduction going on or not. I believe unless someone has shown themselves to be a seducer, it's better to give people the benefit of the doubt, because many offers of affection are not seductions. Learning to relax into the dance gives everyone space to breathe.

One of the biggest traps people fall into is because of our desire to be agreeable, we often find ourselves in situations where we feel like we're being coerced into agreements and behaviors which don't feel right to us. When we feel like we're being pulled somewhere which doesn't feel right, there's probably a seduction going on. That means we have to recognize what seductions are, so we are not pulled in by illusions, coercions, and potentially damaging attitudes and behaviors. Various types of seduction or coercion are always present in any unhealthy relationship. These can take many forms, but none will lead to healthy partnerships or personal happiness.

Why We Like What We Believe We Like

For better and/or for worse, we've all been seduced countless ways by the world we live in. Whether our parents letting us know through their approval or disapproval or what we did or didn't do, or our friends wanting us to keep up with the latest fashion, or agree to things we should not have agreed to, or other social manipulations designed to make us want something or someone, we've all experienced countless seductions. When younger I certainly wanted what I wanted, and was willing to play some pretty strange games to get what I thought I desired. It's not surprising many of these led to disastrous consequences!

Our subconscious mind is directly influenced by our emotions, and defaults to like what it likes and not like what it does not like, regardless of the sanity or lack thereof in those views. These "likes" are often seductions because the unconscious part of our personality always wants more of what it believes it "likes." We learned many of these from our family and friends when we were young, and until we get a grip on our desire nature, we'll want what we want whether our desires are healthy or not.

As a result of every experience helping us learn what others liked and disliked, we grew in what we liked and disliked. During our formative years, we were highly receptive to what brought us praise from our family and friends. We learned all kinds of habits to play for others' approval while being aware of what others didn't like. Everyone goes through this. It's natural to be open to what others offer us which feels good as we meet and part along the road of life.

Over time we learned that while some new ways of expression and interacting brought us what we wanted, other times we found that what we tried to take on was a bad fit and totally against our best interests. Those were the times when our desire mind got seduced by someone else's way of acting, feeling, or thinking, even though it really wasn't the smartest thing for us to do,. How and why does this happen?

It's very human to project our likes onto our world, and be alert to what others like. It begins when we are infants and children, searching for other' verbal and nonverbal cues, where we learn some things bring smiles and praise, while other behaviors, likes, and attitudes bring frowns and disapproval from family and friends. These are powerful cues that influence our choices well into adulthood until we come to a greater self-awareness and have the courage to step outside the expectations and rules of our past.

We Are Taught to Seduce and Be Seduced

Everyone wants to look good to others, since we are seduced by first impressions. I've found everyone shows off their "front porch and living room" in their "house of personality" to others when they first meet. Then you might even get to their "kitchen and bedroom" after a while. That's when you think you really know them. But we don't really know another until we get a good look at their "back yard," as well as their "attic and basement." That's because no one wants others to know what they're ashamed of, or problematic parts of their lives, until they feel safe exposing those things to another.

There is no sin or crime in being seduced. It's part of being human. We all want what we believe we want, and then get it, but then often have to deal with the law of unintended consequences. We also want things which we don't get, and then forget about them only to find at some point we have received what we wanted but not in the forms we thought or expected. As we grow our desires move on, which is why we need to reevaluate our assumptions from time to time, since what we want and need at 30 is not at all like what we wanted and needed at 20.

As we grow into spiritual maturity, we learn to be more conscious in our likes and dislikes and how these help us make our personality into the image of our Higher Self. As we evolve, we become more conscious in our choices leading us to ever-greater states of happiness, joy, and bliss. Then we no longer yield to seductions because we have embraced our "courtship" of our Higher Self, and are becoming a greater Love with each dance step we take.

So let's examine what seductions can look like, how they work, and how they're related to assumptions and projections. By understanding the differences between courtship and seduction, we can identify "symptoms of seduction" and behaviors which will leave us feeling wounded. As we learn to break our attraction to being seduced, we can know what healthy affection looks and feels like and claim our power to be true to our heart and our best interests.

The Difference Between Seduction and Courtship

Knowing the difference between "being courted" and "being seduced" helps us avoid being manipulated. Some forms of courtship may also involve seductions, but they must be harmless and aren't really worthy offerings from or to our Beloved. We are told by the venerable ancient wisdom of the I Ching there is a huge distinction between seduction and courtship shown by how we influence others and how they influence us. We are told any healthy interaction must stem from "reciprocity that stimulates joy," which implies a reciprocal joy will naturally arise from our interaction.

All mutual influences between people are because we are attracted to them and they to us. When we are courted, our Beloved shows us a natural consideration. There is a natural affinity between our heart and theirs, without coercions or manipulations.

Since "consideration" is a keyword for respectful sincere affection, we can infer that seduction involves a lack of consideration. If another is not respectful in their affections, then it's a seduction. This may be demonstrated by a lack of respect for appropriate boundaries, or not allowing us to express ourselves naturally, or them thinking there are parts of us they need to fix. As all of these show a lack of respect for who we are and our ability to know what's in our best interests, it's best to be cautious. A lack of respect indicates a person cannot be a good partner for us.

Signs and Signals of Seduction

Any time there is coercion, a push and pull that seems out of balance, or offers which disrupt your life with associated demands to explain why you aren't going along with them, it's a seduction. Remember that seductions may seem playful, but if you don't go along with them, there are overt or implied threats, whether of withholding of affection, gifts, or even emotional connectedness.

Think "I've done x, y, and z for you, and you don't seem to care." Or "Because I've done a, b, and c, you should be doing d, e or f." Though it seems like these are forms of bargaining, make sure you agreed to the bargain to begin with, otherwise it's a seduction. While reciprocity is very important for a relationship to stay in balance, sometimes one does things the other did not ask for and expects something in return for the "favor."

This is where self-reflection is very important. We have to make sure we haven't invited inappropriate responses through our own verbal and non-verbal cues, since these will lead to misunderstandings. However, when we are naturally ourselves and comfortable with who we are as individuals, we can be authentic without needing to be artificial. There is never a need for us to be anything other than who we are.

Beware of moods. Moods are seductions by the subconscious desire-mind. A good mood is when the subconscious desire-mind has been appeased, while a bad mood is the result of being denied what it wants. You can observe more moods, and moodiness, than usual when a seduction is going on.

These are the times when we must remain objectively detached and dispassionate so we aren't seduced by our own or someone else's desires.

Seductions often involve too much emotional baggage which comes up during the initial stages of getting to know each other. These interactions escalate much too quickly to be authentic. Other times, seductions involve the need for one to "save" another, or "be saved" from something by another. Seductions do not like a healthy autonomy, as seductions are driven by the seducer's power and control issues.

If our inner Lover is unhealthy, we are needy and hope someone will come along to end our feelings of inadequacy and fulfill our lives. If our inner Lover is healthy, we rarely attract destructive or clingy people who get attached and controlling, or those who quickly try to enmesh us in a heavy emotional entanglement or expect too much too quickly. Self-pity is a common way to seduce another into "helping" in ways that don't help. A healthy Lover allows each the space they need, and the time to allow the relationship to develop.

Seductions can feel very exciting, but as many of you already know, the wreckage isn't worth the price. You can spot seductions by noticing if there are demands or expectations requiring you to compromise something you believe in, or you feel coerced into something which doesn't feel right. It may feel like you're spinning your wheels, or something is one-sided and you know something's wrong, even if you can't put your finger on it. A major indicator of seduction is when you interact and wind up feeling fragmented or insecure about your life and experiences which helped you become who you are.

95

The Beloved would never shame you, or weaken you, or make you feel insecure. A true courtship never feels like a hustle. Courtships make us feel like it's the most exciting natural interaction we could have, whereas seductions always leave us feeling more fragmented.

Other indicators of seduction include power games which leave you feeling like something is out of balance or even a sense of increasing powerlessness, or when you struggle with ideas or feelings that aren't ordinarily there when you're happy. Beware of anyone trying to make you feel responsible for something you're not responsible for. While we always need to acknowledge our part in any circumstance, we cannot take responsibility for how another behaves.

If someone insists we agreed to something we didn't, or we're being blamed for not making something happen according to another's expectation when we never agreed to do that, it's a seduction. These are usually accompanied with some sort of offer from them, and even a statement about how much they've done for us. We just have to be clear if it's a cry for acknowledgement or a manipulation.

"Gaslighting" is a seduction tactic of those who are trying to get us not to believe what we know is true, or believe in something we know isn't true. Gaslighting may take form as someone trying to persuade us something we remember or experienced isn't true, and won't discuss facts except to dismiss ours. Often there is a misrepresentation, or a hidden agenda in a seduction. Lies and deceptions justified by one to the detriment of another is always a seduction,

Seductions are never harmless, since there is always some form of manipulation involved. Once we get beyond seducing and being seduced, we neither manipulate nor can be manipulated. As we cultivate a measure of detachment, dispassion, and discernment it allows us to generate whatever good we choose, for us, another, or our world. We get to live the life we want to live. No one has the right to try to impose their rules or assumptions on us.

No relationship can last where one is undermining the other, creating dependencies or self-doubt, or diminishing the sense of love we have for ourselves. When we feel these are happening, if we look below the surface we usually find at least one type of narcissistic behavior fueling the seduction being forced on us.

Narcissism is not Self-Love. It is vanity attached to a perception which exalts the ego, preventing any true feeling of love. That said, Self-love is not necessarily narcissism. We are allowed to love ourselves in countless healthy ways, and as each of us has the archetype of the Innocent in us, we all are learning to master lessons of acting with enlightened Self-interest. As we dance down the path of Life, we learn about both higher Love and lower desires. By knowing the difference between how these feel to us, we can see patterns, and by being conscious in replacing lesser desires, we stop being seduced into attachments and affections that leave us feeling badly.

Should You Marry If You're Not Sure They Are the "Right One?"

We often find ourselves with someone wondering if they're "the One." While it's natural to want to marry someone we believe we love with all our hearts, marriage shouldn't be a consideration until we have a secure friendship. That means actually getting to know someone through both good times and bad. We believe we know why we want to be with someone, but before we can trust them with our heart we must see their weaknesses as well as their strengths.

We must learn to beware of people who are childish, selfish, petty, angry, or vindictive. We can spot them through their bad attitude. Beware of those who show up who resemble people from your past who were negative or destructive. They are the manifestation of images you never let go of in your subconscious mind. Of course, sometimes we are already in a relationship with someone when we unexpectedly find them showing negative traits, some of which resemble the behavior of people we used to know, while others make it clear we didn't know something crucial about the other person. That's when we have to make a decision how to deal with, or get distance from, those negative traits. When people break up, it's usually because of the unexamined negatives and not what attracted them initially.

Beware of paternalistic attitudes. Your mate is your partner. Not your dad, not your mom, not your boss, nor yours to boss around. While every relationship requires us at times to "go along to get along," after a point the relationship either works or it doesn't. If the other person can't figure it out, or resists a plan to move it forward, then one fact is clear: it takes two to make a relationship, and either they're into moving forward or they're not. This is where we learn not to defer to external authority in our process of making autonomous choices in our dances with others. We're all learning to be whole and complete unto ourselves, as much as possible.

Many misunderstandings can be avoided by learning the areas of harmony and friction between our personality and another's so we can take differences into account about how we each deal with what is easy and what is difficult. Even these will change over time, so it's not like where we are compatible, or incompatible, are set in stone. We can be perfectly harmonious in one area at one time and not another. We can like the same things at one stage but not another. How each exercises their free will when confronted with major decisions related to changing patterns determines whether they'll make it as a couple over the long run.

I once heard it said that marriage is not for the weak, the jealous, the selfish, the lazy, or the insecure. Obviously, weakness and insecurity will bring down any relationship, since the center will give way quickly when difficulties arise. Selfishness is incompatible with the open sharing of selfless love which comes forth in a long term healthy marriage. When someone is lazy they cannot be a true equal with anyone else. This creates an imbalance in relations, since marriage, being ruled by Libra, is a contract between equals. Libra is the sign of equality, fairness, and justice. Where these are not present the relationship will eventually confront difficulties.

Certain questions must be asked before we give ourselves over to believing we could have a long term relationship with someone. Among these are: Are they violent? Do they lose their temper inappropriately? Are they selfish? Do they take responsibility for their behavior, or blame externals? Are they affectionate and respectful? Do they take care of their lives, or expect others to take care of them?

Beware of threats to leave if you cannot satisfy their demands. There may be feelings of guilt and/or regret from being unable or unwilling to give them what they want, but the only thing which matters is your ability to claim what's true for you and what's not. While it's very human to second guess many of our perceptions and decisions, just remember how bad it's already become if you're even in that situation to begin with. While breaking up is hard to do, by the time we're considering ending the relationship, it's probably long overdue!

I believe where there has been love, that must be the focus even if you're considering breaking up. I've also found that there's no way to "go back" to the way it was. Because we can only go forward, any relationship which needs renewing must focus on a shared future which will look different from the past. If it doesn't you can bet that at some point the unfinished problems from the past will again bring one or both to a point of crisis.

Jealousy

The "deadly sin" of jealousy is always a disaster and the ultimate deal-breaker for a marriage, or for any relationship. It's said to be a "deadly sin" for a reason. Like the other deadly sins, jealousy will kill anyone who embraces that path to self-destruction.

Jealousy is toxic, leads to very bad interactions, and is entirely the problem of the one who is jealous. No one can "make" another be jealous, or make a jealous person get over it. Either a person chooses to be jealous or not.

Of course it never bodes well for a current or future marriage if one or both flirt with other people or indulge in inappropriate or dysfunctional interpersonal behavior. Why would anyone want to encourage jealousy, even as a game? A heart divided can no more stand than a house divided.

Jealousy is driven by insecurity coupled with possessiveness, and cannot be blamed on any thing or person. Jealousy destroys trust, and it can never be "cured" by anyone or anything except the one who is jealous. Each of us has the power not to be jealous if we choose not to be jealous. No one gets over jealousy through either repression or acting it out.

Getting over jealousy usually manifests as a relief from a toxic personality trait that is not helpful in any way, shape, or form. It's like setting down a horrible burden which eats up a person from the inside, and will literally drive people crazy, to the point of suicide/homicide. Jealousy alone WILL break a marriage. Add violence and/or aggression, and it's a toxic disaster.

Where two hearts are committed without reservation, there can be no jealousy possible. Even to be accused of thinking of another is ridiculous, since hearts at peace with one another are not yearning for anyone else. That is the gift of maturity, since it allows trust to develop over time. While there may be uncertainty at the beginning about whether the relationship will develop into a long term love, as time goes by each should feel more comfortable and at peace in the love you share. Even if both have had horrible marriages or relationships in earlier times, where love is true there is no mistrust or suspicion in the mutual love and affection each has for the other.

It doesn't matter what's happened in a person's past. We are entirely responsible for our actions in the present. Simply because we or our beloved had to deal with betrayal from another in the past does not justify suspicion in the present.

Any healthy relationship will have all kinds of friends. Each will have their own friends, and the couple will have friends as well. In a healthy relationship each will have as many friends as suits them, since true friends rarely create tension in healthy relationships. While there may be feelings of concern due to rough patches and misunderstandings, there is no place for jealousy.

When A Chapter Must End

All relationships begin with a lot of hope, and over time either people become close friends or indifferent to each other in many small and large ways. This is a universal. All relationships change over time, and because we do not control anyone else's responses and can only manage our own, we can love with all our heart but cannot make another stay if they are determined to go, or their destiny forces them to go, even if they don't want to.

We all have known the pain of losing a loved one more than a few times. When we lose a loved one, it's natural to feel the pain of having to walk on into the unknown, whether we want to or not. As one who has known terrible tragedies affecting several long term relationships, people I loved with all my heart, I can truly say the only thing to focus on is how your ability to love as grown.

If we dare to love, we all go through certain universals. We begin in ignorance, with our desire mind and programmed images dominating our search. The pleasure/pain duality of human life leads us into things we think we want but don't turn out the way we think. Many times our first marriage was a mixture of two people not having a clue, teaching us what we do not need to tolerate any more. This is where forgiveness allows us to redeem many good things in our lives. I believe some relationships are of our karmic past, while others are karma we make in the moment. Many things in life have to be chalked up to "it seemed like a good idea at the time." And hopefully we learn what we love and where we don't ever need to go again.

When we leave old relationships behind, it's good to remember we ARE the love we seek, we have the power of opening to better attitudes and feelings which could bring us face to face with someone perfect for us, and our ideal partner is in our chart, so all we have to do is find the right "open mindedness" to shape our expectancy without encumbering things by fixed assumptions. This is why cultivating friendships helps us when we hit forks in the road, because we have a working partnership with an ability to discuss and explore things. We begin all relationships with a maximum of hope and potential, but over time we actualize what we can and are left with either a sense of adventure as we dance down the road with our partner, or we wind up wondering "what's next?" or "where's this going?"

There is wisdom in not wasting time and energy on something beyond our control. Again, we do not control anyone else's responses. The best we can do is respond wisely and respectfully toward them. Many times we wish we could continue as friends, but each has their own understanding of what that means, and with the memories of all which cannot be "unheard," sometimes hoping for a friendship is unrealistic. When both have been heavily invested in the relationship, it's natural to want to believe there's still something there. While friendships after breakups are rare, they do occasionally happen, but I've seen they're all based in a healthy respect for each other's autonomy, knowing it won't be the same as it was.

We always love those we love; however, because this world is impermanent, we often find ourselves loving someone with all our heart, but they are no longer there for whatever reason. As we cannot live in an indefinite and unfulfilling relationship, if another is choosing not to relate to us in healthy ways, regardless of how noble our intention, when a chapter ends we ultimately must walk on, since that's what evolution is about.

These are times when we must detach from the past so we don't allow the thief of our past to steal our present. We can never "go back." We can never revive any relationship of the past, because we can only move forward to new ones, sometimes with people we used to know in a different way, and sometimes with completely new people.

Each relationship holds a promise, yet will never be entirely as we hope; however, it could better than we can imagine, in that each opportunity we take to grow in our love paves the way to more loving relationships in the future. I learned a long time ago that if we cannot "make a happy life" with one, there is surely another with whom we could "make a happy life." That's why a positive attitude about our life and love guarantees us better relationships in the future, since all of us want a happy life with someone who we positively love and who positively loves us.

This touches the heart of the matter of being fully human, eternally learning to navigate life while also learning to feel all there is to feel so we can bring forth "the better angels of our nature." While endings can be painful, we do not need to suffer, since we are as surrounded by Life, Light, and Love as a fish by water. We are always within a loving web of Light/Life if we learn to see it, feel it, embrace it, and swim in that vast ocean of loving light. It's all a matter of finding the right point of view.

All of humanity is a unity and we all share the effects of each other's joys and sorrows whether we realize it or not. We all feel what is happening in the collective field. We just have to be clear about what we're picking up from the field which is distinct from our experience of that confusion, fear, and all the other collective energies. Then we can view those feelings as in the atmosphere, but not take them personally.

Even when things are difficult, there is a value because with difficulty comes striving, and with striving comes unimagined possibilities. As we become clearer about what love is and is not, we learn much about what love ought to be, and the joys and sacrifices of commitment, as well as how important independence and stable foundations are. As we grow in awareness, we will of course feel all there is to feel. Our task is to use every difficulty to cast off our fears, our vanities, our obsolete desires, and any need we may have to replicate sensations which we no longer need to experience. As we practice forgiving and release our hurt feelings and any bitterness or need to cling to fantasies, we find we are feeling stronger in our autonomy.

The Value of Autonomy

All healthy individuals need time and space to contemplate what they need to in solitude, as well as time and space to interact with loved ones and friends. All Beings feel the need for "freedom" and connectedness. What better way to demonstrate loyalty and affection than to be with someone wholeheartedly while still claiming the power, love, and wisdom of our autonomy?

Regardless of outside pressures, we either choose to be autonomous in our relationships or we don't. We choose to continue to learn and grow or we don't. Either we trust each other or we don't. Either we respect each other enough to know each must find what is best for them or we don't. A true friend encourages our autonomy, with a natural trust and respect. So will our Beloved.

Without love, trust, respect, and spontaneous affection there can be no lasting partnership. Either we offer our hearts to each other without controlling demands, or we put doubt and discontent over the blessing of a contented heart.

In my experience, even though a couple is severely tested through difficult periods, whether in terms of outside seductions or even worse things, they can come through everything more dedicated, more in love, and more absolutely clear about the love they have for each other. No external thing can introduce doubt in a relationship where both hearts are secure.

When confronting a lifelong commitment like marriage, many feel fear to some degree or another. Uncertainty is more common than most would like to admit. Our Beloved will never try to provoke or instill fear in us. The last thing anyone should feel is that their Beloved is afraid of them, or they feel fear of their Beloved. A true partner is one who can be the other's comfort, strength, support, defender, (and sometimes challenger), always from a loving and respectful approach.

Even if one is afraid of something for whatever reasons, a true friend and partner would never want us to continue fearing anything. While most of us must get over fearing whatever we've learned to fear, we must never give our Beloved anything to fear. A marriage built on the fear of how another could behave cannot last.

When two beings suited for each other are ready, nothing can strain the bonds of love they share. Though the way be thorny, rough, difficult, perilous or uncertain, where there is true love there is an eternal bond.

Ultimately, any two people are friends or they are not. It takes two to make and keep a friendship. Friendship never wavers in its love, and where there is no friendship, there can be no lasting relationship, regardless of vows and rituals. We must cultivate the friendship first, and let the romance follow. That gives us the strength of a loving friendship to rely on even when the rest of it gets strange or outer circumstances become difficult. As we cultivate the friendship, our past, any dysfunctional elements of personality, as well as personal baggage in our lives and theirs are all revealed. Then we see if we are suited for each other.

While we may have a strong attraction to someone, even be with them awhile, it doesn't mean they are the "perfect" person who could fulfill our hopes and dreams. As I pointed out in "The Square of Right Relations," our ideal mate is one who is good to and for us, and we will be good to and for them, a person who will bring out our strengths and call us to become a better person.

As We Embrace A Greater Love, We Become A Greater Love

As we become more authentically our Higher Self, we will naturally express our love and wisdom in our actions, feelings, and thoughts. As we live the love and wisdom of our Higher Self, we find it's directly related to our ability to love God, our Truth of Being, and our community of loving Souls. When we're oriented toward our higher Love, we cannot be seduced by anything which is not loving or wise.

As we become more loving, wise, and intelligent in our relationships, our magnetism attracts others who are also these in their own ways. Despite the occasional friction which is inevitable between two people, the more we treat ourselves with respect, love, affection, and friendliness, even in our human fallibility, the easier it gets to offer them to others on a consistent basis. It really is true that as we learn to love and respect ourselves, we can learn to show love, respect, and affection to others. Over time we become more natural in our heart's expression, leading us to all kinds of interactions. While there's always more to learn, by choosing to be honest with ourselves and others, we naturally spot seductions, since they are dishonest.

When we have a healthy Lover archetype, we are free to be ourselves, and welcome others to be themselves. We can enjoy the relationship freed from the snares of ego, since we understand healthy and reasonable boundaries and can express a greater Love, both personal and impersonal.

As we change old patterns that attracted the lesser, we begin to live a different way of relating to ourselves, others, our world and experiences, as well as life itself. Then we are the Love we once sought, and can BE that greater Love in our world. As we live our higher Love, we attract truly loving friends and companions so all may find what they need to nourish and strengthen their Soul connections.

To Live Is To Be In Relationships

Ultimately, the Lover archetype teaches us about the dance of courtship between our lower self and the Higher Self, and we play out this dance through relationships which mirror both of these parts of our inner nature. As we embrace the courtship of the Higher Self we transcend our suffering and can dance with others, seeing all our past and present relationships as opportunities to know what helps our love grow.

Please take some time to review how throughout your life others have offered you healthy affection, and how you offered it to them as well. Consider all you have liked and loved, and everyone and everything that inspired you to give and receive your tender affections and a higher Love. These were the times you were the Lover, doing a timeless dance with a form of the Beloved showing you the infinite ways Love can reappear in your life. We have the power to re-shape who we attract in the future, but we must be clear and specific so we attract more perfect relationships in the right way and time.

When we're clear, we have a very powerful "attractive focus" which operates on many levels. Here I'll offer you something I've recommended to countless clients and friends, having seen it work over the years. It is a way to get your "attractive focus" centered on the best you can imagine. The first step is to do a thorough self-evaluation, and make three lists.

The first list is all the good traits you've ever known throughout your life in the gender you wish to attract. The second list are all the traits you do not want in your next partner. The third list are the traits you haven't experienced yet but you'll like to see in a mate. That's your "stretch list." Then study those lists. Contemplate what you're asking for.

Make sure that your list of good traits couldn't lead to a form of a bad trait. Wanting a hard worker is good, but not a workaholic. Attracting someone who is detached and dispassionate is good, but they also need to be caring and concerned at the same time, if only in their own way. You will find that you really want certain core traits which will affect what you add or remove from your lists. These changes will show your heart's desire and what you believe will fulfill you. We all can attract what is good for us.

Remember that the higher a Being you are, the higher your consciousness in welcoming the one who could be your greatest love and greatest adventure. Know that they may not look like anyone in your past, but they will promise all the good that could be. All we need to do is get out of our own way, stop "desiring" and "fearing" and believing "it's going to be this or that way," and go to the source of our innermost being, asking our heart for the wisdom to recognize our Beloved.

This always involves letting go of a lot of expectations, since we never know where we might have to be or go to meet the Beloved. Until the Beloved appears, never play games, never be seduced, and never settle for anything less than the best. Our goal is to dance with the Beloved. Ask, be patient, and we always attract exactly what we need to grow in our love and wisdom.

CHAPTER SIX

ASTROLOGICAL FACTORS
IN COMPATIBILITY

Synastry, Compatibility, Composite, and Marriage Charts

Astrology shows us how any two people are both compatible and challenging. (Yes, there's always both harmony and friction in any chart comparison.) There are two main techniques to evaluate harmony and friction between two charts. One technique is called Synastry, which is when we look at how the planets are placed in each other's chart by sign and aspect. The other involves the Composite chart, which shows how two or more charts blend together. The personal chart is the "I." The composite chart is the "We." The composite chart is most commonly found by looking at the midpoints between the planetary positions in the two charts.

Briefly, synastry is how one chart influences another and the composite chart shows the sum of the two beings which creates a third entity. While synastry gives us a tremendous amount of information of how 2 charts are compatible, comparing each chart to a composite chart gives an added dimension of interactivity. This chapter will offer insights about key factors in each of these techniques.

A third important factor in seeing how a relationship will develop involves a chart for the time two people meet. A chart drawn for the time, date, and place when two people first meet always gives us an interesting snapshot of what is going on in each life, and what will follow. That point in time initiates the relationship and allows us to see the future shifts and changes for each party in the relationship and when they will happen. As an aside, this technique is good for showing us how any relationship will develop, whether we are looking at a romantic relationship, or business relationship, or friendship. Each of these chart reading techniques requires different astrological skills than simply looking at natal charts. Anyone considering a long term commitment should have a thorough compatibility session, examining synastry, the composite strengths and challenges, and factors indicated in the time for when they met.

Besides the overall compatibility between two charts, if two people are considering a marriage, it's extremely important to find the best time to marry. The marriage chart, marking the beginning of the formal marriage contract, gives us a sense of how the marriage will develop, and when the challenging times will happen. The time when we commence the ceremony culminating in each saying "I do" shows us the cosmic patterns as we launch one of the most important journeys of our lives.

Because a marriage is a contract, the same principles for the timing on signing a contract are in play when finding the right day and time to marry. During a year, there are always several times which are perfect for a couple to ensure the best possible journey and outcome of the union. Because finding a good time to marry requires a different approach than looking at natal charts, it's important for the astrologer to have specific expertise in that particular field.

I use both synastry and the composite chart when I do comprehensive compatibilities. Because both of these techniques involve the natal charts of the people thinking about becoming a committed couple, another crucial factor in beginning a relationship involves looking at the natal charts of each to see if their planets and houses indicate it's a natural time for that. This is also useful to see when we might meet someone who could be our perfect partner. This involves looking at the appropriate houses and their rulers, since different marriages are ruled by different houses, which I'll explain in the section on marriage charts.

Synastry

A synastry analysis between two charts shows us where person A's planets fall in the chart of person B, and vice versa. Chart A on B shows how A will impact B. Chart B on A shows how B will impact A. This gives us specific information about how each impacts different areas in the other's life, and allows us to see how each person's planetary personality traits relates to the other by signs and aspect. We can also see how these relate as house rulers in each other's charts, revealing areas of harmony, friction, and growth.

Synastry shows us many intricacies between people, and where common ground can be found. However, because each grows and evolves (as shown by how and when the planets progress), our personality traits change over time and we wind up attracted to different things and people. As a result of our choices and changes, we find ourselves liking or not liking what has been, and seek new people and experiences.

In a thorough synastry comparison, we evaluate six things:

1. The sign qualities between the same planets in the two charts. Different signs have different element and mode qualities. Fire signs have a different relationship with Water signs than with Air signs; Cardinal signs have a different relationship with Fixed signs than Mutable signs. This gives us important clues about the similarities and differences in how each expresses those parts of their personality.

2. The aspects between the same planets in two charts. This indicates where each planet stands in the "phase relationship" which those aspects indicate. Obviously a harmonious sextile or trine between two Suns or Moons is favorable, but I've also seen how two people with Mars in square help to serve as a check and balance on each other's Mars function. A square between two Venuses is not a deal breaker in a relationship as long as each honors the other's ways of liking and appreciating things.

3. The aspects between all of person A's planets and all of person B's planets. This lets us know (for example) how A's light (Sun) relates to B's habits (Moon), or A's fears (Saturn) relate to B's way of processing and communicating information (Mercury.) If A's Mercury is square B's Mars, how A expresses their ideas may at times aggravate B, but this contact could just as easily lead to A's ideas being spurs for B to act, or B's initiatives help A frame things differently in terms of possibilities to act.

4. How A's planets fit into B's houses and how B's planets fit into A's houses. This level of analysis

also gives us insights about how A's planets ruling B's houses influence B's way of dealing with those houses, and how B's planets ruling A's houses influence A's way of dealing with those life areas.

5. How A's progressions relate to B's natal and progressed positions and how B's progressions influence A's natal and progressed tendencies.

6. Because the signs span the personal, interpersonal, and transpersonal phases of expression, and the houses show us these phases of activity in all the areas of our lives, by seeing how the signs are placed in each chart relative to the Ascendant, we can know each person's emphasis in their relationship.

As giving examples of all of the above would become a book in itself, we'll stop at this point and take a brief look at how our spiritual planets play a big part in how synastry works to help us transform our lives and relationships to their highest spiritual potential.

How Do Our Spiritual Planets Affect Others?

The art of synastry shows us how our planets affect others and vice-versa. While our seven visible planets affect other people's charts in countless way, we also have a transcendent influence on others, and they on us, often without any conscious intention on our part.

As we discussed earlier in this book, any time someone's Uranus, Neptune, or Pluto conjuncts planets in our chart, or our spiritual planets conjunct one or more of theirs, major transformational energies are set into motion by the contact, and will be a predominant energy in the relationship. Because these planets represent broad transpersonal influences, symbolizing generations and subgenerations, they are beyond ego. Because spiritual transformational forces are "nothing personal," these contacts often are misunderstood, especially if one or both do not have some form of spiritual practice.

Any time our outer invisible planets contact the personal planets in the chart of another person, they and we are impacted in ways that are beyond ego controls. Depending on the level of awareness, some get unnerved, some get threatened, some move forward despite the uncertainty of dancing into the unknown transformational energies we're releasing within them, and some enthusiastically embrace the Mystery of our dance together. When we stimulate another's spiritual inclinations or they stimulate ours, life changing transpersonal forces are set into motion.

The placement of our Uranus shows our uniqueness, and awakens others' uniqueness when our Uranus conjuncts one of their personality planets. Of course, they also awaken us in some way, depending on the planetary contact and how open they and we are to Uranus' influence of awakening, revolutionizing, and individuation.

Neptune shows our openness to collective consciousness on vast levels. As we embrace the spiritual expression of Neptune, we become more emotionally aware, more empathic, and more able to identify vast collective feeling states. As we grow into that energy it becomes a stronger force within us. When our Neptune conjuncts a personal planet in another's chart, we become that collective gateway, or they become that gateway for us. We may inspire them, we may turn them on to collective consciousness, we may confuse, mystify, or enchant them, or we may help them know what feelings are theirs and which are just in the collective atmosphere.

Because we are not separate from our planetary expressions, all the planets symbolize parts of ourselves as they exist simultaneously. We have a spiritual component and a worldly component, and our lives are a journey of discovering we are a Soul/Spirit which loves and learns from what awakens via Uranus, what unifies us via Neptune, and what purifies us via Pluto. As we get our body, feelings, and mind integrated, we can more easily express our Higher Self and become the vehicles through whom Uranus, Neptune, or Pluto (or a combination of them, since they always work together to a single Divine purpose) express in our world.

Being a Conscious Awakener

Having discussed Uranus and Neptune, let's turn to Pluto. We all have Pluto somewhere, and those contacts make for some VERY intense people and interactions. Pluto is intense, "beyond ego controls," and distributes the seeds of the future. Pluto is present when people are stuck in their private hell, as it is "the Lord of the Underworld" in each of us. Pluto contacts challenge us not to be frightened of our need for purification, elimination, and/or regeneration. A Pluto contact between two people will help one or both get to the hidden core of things to sprout them or kill them out, always with an element of extreme intensity.

Pluto can be a major factor in relationships since it, along with Neptune, indicate generational and subgenerational energies which affect hundreds of millions. An example of this is everyone with late Cancer or Leo rising has the entire Pluto in Leo generation's Pluto near or in their first house. While a transpersonal planet (Uranus, Neptune, Pluto, TransPluto) will have its influence, it doesn't qualify as a specifier of individual partners, since these planets are "nothing personal." Otherwise we'd be attracted to hundreds of millions with that position, which is clearly not the case in the real world.

The outer "invisibles" symbolize divine force, the eternal triad of "God" with the added dimension of a vaster redemptive force of Divine Mother symbolized by TransPluto. While these may affect us personally in life changing ways, these divine manifestations aren't really personal in the same sense as the "Seven Sacred" visible planets are. Of course, when one or more of our partner's transpersonal planets occupies an important placement in our chart, they bring that divine energy into our lives in their own ways, just as we do theirs.

Because Pluto strips us down to the core, people with Pluto contacts go through intense purifications. Uranus contacts send us out over the precipice while Neptune dissolves us to the point of wondering if we'll get lost at sea. Transpersonal divine contacts offer us and others the transformations of a lifetime so we can become the beauty of divine expression in our own unique, collective, and authentic style.

However, we must keep in mind that because they're invisible planets, they often are not "seen" by those who are influenced, unless they have awakened their "spiritual sight." Because outer spiritual planet contacts can be misunderstood, they frequently trigger a spiritual crisis in another. These are times when we need to have healthy Saturn responses, since spiritual crises often have an element of fear, and fear is ruled by Saturn.

If one of our spiritual planets makes a contact with a planet in another's chart, then we must use Saturn's wisdom, maturity, and patience to understand healthy limits and boundaries needed in that interaction. Especially if we find ourselves dancing with someone who hasn't learned healthy responses to challenges, we have to embody Saturn's virtues. When one is triggering a spiritual transformation in another, it always involves forms of individualization, relatedness, and their seed power of eternal renewal. While the reactions can be extreme, if we're help mates or Soul Mates we can open them to greater possibilities of a more genuine and healthy self-expression, and in doing so, assist the transformational process.

Whether we're dealing with Uranus, Neptune, or Pluto, the impact between these in charts is fairly intense, and sets forces into motion which change both of us forever as a result of having to "walk between worlds." We all occasionally serve as vehicles to a vaster understanding of things unknown to others. The more we live our Higher Self, the more likely this is to occur.

Regardless of planetary contacts, each must learn to choose what in their hearts they know is right for them. That's why as we dance with others through life we cannot take it personally if another just doesn't get it. All we can do is take responsibility for learning to love the best we are able, and allow others the space to grow at their own pace.

Now let's turn to the Composite chart and how it dovetails with synastry.

Composite Charts

The composite chart is a unique chart of the blending of our energies with another, and is derived from the midpoints of the same planets and angles between two charts. Those midpoint placements indicate the "middle ground" where our planetary energies meet and merge with another's planetary energies. The composite overlay on each chart shows how the interactive being impacts each individual.

Many times individual charts may also have significant points or planets in the composite chart, and as a result one person may be more the composite Moon, whereas the other may be more the composite Jupiter or whatever other planets synch with the points in the individual charts. Even the individual progressions can come out as composite positions, which show more a passing connection than a permanent one.

One example of finding the "middle ground" between two planets would be if one has a Sun in Aquarius and the other has a Sun in Gemini the composite Sun will be in Aries, the sign equidistant between Aquarius and Gemini. In another example, if one person's Moon is in Sagittarius and the other Moon is in Aquarius, the composite Moon is in Capricorn, the sign in between Sagittarius and Aquarius.

Composite positions are important because they're a product of the angle between the two planets, the "harmonic point" midway between the two. While usually the composite chart gives us planets equidistant from the same planets in the chart of person A and person B, sometimes Mercury or Venus can wind up on the opposite side of the chart from the Sun, which in regular astrology is impossible, since these two planets are always near the Sun. When this happens, it's better to toss out the position calculated by the software and find the midpoint of the other angle between the planets, which will always be within a sign or two of the Sun.

While the angle between any two planets is important in and of itself, sometimes it takes on an added importance if the midpoint also yields important aspects to the two planets. For example, if one has Jupiter at 26 Pisces and one has Jupiter at 18 Gemini, then there are 82 degrees between them, which is a fairly powerful spiritual aspect called the binovile. That puts the composite Jupiter at 41 degrees distance between the two natal Jupiters, generating a different spiritual angle (the novile) between each and the midpoint. In this example the composite Jupiter is at the 7th degree of Taurus. That means any transit of that midpoint creates a multi-point "spiritual resonant field" impacting other planets in each chart.

There are several other methods for calculating midpoints (using time, for example), but that's beyond the scope of this section. For all practical purposes, the longitudinal point midway between any two planets will always yield valuable information about the "third being" who exists in a place equally accessible to each of you.

In another example, if one has a Venus at 14 Taurus and the other has Venus at 26 Cancer, there are 72 degrees between them. This is an angle called the quintile which promises specialization and unique gifts, and generates a midpoint at 20 Gemini. This midpoint is 36 degrees from each Venus, and this angle (the decile, or semi-quintile) is also one of partly developed specialization and unique gifts. So each Venus will have a "specializing" factor come up when 21 Gemini is transited. For the person with Venus at 14 Taurus, it will always involve a "waxing" or emergent energy, because Gemini can only make waxing aspects to Taurus. For the person with Venus at 26 Cancer, it will always involve a "waning" or completing energy in specialized circumstances, because Gemini can only make waning aspects to Cancer.

All our planets make midpoints with all our other planets, so we and any potential partners already have several in play before we meet. We then set more into motion when we decide to attempt to create a relationship. Add to this the various aspects made to our other planets not involved in creating the midpoint, and you can see there are many things going on simultaneously when looking at a composite chart! Obviously, midpoints have a resonance all their own, and there is an entire field of study devoted to how all midpoints blend two or more energies, and are triggered by various transits and other astrological timing factors.

Marriage Charts

As noted earlier, the Marriage chart, done for the time of initiating the marriage ceremony, is a crucial roadmap in a marriage. When we say "I do," we begin the adventure and give new momentum and energy in our relationship. Here we encounter the question of whether to do the chart for the commencement of the ceremony or the moment vows are exchanged. I have always set the chart for the time it begins, since in that chart we should see the outcome leading to "I do."

The Marriage chart should be seen in the same light as the timing on launching a business, starting a project, or signing legal papers. A successful relationship will always involve a combination of resources, tools, and skills, as well as the best time for beginning a partnership, project, or new initiative.

The branch of astrology dealing with launching events, marriages, signing contracts, planning travel and medical procedures and other actions is called Electional (or Inceptional) Astrology, and is an art in itself. Each moment has its special qualities and challenges, and it's always good to launch our boats on a favorable tide. That said, it is equally important to remember that it is impossible to counteract "real world" conditions, even if these can be seen in a person's chart as well as the chart for when two people meet.

A marriage chart is actually an Inceptional chart, in that a marriage is the inception of the contract of partnership. The casting of marriage charts is a specialized branch of Astrology showing the past, present, and future of the individuals, as well as the composite unit. A marriage chart must be a favorable time in itself, while also being favorable in the chart of the two who are marrying. A marriage chart begins a voyage and shows the factors affecting the voyage, as well as crucial junctions where free will and destiny will intersect.

125

Important Factors in Marriage charts

In finding a good marriage chart, it is most important to make sure certain chart rulers are in harmony with other chart rulers, especially houses related to marriage, home, and other life areas important to the couple getting married. Different ages bring different priorities. For example, while young people often want a chart favorable for having and raising children, that will not be as important to an older couple who are not going to have children. People who want to live in one place for the rest of their lives probably shouldn't marry with the Moon in Gemini, Virgo, Sagittarius or Pisces, since these are all "mutable signs" and dualistic in nature. If the Moon rules the home and it's in a dual sign, it often produces multiple homes, or multiple bases of operation.

Once we find some potential marriage dates, then we have to find which of those dates are in harmony with the specific house rulers and other major players in each individual chart. This is where general astrological knowledge may or may not be helpful. We cannot assume a given position or angle is good in and of itself, since any astrological position could have both positive and negative expressions.

That's why there is no universally good date where there will be no friction in the marriage. Every chart has its challenges. If obsolete ways were not challenged in a marriage, we'd never grow. We cannot expect things to stay harmonious and rosy in a marriage at all times; this would be contrary to human nature. We grow together by the trials we meet, as long as we are open to becoming "we" rather than "me." A good marriage chart can help each come to move toward the best for each and both, but only if both are willing to cooperate in the journey. One sided relationships never work in the long run. Only those that allow healthy bonding and healthy room to grow will succeed.

I've also found after doing countless marriage charts, a curious thing happens. Once the date is set, each of the pair begins to grow and evolve into what the chart indicates for the marriage. So for example, if a marriage chart features Sun in Leo and Moon in Sagittarius, each will begin to grow into that Fire trine relationship. Everything in a marriage chart calls each to become the best expression of those planetary factors.

Always pay attention to the position of the Moon and ruler of the Moon, as these factors indicate the "personality" of the marriage and the day to day feeling atmosphere of the marriage journey. As the Moon generally rules the home, if the marriage begins with Moon in fixed Taurus it will be a much different experience than if the Moon is in mutable Gemini!

I've found the ideal marriage dates always have strong contacts with the charts of the couple. Which marriage planets contact which natal planets in each person's chart are good markers for describing the role each will play in the marriage. Again, this is where the factor of the planets' dispositors (rulers) make a huge difference, since getting married with a Moon in Sagittarius will have a much different quality if Jupiter, ruler of the Moon, is in Pisces rather than Aries.

This is why each marriage chart must be carefully crafted, taking into account many different factors. If the Moon is in a water sign, the couple may wind up living near water; it is easy to see how if one or both don't like watery environments, the marriage should not have the Moon in the water signs of Cancer, Scorpio, or Pisces. If the couple wants to do traveling, and maybe even have a home in two or more places, then as noted earlier the Moon in Gemini, Virgo, Sagittarius or Pisces will work better than if the Moon is in fixed Taurus, Leo, Scorpio, or Aquarius!

Obviously there are many days in a year which indicate the possibility of a long and happy marriage. However, an important factor in a marriage chart is the time of day, since that determines the signs on the houses and therefore affects the rulers of those houses. This is a consideration if you don't want to explain why the wedding ceremony had to begin at 7:28 am or maybe 8:34 pm on the marriage day! Most days even an hour makes a difference due to sign and house rulership changes, as what is good at a certain time may not be good if begun an hour earlier or later. This is also why many choose a civil ceremony at the best time and day, and then have another ceremony and reception later on when it's more convenient for people to attend.

The 7th House

The 7th house is the house of marriage and all equal partnerships. While it has others associations beyond what are covered here, this section will focus on the many things it reveals about our mate, which sets the foundation for what you will read about some of each sign's mate qualities.

By understanding the qualities of our 7th house signs and planets, we'll get clear about the qualities of our natural mate. The sign on our 7th house cusp is very important in showing the qualities of our mate. So are any planets we have there. Here I want to dispel a superstition. If the 7th house has no planet in it, it doesn't mean that person won't marry or potentially find their perfect partner! This is also true in synastry. We don't necessarily need to have 7th house placements to be perfect partners.

The lack of a planet in the 7th house has nothing to do with whether our partnerships are vibrant, healthy, or viable. That's entirely up to us, whether we have the Moon or Jupiter or Saturn or Pluto in the 7th, or no planets at all. It's the same for frictional contacts between our 7th house ruler and someone else's 7th house ruler.

An empty 7th puts the emphasis on the ruler of the sign on the 7th house cusp, which in turn is given texture by the ruler of the planet ruling the 7th. There is a lot to be known by looking at the planet ruling the 7th, both by sign, decan, house position, and aspects. There is even more to be learned from looking at that planet's ruler. Even with an unoccupied 7th house, we can have varied and profound healthy experiences with others which lead us to ever-more ideal relationships.

If there is a planet in the 7th house, everyone who is our equal will in some way embody some quality of that planet. Our perfect mate will be an embodiment of the best of those planetary traits. They can come out in countless ways, whether by planet emphasis, sign emphasis, or dispositor emphasis. If there are one or more planets in the 7th, naturally there will be similarities in our many life partners which seem to correspond to those planets. However, while some qualities will be similar, it's also true that we meet each one under completely different conditions since there is no way that two circumstances are ever completely the same.

All planetary contacts between charts can manifest as a force for good if we choose. Saturn can be a drag on our line, or a path to authorship of our life. Jupiter can bring blessings or extravagant crashes. Even though a Uranus, Neptune, and Pluto contact between charts can bring upheaval, chaos, or even a sense of the unreality of an experience, they also bring us face to face with our Higher Self, which is always a good thing!

Different Relationships are Ruled by Different Houses

In finding a good marriage chart, here are a few pointers to consider. First, make sure that the natal chart rulers of the two people getting married are harmoniously aspecting each other, and if possible, the mutual rulers of each person's marriage house (7th house). Favorable Sun, Moon, and Venus contacts usually assure a basic level of harmony, attraction, and mutual affection. Of course, Saturn will be prominent in any healthy long term relationship, since it rules the qualities of maturity, healthy boundaries, and both a sense of contentment and a good attitude about the responsibilities which come with any partnership.

However, here we run into some distinctions. A partnership not formalized by a marriage or other contract is technically not a 7th house relationship. Love affairs are ruled by the 5th house, not the 7th. If there is no formal legal contract between two people, no matter how long they've been together, their relationship is shown by their 5th house and not their

7th. Again, contracts are governed by the 7th house, and marriage is a contract, both written and verbal.

While "marriage" in general is always ruled by the 7th house, subsequent marriages are shown by different houses. These days, more people are marrying more times in a life than ever before in human history. So what do we look for if someone has been married before?

The first marriage is ruled by the 7th house, as are all partnership circumstances throughout the life. The second marriage is ruled by the 9th house, the third marriage by the 11th house, and so on. Of course, 7th house factors must still be taken into consideration, but with an eye to the specific house governing the specific marriage. When looking at a second marriage, I have found that it always involves the quality of planets in the 9th, the sign on the 9th, the ruler of the 9th, and other factors that are equally as important as the basic 7th house indicators. It's like the 7th house shows our basic inclination, but the 9th house shows how we evolved in our view since the first marriage.

This is a crucial factor for those who want a good wedding date. In planning a second wedding, then that person's marriage significator is the ruler of their 9th house and any planets in that house, and the 7th becomes more of a secondary general influence. However, if they are marrying someone who hasn't been married before, then the previously unmarried person has the 7th house as the governing influence in their view of marriage.

I'll close this section by reiterating that after many years of finding the "best marriage day" for countless couples, there is never a time when one or more difficult aspects aren't happening. However, despite difficult aspects, we can still create an ideal marriage if the relationship is founded on affection, respect and heart-centered Love.

Our ability to be loving, wise, and intelligent is superior to any external condition or influence we confront in relationships. We always have the power to choose to express our Higher Self in positive ways despite our challenges. We may not be able to control some events. We may not be able to control the responses of others. But we can always choose to see and live the Higher Way which is right for us.

Astrology Can Help Relationship Problems

Many of life's problems can be solved if we find the right approach. Besides our unresolved personal issues, all too often worldly pressures push our personal buttons in ways which impact our relationships. Many times, due to being under a lot of stress, some try to relieve it by being unkind to others, including their loved ones. Obviously this is not a satisfactory way to maintain and preserve healthy intimate relationships, as being unkind creates more problems and hard feelings.

This is where planetary attractions do not override "real world" circumstances. If two people are not loving, kind, friendly, respectful, and affectionate toward each other, at some point the lack of these will be a deal breaker. It doesn't matter if their Venus conjuncts your Sun, or their Jupiter is on your Moon. As I offered earlier, if A is striving for something different than B, eventually it will end. And, as I also offered earlier, the only relationships which last are those which are based in friendship, autonomy, respect, and harmlessness. As we learn to live these qualities the best we're able, even when we have an occasional conflict, we still can work through a lot of life's rough patches.

We all have a personality with its quirks, and none of us were raised by saints or sages. While our lessons can be seen in our synastry contacts, we are the ones who decide whether our planets express in healthy or unhealthy ways. And it's a fact of life that we don't control others' behavior since no one gets to violate another's free will. Ultimately, we cannot blame a planet in a house for our responses since we choose how we will express all our planetary energies. We are not limited by our planets! We are the determiners of our fate, "the dispenser of glory or gloom unto ourselves" in every way, as we are told in "The Three Truths" from the venerable Light On The Path.

Difficult feelings must be dealt with in productive ways if we don't want our relationships to crash. Loving-kindness and a willingness to be reasonable are essential if we are to meet another on common ground. In decreasing hostility while acting with integrity and knowing what we stand for, we allow our higher spiritual power to express itself. As we tap into that power, we transcend all the temporary problems caused by attachments, aversions, illusions, and habits of acting, thinking, and feeling which perpetuate conflict.

In dealing with problems, we need a proactive grounded optimism so we're always open to the love we share. Indifference or disrespect both create problems since it takes two to make a healthy relationship. If one party does not want to make a positive effort, then we may simply have to walk away, if only for a while. This is where we must remember if we can't make it better, then don't make it worse.

Because we cannot "unsay" something, it's better to hold back and be silent before we damage a relationship by thoughtless words. Of course, for the sake of the relationship, both must make an honest effort to deal with their pressures in healthy ways since not discussing problems won't help us understand what's happening and how to deal with it.

In a previous chapter I offered that every part of the life is governed by an astrological sign and each sign is in conflict with three other signs, as well as in harmony with at least four others. The signs give us the key to the causes of disputes as well as ways to resolve them. If we know what sign energies represent the conflict, we can easily see what is needed to lessen or block the cause of the conflict and invoke the energies needed to stabilize and harmonize the situation.

These complex relationships between areas of our lives show us why so many things create conflict in this world, and also the way beyond the conflicts. All conflicts arise because some signs are not in harmony with others, showing some areas of life do not interact easily with others. Conflict is the way we recognize what we believe, what we know, and where we respect our knowledge but also value the knowledge of others.

Using Astrology to Resolve Conflict

Conflict is a challenge to bring forth the power of our Higher Self to find a compassionate higher view of the factors in the conflict, and by using astrology, we can know which astrological energies will resolve the problem.

For example, if the problem involves money or possessions, how to view them or how to use them, we are dealing with the energy of Taurus. Taurus is opposed by Scorpio (desire and fixed interpersonal feelings), and squared by Leo (pride and power) and Aquarius (willfulness and detachment). However, these signs when used positively can resolve Taurus disputes, since Leo and Aquarius can put the brakes on the conflict, while Scorpio can counter the conflict as an equal force and bring a greater awareness of the problem.

If a dispute involves Taurus energy, the solutions to problems involving money or values involves some type of letting go to create space (Scorpio), or perhaps as love, affection, and putting the heart's priorities first (Leo), or friendship and a commitment to a greater set of shared goals (Aquarius).

While these all challenge the basis of a Taurus dispute, the key to finding the best possible outcome is to reference the signs in harmony with the sign characterizing the dispute. In our example, Taurus is in harmony with Capricorn and Virgo. Thus financial issues can be understood clearly if we figure out who is responsible for what (Capricorn), and what practical adjustments must be made to restore the "health" of the finances (Virgo).

The signs in sextile to Taurus are Cancer and Pisces. These signs show how to make productive effort to move the oppositional energies of Taurus and Scorpio into a positive expression. This means that in all disputes involving money or values, productive movement is found by sensitivity to needs and

135

renunciation of fear or old habits (Cancer), and compassion, foresight, forgiveness, and accurate intuition (Pisces).

In the case of a betrayal of some sort, we are dealing with the energies of Pisces. These disputes are not helped by criticism and worry (Virgo, the opposing sign), talking in circles (Gemini - square), or justifying a dualism (Sagittarius - square.) Betrayal can be countered by looking at dualities and loose ends in what we're being told (Gemini), looking at the details and inconsistencies in what we're being told (Virgo), and any tendency for the other to "run away" from the dialog (Sagittarius).

As with the previous example, issues of betrayal require that we come to a clearer understanding through signs in harmony with Pisces, those being Scorpio, Cancer, Taurus, and Capricorn. When there has been a betrayal, we can make progress by invoking and manifesting the virtues of Earth and Water signs. In these signs we find a sensitivity to needs, values, responsibilities, and loyalty. We find tenderness, clarity, simplicity, and responsibility, with a willingness to regenerate by being clear about what must not corrupt the integrity of the relationship.

In another example, any dispute related to a miscommunication, interpretation, clash of ideas or perspectives involves a Gemini problem. If we're in conflict with another around issues of truth, philosophy, ethical behavior, or religious differences, we have a problem involving Sagittarius energy.

Any Gemini or Sagittarius problem can be harmonized by using Aries, Libra, Leo, and Aquarius energies in productive ways. These approaches may involve such questions as: What is the truth or essential nature of both the lower and Higher Self in each view? What is fair, balanced, and reasonable? How can we play with these ideas creatively so that each sees the truth of the heart? How dispassionate and impersonal can we be in examining the larger context of the idea, interpretation, or perspective? Is this view leading to the greatest good for the greatest number, or is it limited?

These are just a few examples of how astrology can help resolve many problems Also, because some time periods are more difficult than others for everyone, many times problems will pass if we don't do anything to aggravate them. This is where knowing astrology can help us stay calm and keep a steady course as we navigate the storms of life.

All challenges are useful in helping us resolve old karmic patterns, and move into a more effective expression of our Higher Self. Once we learn how to view problems and implement the corrective energies, we move beyond getting trapped in old patterns of conflict, and so shift our future karma.

Even though some people are more inclined to create problems than others, we never have to lose our self-control, since that is not helpful. As we become more at ease demonstrating our Higher Self in life's disputes, we learn how easy it is to avoid unnecessary conflicts before they arise. It is safe to say that in all relationships, if each is living their Higher Self the best they are able, all disputes can be resolved, despite the differences. Those who love will always want to reconcile any conflict so love may prevail.

Who Are We Attracting and Why?

To find our perfect mate, we have to get clear about why we're attracted to the people we are, and how relationships might be influenced by projections of what we believe we're looking for, or a compensation for what we haven't known.

As I offered you in chapter 3, "planets are people." The planets in our chart are associated with people in our lives, which is why when we outgrow an old form of planetary expression, we move on to the next level of learning about that expression, attracting new people we will learn from. Why a person plays out as one or more of our planets is part of the Mystery of our unfolding Self-realization. By our attractions we come to know ourselves.

We change how our planets manifest as a result of our choices in life. We have our inner response to our planets, and project those energies into our world. Karma being what it is, like the proverbial stone thrown into the pond, once the ripples or our planetary expression hit the edge of the life field we're in, they inevitably return to center.

All our relationships fulfill certain planetary positions and patterns in our charts. As we move from relationship to relationship, our journey shows us how we invited that energy into our lives, and what motivated that attraction. When we understand the place of various relationships, we ultimately find the gift of objectivity. As we observe that which moves us toward or away from others we find opportunities to do the many small self-redefinitions required to make our relationships more ideal.

Our first marriage is usually a hope and a dream involving a lot of projection of images (conscious and unconscious) based in cultural expectations learned from our family and social matrix. Often the second marriage is a reaction to, and compensation for, what was and was not fulfilled in the first.

Many times the unconscious factors in our first marriage make it clear over time that we really don't know each other, don't speak the same language, and don't have the same hopes and dreams. If our value systems diverge too radically, then it's almost impossible to find a harmonious common ground.

In my own life, after my first marriage ended, I bounced around, not having any idea what I wanted. After a period of reflection (coinciding with my first four years of astrological and metaphysical studies) I chose my second marriage for all the right reasons. Of course there were similarities between my first wife and my second wife, both astrologically and other ways, which made it clear they had some similar energies. The second fulfilled everything I never dreamed of in the first, but after some years, due to forces beyond our control, we parted.

That led me to take a look back at every partner I ever had, and I began to note patterns. Some were healthy, some were unhealthy. Then I chose to change those "patterns of attraction," consciously refusing the old tendencies, and "sat with the emptiness" until my energetic field was cleared. That ultimately led me to entirely new types of relationships. Those people looked differently, thought differently, and behaved differently than those I had been with before.

Over time those potentials played out and I found myself again examining my relationship patterns to see what needed to change and what didn't. As a result of my willingness to grow, not get discouraged, and keep my focus on attracting good people into my life, my choices have brought me to the happy, contented, and fulfilled space I'm in right now. Once we stop projecting our wants and needs on to others and examine why we believe we want something and what purpose it serves, then we can begin to negate the power of our unconscious patterns and turn to crafting "the art of our life." When we realize what has been fulfilled, whether good, bad, or ugly, then we can shift to a new way of seeing the best potential.

As we grow. we drop many comfortable assumptions. As our lives and relationships evolve, neither we nor others are the same people as we were back when we met. As a Great One once wrote, "The Moving Finger writes, and having writ, moves on: nor all thy piety nor wit shall lure it back to cancel half a line, nor all thy tears wash out a word of it." That's why there's no point in going certain places, and no point in saying certain things, even when we're right and it's true.

By observing "that which moves and that which doesn't," we can come to know whether we and/or they are operating from unconscious patterns of need, desire, or projections. Of course, not all projections are unhealthy, since the greatest love story on Earth is still a movie that must be played out by the lovers on the stage of Life and appreciated by those who watch and applaud in the theater of Life!

If both people in a marriage choose to individuate and craft an ongoing friendship, then it doesn't matter what has gone before, since a marriage based in an ongoing friendship can succeed in extraordinary ways. This transcends planetary contacts, since those expressions will always be infused with love.

Any planetary contact can bring pleasure or pain, bondage or freedom, upheaval or temporary stability, chaos or order. Since life is but a dream, and we're all flowing through the dreamscape we call Life, it's no wonder that sometimes worldly events seem unreal. That's because our true Self is beyond time. We are Eternals learning to navigate Life by perfecting our personalities. As we examine the patterns of what we've attracted and why, we get a sense of how we've grown in wisdom in who we want to be with, and how we've steered our "ship of personality" from unconscious difficult relationships to healthy conscious relationships.

As we see which patterns have moved us between pleasure and suffering, we come out of being moved by unconscious imagery and have more of a sense of our power to choose our responses to relationship in a conscious way. Then we're no longer unconsciously accepting others' projections, nor seeking fulfillment in outer forms. We are living our loving wisdom, which is the only authentic way to be.

And now, the chapter on the qualities of mate signs!

CHAPTER SEVEN

THE NATURAL MATE FOR YOUR SIGN

Now we turn to the heart of the matter, the natural mate for each sign! This chapter was originally the core material for my Professor Robert's Mojo Love Reports, and offers many qualities of the natural mate sign for all 12 signs of the zodiac. As with the originals, I encourage you to read both your Sun sign and your Rising sign, since together they will give you a comprehensive picture of many possible traits of your natural mate.

As well as natural mate signs, there are always other factors in play when trying to figure out the qualities of our perfect partner. Some of these include planets we may have in our 7th house, the ruler of our marriage house(s), their dispositors, their decan location, and planets which conjunct them. When we add progressions which affected our 7th house, its ruler, or planets there, we then have a comprehensive map of what qualities our natural mate will have, and how our likes and dislikes evolved over the years as various affairs and friendships played out in our lives.

Of course this involves the archetypal "Masques" we wear as we dance with others in various types of relationships. You will recall from Chapter 5 there are six archetypal energies we embody, depending on which signs are active in any given interactive dynamic, and each archetype involves two signs in opposition to each other. To refresh your focus, they are the Lover/Relator

(Aries/Libra) with its focus on the "I-Thou;" the Warrior/Guardian (Taurus/Scorpio) with its focus on stability; the Questor/Magi (Gemini/Sagittarius) with its focus on experimentation; the Innocent/Primal (Cancer/Capricorn) with its focus on self-interest; the Ruler/Orphan (Leo/Aquarius) with its quality of nobility; and the Healer/Shaman (Virgo/Pisces) with its focus on finding new quality of life.

As I offered that chapter, a healthy archetype will express the best of itself and its complementary sign on the other side of the zodiac. A healthy warrior is a healthy lover, and vice versa; a healthy healer is a healthy magician; a healthy ruler is an innocent who instinctively does their best. As we have all the signs in our chart, we have all the archetypes within us, with each taking its place on the stage of our life depending on what energies are in play in a given activity or relationship.

Throughout our lives, we have many different types of sign energies we get along with, and each sign holds within it the mystery of its mate sign. This section focuses on the natural qualities of the signs opposing our Sun or Rising signs. Some of these qualities may be subtle, while others are obvious. Some may be in the foreground when we meet someone, while others may be in the background. Over time these and other "mate sign" traits will teach us about our partner by how they respond to the challenges each sign brings to us.

By understanding how the signs might manifest in a given house, we can learn why we attracted certain people with those patterns. What you're about to read will take you on a journey through the traits of the natural mate for each sign, giving you a sense of the vast sweep of what there is to learn using this technique. Have fun, since everyone who ever got a Professor Robert's Mojo Love Report told me how accurate and enjoyable these are. So let's begin our exploration of the traits of the natural mate for each of the twelve signs!

You have a **SUN in ARIES** (the following descriptions are also true if you have an Aries Ascendant)

If you've ever investigated astrology, you probably already know your ideal mate will have a heavy Libra influence, since that sign naturally complements your own highly energetic nature. Of course, this could mean a Libra Ascendant, Moon in Libra, or any number of other types of Libra influence, whether natal (birth chart) or progressed (how the natal evolves over time).

This indicates your ideal partner will usually be good looking, firm but fair, and have some form of artistic talent. They will always try to live up to their ideal of a form of perfection, beauty, or well-polished grace and charm. They will be reasonable, agreeable (sometimes TOO agreeable!), with classic features and probably a dimple in their cheeks. Needing a well-rounded approach to knowledge leading them to a moderate take on things, they will be great conversationalists, always willing to explore many different points of view without feeling like they have to decide on any one, and will have many varied types of acquaintances in their lives.

In many ways, their life will seem like a Hollywood movie, or a heroic epic, with all the dramatic elements which assure everyone a grand story lived in grand style. Highly theoretical and always up for a visit and/or discussion about almost anything, they will have big ideas, but will also be a bit ambivalent about what they really mean and what they should do about them. This is where your ability to anchor the idea in an immediate action to move things forward can help them. You are here to show them how to move their theories into practice, and assist the decision-making process by "cutting to the chase."

Your Venus sign is very important in showing you the type of person you'll do best with, since Venus rules Libra, your natural mate sign. As you know from what you've read already, Venus also shows the energies we'll like the most, since Venus rules our ideal of beauty. So in your case, Aries, this double Venusian influence gives your Venus sign attraction even more power, since the ruler of your natural mate is the planet of love itself! The sign your TransPluto occupies also symbolizes a higher, invisible aspect of your ideal mate's character. Most people currently alive were born with this outer planet in Leo. You can find out a lot more about who and what attracts you in the next chapter detailing how Venus operates in the signs.

Your ideal mate will have gone through losses and defeats and come out stronger as a result. They will have an appreciation for the hidden value or usefulness of things. They will easily embrace getting rid of things when they are obsolete, yet will want to discuss and weigh possible alternatives before doing anything drastic. They will have strong magnetism and an open point of view that attracts resources to them, and value education and experimentation in a big way. They are natural teachers and communicators, pretty positive in their offerings, and highly disciplined when there is a need.

Their family will have had a lot of rules of conduct, some of which were too rigid. This is behind any imbalance or tendency to unfairness you may find. Your mate will come from either power or poverty, and have the ability to work and talk their way into positions where they can take on responsibilities effectively. They will be visionary in their expression, love to play and do creative projects with their friends, and will be impersonal and progressive when it comes to children. More than most other signs, your mate is highly susceptible to other people's psychic states, and need to monitor subconscious tendencies to get to the roots of health problems.

Your natural mate will avoid conflict and be a peacemaker, probably quick to say yes and then have second and third thoughts shortly thereafter. You may need to give them time to change their mind so that you don't wind up in unnecessary conflicts. Their pace will be slower than yours, and much more theoretical and interactive than your own natural tendency to act first on your own initiative and discuss things later on. So slow down and dance a little, and learn your mate's rhythms and ways of weighing and balancing things to come to a well-rounded view.

They will desire to enjoy the finer things in life, but sometimes can be too indulgent. They will be fixed, simple and direct in their attitudes about society's values, probably be fairly well off in the credit department, stable and secure in what they have available to draw on. As a result of losses and defeats, they get resources of concrete value, and have a slow but steady process of self-regeneration.

There will be a need for genuine selflessness when it comes to shared values and resources.

Your mate's philosophy will have some dualities and facets that may be difficult for you, given your more straightforward approach. They will be as freedom loving as you are, but with a much stronger need to read, write, and speak their ever-evolving truth in numerous ways. They will be open to discussions about ethics and philosophy where many different points of view are exchanged, and will ultimately come to their larger vision through interactions with people who represent an ideal of brotherhood and sisterhood to them.

They will be very sensitive to their public standing, but will follow their personal needs and habit patterns even in the face of social disapproval, which they usually avoid at all costs because they are really somewhat timid and insecure publicly. Their profession may involve land, supplies, trade, families, children, or something related to dealing with the general public. They really would rather work at home, are proud of their friends, and have noble and shining ideals. Their creativity will come out in teamwork, or group projects.

They are concerned about little things that almost no one else would notice. For their best physical and psychological well-being, they need a practical discipline keeping them on a regular routine. They may have a problem with nervous conditions, but can usually work their way back to health. Excessive criticism is a signal something is ending. Whether directed at them, or received from them, nitpicking and excessive focus on all the little things which are wrong about someone or something is a

148

sure sign it's time to close an old way of relating, and begin a whole new dialogue.

They will be motivated by specific practical ambitions, probably always have more than one thing going at a time, and may run the risk of getting too narrow in their vision of what is possible for them. Any lack of a greater vision and future will be their sorrow or self-undoing, as will excessive criticism and worry. You can assist them in seeing immediate effective possibilities so they can take some action moving them beyond doubt and skepticism. Then they will be able to move through completing an old self-image into a more perfect picture of what they could be.

OTHER FACTORS

As could be inferred from earlier paragraphs, if you have a Sun in Aries or an Aries Ascendant, you will be attracted to certain sign energies more than others. Because you are a Fire sign, you will be attracted to others with the Fire element strong in their chart. You would do very well with someone with a Moon or Ascendant in Leo or Sagittarius, since these are the other two Fire signs. You will also be very attracted to someone with Venus in Aries, and they to you. You will naturally like each other, and could become very good friends fairly quickly.

You will almost always do well with any of the Air signs, those being Aquarius, Gemini, and as I said earlier, Libra. Here someone with a Moon or Ascendant in Aquarius or Gemini would be very compatible for you, less so Moon in Libra if you have a Sun in Aries. Someone with a Libra Ascendant would exert a very strong attraction on you. All the Air signs will bring ideas and people stimulating your inspirational tendencies, and give you much needed interaction and opportunities to express your forever creative vitality.

People with strong Capricorn energies bring growth to your solar energies, but also difficulty. Your worldly ruler, Mars, finds its "exaltation," or sign of greatest growth, in Capricorn. Therefore, Capricorn energies challenge your discipline, and force you to be more deliberate, more efficient, and more organized in how you naturally express your light and power. However, this sign also "squares" your Aries energies, indicating potential conflict through differing points of view with a need to learn correct forms of practical, responsible, mature, balanced, and measured action or non-action.

Someone with Cancer energies may be challenging because that sign also squares Aries, with the same effect as above. Also, your ruler Mars doesn't do well with those sign energies, because they are usually too emotional, changeable, and subjective, and Mars needs practicality, discipline, and objectivity. Still, Cancer grounds you and can satisfy your basic needs, even if things get unsettled from time to time. They challenge your sense of balance, maturity, organization and self-discipline.

You naturally do well with Scorpio energies, since there is harmony due to you both being ruled by Mars. You are naturally comfortable with each other's intensity, and can usually keep up with one another admirably. Because both of your signs are quick to do battle, Scorpio will teach you to choose carefully what to say and how to say it, not going where you don't need to go. This will naturally lead you to greater flexibility, communicability, and a more ordered sense of service.

You have a **SUN in TAURUS** (the following descriptions are also true if you have a Taurus Ascendant)

If you've ever investigated astrology, you probably already know your ideal mate will have a heavy Scorpio influence, since that sign naturally complements your own highly durable nature. Of course, this could mean a Scorpio Ascendant, Moon in Scorpio, or any number of other types of Scorpio influence, whether natal (birth chart) or progressed (how the natal evolves over time).

Your ideal mate will be intense, magnetic, strong, determined, powerful, and ambitious. It is very improbable that they will be seen as ambivalent, wishy-washy, or superficial, unless there are overriding planetary factors specifically indicating these qualities. Your natural partner will have the power to draw whatever they want to themselves, for good or ill, and know when something has become obsolete. Their gift is knowing how to turn defeat into victory, and loss into forms of regeneration. They will be keenly discerning, with an ability to get behind other's inhibitions and draw forth secrets that may make others uncomfortable. Direct and to the point, they are hard to fool, and need to learn to relax around the natural boundaries that are set by people and circumstances whether they like it or not.

Your love will be a natural detective who will scrutinize everything and everyone, and usually will not be interested in superficialities. They will frequently push the envelope, taking things to the very edge, and occasionally go too far. Then they'll wind up over the edge in the interests of winning at all costs, which of course will conflict with your own gentle and reasonable nature. You're here to teach them to take it easier, be kinder and lighten up, showing them how not to be so discontent and possessive, so everyone can enjoy life.

Your Mars sign is very important in showing you the type of person you'll do best with, since Mars rules Scorpio, your natural mate sign. The sign that your Pluto occupies also symbolizes a higher, invisible aspect of your ideal mate's character which will attract you. As you know from what you've read already, Venus also shows the mate you'll like the most, since Venus rules our ideal of beauty. It is also the planet ruling your Sun sign, an even more powerful influence. Being ruled by the planet of love itself, you are one of the most romantic signs of all! You can find out a lot more about who and what attracts you in the next chapter detailing how Venus operates in the signs.

Your ideal mate will have a big vision when it comes to money and possessions, but may be prone to waste through lack of paying attention, extravagance, or getting too spread out. They may also need to learn not to gamble or take unnecessary chances with what they hold valuable. Often thinking they have things all figured out, they will be able to justify everything they think and say. However, they may also occasionally suffer from a hard or narrow vision based in a parental attitude or rules of communication they learned in childhood. This is where your own calm sensitivity and sweetness can be a big help to them.

They had a very unusual childhood or early upbringing, which may have involved excessive idealism, or strange conditions, or an exceptionally smart or progressive parent who was highly impersonal and probably inflexible in the way they related to their family. Your mate will seek seclusion when being creative, and may be prone to strange forms of recreation, or strange moods when having the most fun. They will have an unusual telepathic connection to their eldest child, or be the despair of their children due to a subtle form of extremism. If the latter, your natural moderation will bring a balance to the family dynamic.

They will like to work independently, but be very loyal when they are in service to someone. They will usually be found working at something where they can take the lead, or work as fast and hard as they feel like. Your mate may love to be immersed in sensory pleasures, and this is where the two of you will have to come up for air, and come up with new routines of pleasure, to avoid getting stuck in a rut too deep for long-term comfort. Your ideal mate will desire an ever-deeper union with you, others, and even their own experiences, and should cultivate more appreciation of what they experience so that they don't fall into discontent while holding on to unfulfilling patterns.

You both need to cultivate non-possessiveness and detachment, since you both share a fixed determination to hold on to what you value at all costs. Your ideal mate will need new ideas, new attitudes, new information, and new perspectives to regenerate their lives from time to time. Argumentative and dualistic inner conflicts will prove self-destructive. Help your mate to become more impersonal regarding their losses, seeing how nothing can be lost unless it is no longer true for you.

Your mate will have a very traditional philosophy, somewhat sentimental and mostly concerned with basic needs and primal patterns within a family context. They will always be searching for a vision of how to provide for future supply of needs and must be scrupulously honest in their methods while learning when to let go, not trying to hold on to too much. They will want to feel the future as an intensely personal process of self-unfoldment.

They will be very proud of their public standing, and often seem to be more of an actor in the presence of a public than the vulnerable and deep person you know them to be. Your natural mate will want to be the center of attention and shine on the world stage, and their best professional tendencies involve art, children, entertainment, or something where they can appear their best. They can definitely charm the public, but must not become huffy or sulky when their fragile pride is wounded, and learn how to share the spotlight with grace.

Your mate may be very analytical or critical of their friends, expecting them to fulfill a host of minor details and functions to prove they are worthy of friendship. Your mate will never be completely secure about their goals and ambitions, and should be striving to learn that we are here to serve the greatest good in the moment to bring forth a more perfect world. Any lack of balance or fairness will be their sorrow or self-undoing, so assist them to see a well-rounded view of things, so they become just and balanced as they break through one barrier after another in their quest for ever-more intense interactions with their world.

OTHER FACTORS

As could be inferred from earlier paragraphs, if you have a Sun in Taurus or a Taurus Ascendant, you will be attracted to certain sign energies more than others. Because you are an Earth sign, you will be attracted to others with the Earth element strong in their chart. You would do very well with someone with a Moon or Ascendant in Virgo or Capricorn, since these are the other two Earth signs. Virgo actually presents a mixed bag for you, since Virgo is in fundamental harmony with Taurus' Earthy nature, but your ruler Venus does not do very well in that sign, due to excessive worry and narrowness of view. However, you will be very attracted to someone with Venus in Taurus, and they to you. You will naturally like each other, and could become very good friends fairly quickly.

You will almost always do well with any of the Water signs, those being Cancer and Pisces, and as I said earlier, Scorpio. Your ruler, Venus, is generally attracted to Cancer and Pisces energies, though this may change somewhat if your chart indicates contrary influences. Here someone with a Moon or Ascendant in Cancer and Pisces would be very compatible for you, less so Moon in Scorpio if you have a Sun in Taurus. Someone with a Scorpio Ascendant would exert a very strong attraction on you. All the Water signs will bring you deep feelings and experiences stimulating your social tendencies, giving you much needed interaction and opportunities to express your durable and sweet stabilizing influence.

People with strong Pisces energies bring growth to your solar energies, helping you broaden and deepen your emotional expression. Your ruler,

155

Venus, finds its "exaltation," or sign of greatest growth, in Pisces. Therefore, Pisces energies challenge your comfortable inertia, and force you to be more compassionate, selfless, and empathetic in how you naturally express your light and power. Since this sign "sextiles" your Taurus energies, it will help you learn flexibility, subtlety, non-possessiveness, and a more universal point of view. Pisces helps you get outside your private world and opinions and learn a more fluid and intuitive approach to life as you move through subtle, complex, and vast feelings. Though unsettling to your simple and direct way of approach, it is still a very productive learning experience for you any time you find yourself dancing with Pisces energies.

Someone with Leo or Aquarius energies may be more difficult because those signs "square" Taurus, indicating challenge, conflict, and the need to learn correct forms of gentle, noble, or impersonal action or non-action. Also, your ruler Venus doesn't do well with those sign energies, because they are usually too hot or cold and unwilling to bend, and Venus needs compassion, forgiveness, and a universal view to do its best. Leo and Aquarius are as fixed and unmoving as you are, and show you the circumstances where inertia alone will not get you what you want. Still, Leo grounds you and can satisfy your basic needs, even if things get unsettled from time to time. You naturally do well with Libra energies, since there is harmony due to you both being ruled by Venus. You are naturally comfortable with how agreeable, moderate, and enjoyable each of you are, and usually enjoy each other's company quite admirably.

You have a **SUN in GEMINI** (the following descriptions are also true if you have a Gemini Ascendant)

If you've ever investigated astrology, you probably already know your ideal mate will have a heavy Sagittarius influence, since that sign naturally complements your own highly energetic nature. Of course, this could mean a Sagittarius Ascendant, Moon in Sagittarius, or any number of other types of Sagittarius influence, whether natal (birth chart) or progressed (how the natal evolves over time).

This indicates your ideal mate will be freedom loving, independent, and keep their eye on other, greater possibilities just around the corner. They will be well educated, even though it may not be in a traditional sense. Clever and future-oriented, they'll always have something going and try to live life as a grand journey opening wider horizons and possibilities. They should have a great sense of humor, but occasionally will become contrary or grumpy due to their sense of irony or absurdity turning cynical at times. They are philosophers and raconteurs with a very vivid imagination going in many directions at once, and life with your mate will be several grand adventures rolled into one. They may be hard to pin down, and won't be much for traditional bonds, but will always respect your right to do your own thing in your own way. They'll probably have prominent hips, curly hair, and/or a high forehead.

Your Jupiter sign is very important in showing you the type of person you'll do best with, since Jupiter rules Sagittarius, your natural mate sign. The sign your Neptune occupies also symbolizes a higher, invisible aspect of your ideal mate's character. As you know from what you've read already, Venus also shows the mate you'll like the most, since Venus rules our ideal of beauty. You can find out a lot more about who and what attracts you in the next chapter detailing how Venus operates in the signs.

Your ideal mate will have gone through many ups and downs financially, mostly due to the values they were raised with. They should have a knack for landing on their feet and doing well despite conditions. In fact, your love may be extraordinarily lucky at times, and even though very generous and seemingly a bit cavalier about money and things, they're always examining the balance sheet, even though it may come out like a joke. They can be extravagant, but it usually serves a purpose. Your mate will spend a lot if it helps to position them for future opportunities, but must beware of gambling on unsound impulsive hunches or treating cheaply that which they should hold as precious.

They will hold some very progressive and advanced views, and will have a natural gift for seeing the big picture by putting all the various pieces together within a larger vision. They can help you with your natural tendency to be scattered in your opinions and ideas, and will stimulate your imagination without any need to control or confine your curiosity. Your mate will be able to handle and even appreciate your tendency to question and examine everything.

They will have some strange memories of their early childhood, which will seem in some ways to be as much of a prison as a vehicle for exploring the joyous freedom they've lived their entire lives. Still, they were very protected, even if things really were as weird as it seemed. There is much from their past they consciously need to forgive, regardless of how much they say they've done and how light they make of it. Ultimately, your ideal mate will be more into moving toward a better future than going back into the past.

Your beloved will want to play spontaneously, like there's no tomorrow, and need lots of variety where their fiery intensity can blaze while moving in and out of experiences very quickly. They could have a great storytelling talent, creating unique forms of self-expression, almost effortlessly and spontaneously. However, occasionally they can be too abrupt or abrasive with children. Natural teachers, they have a way of making things simple, grounded and practical when working for others, but can become obstinate and need more patience while capturing the resources that will secure the next step in their movement.

Your Beloved may not seem like the model of consistency or responsibility, so it will be up to you to manage the variety they need in your relationship while honoring their need for a sense of freedom. Of course they should be faithful, and will be, as long as there is enough variety and change in the forms of your relationship so they can live their freedom to be themselves in a variety of ways. As you express your natural adaptability, they will continue to stay fascinated with the different people you seem to be, and will naturally be excited to dance with the various facets of you.

They will acutely feel their losses, despite how easily they seem to toss them off. Your mate will need more of a sense of society's values so they can understand how to fulfill their specific needs in the moment. If you can assist them to become more sensitive to their society and its values, they'll

159

magically receive all they need. Your love will have a noble and dramatic way of expressing their vision, truth and philosophy, and will find their light as they travel, both in outer and inner space. Your mate is a teacher with a natural rapport with children, so they learn from them like no other source.

They will probably do better working for others than for themselves, but will always need freedom to do as they need to do. You will be able to help them manage the details around their profession, since your natural mate will tend not to pay much attention to the small things accompanying success or failure in most enterprises. They will also need good helpers and assistants in their profession so that they don't get stressed trying to manage all the things they really don't care about.

Your Beloved is very idealistic, and wants to be perfectly fair and even-minded when it comes to making decisions. They believe they hold a more idealistic image than most of humanity, and are looking for friends who fit a certain image. Thus they may get into friendships with people who are superficial, unreliable, or insincere. Of course, they may also be quite well known in their own sphere, and will always be good looking.

Your love will be motivated by forces seemingly beyond their control, with desires which may not be able to be fulfilled, at least in this world. If they're self-destructive, it's because they've pushed it to the edge and jumped over rather than anything you or anyone else said or did. If they can learn how to let go of dark feelings fixed in their subconscious, they'll clear out a lot of stagnant material from their ego and focus their magnetism to bring them the deeper feelings they want, along with the freedom and opportunities to move into the future.

OTHER FACTORS

As could be inferred from earlier paragraphs, if you have a Sun in Gemini or a Gemini Ascendant, you will be attracted to certain sign energies more than others. Because you are an Air sign, you will be attracted to others with the Air element strong in their chart. You would do very well with someone with a Moon or Ascendant in Libra or Aquarius, since these are the other two Air signs. You will also be very attracted to someone with Venus in Gemini, and they to you. You will naturally like each other, and could become very good friends fairly quickly.

You will do almost always do well with any of the Fire signs, those being Aries, Leo, and as I said earlier, Sagittarius. Here someone with a Moon or Ascendant in Aries or Leo would be very compatible for you, less so Moon in Sagittarius if you have a Sun in Gemini. Someone with a Sagittarius Ascendant would exert a very strong attraction on you. All the Fire signs will bring energy, inspiration, and people stimulating your natural openness and curiosity, and give you much needed vitality and light to express your forever creative mind. However, your ruler Mercury doesn't do well with Leo energies, because they are usually too personal, combustive, and centered in their own powerful, natural self-expression. Mercury needs impersonality, reasoned understanding, and detachment, as well as innovative or unique rather than traditional points of view. Mercury also is challenged by Sagittarius energy, as it finds itself too hot and scattered over too much

161

information, and Mercury needs ordering, structure, and prioritization to come to a consistent, integrated vision to do its best.

People with strong Aquarius energies bring growth to your solar energies, as well as understandings and ways of being that will be natural to you. Your ruler, Mercury, finds its "exaltation," or sign of greatest growth, in Aquarius. Therefore, Aquarian energies challenge your ability to synthesize your many ideas and points of view into a comprehensive, interconnected larger understanding. People with planets in Aquarius help you become more progressive, innovative, and unique in how you naturally express your light and power. Since Aquarius "trines" your Gemini energies, a mate with these energies strong in their chart will help you through a natural harmony and understanding to learn to synthesize your many ideas and points of view into a comprehensive, interconnected larger understanding. People with planets in Aquarius help you become more progressive, innovative, and unique in how you naturally express your light and power.

Someone with Virgo energies may be difficult because that sign also "squares" Gemini, as does Pisces. These squares indicate challenge, conflict, and the need to learn correct forms of gentle, noble, or impersonal action or non-action. However, Virgo grounds you and can satisfy your basic needs, even if things get unsettled from time to time. You naturally understand Virgo energies, since there is harmony due to you both being ruled by Mercury. You will be naturally comfortable with each other's mental restlessness, curiosity, and analytical-evaluative styles, and usually have the ability to keep up with one another admirably.

You have a **SUN in CANCER** (the following descriptions are also true if you have a Cancer Ascendant)

If you've ever investigated astrology, you probably already know your ideal mate will have a heavy Capricorn influence, since that sign naturally complements your own highly sensitive nature. Of course, this could mean a Capricorn Ascendant, Moon in Capricorn, or any number of other types of Capricorn influence, whether natal (birth chart) or progressed (how the natal evolves over time).

Your Beloved will be organized, responsible, determined, authoritative, mature, someone who never misses a thing, but may suffer from occasionally being too conservative, too pessimistic, or trying too hard to control outcomes. People who are somewhat older or younger than you exert a strong attraction to you, as do those who physically or psychically resemble an elder from your childhood, or an old childhood friend who impressed you with their confidence. Your mate's naturally calm disposition will help you decrease your own nervous concerns and insecurities, and they'll be able to help you take a broader, more patient view.

You'll feel safe with your ideal mate, since they'll be the picture of predictable or responsible behavior, always willing to do the right thing, saying whatever is needed to establish control of situations. They may wait to say something, but when it finally comes out it will definitely be important. Being instinctively cautious, they'll often play it safe and try to take the long view. Your mate will be a natural diplomat, and will have the ability to rise to a position of great influence if they can just find their place in some social system or organization.

Your Saturn sign is very important in showing you the type of person you'll do best with, since Saturn rules Capricorn, your natural mate sign. The sign your Uranus occupies also symbolizes a higher, invisible aspect of your ideal mate's character which will attract you. As you know from what you've read already, Venus also shows the mate you'll like the most, since Venus rules our ideal of beauty. You can find out a lot more about who and what attracts you in the next chapter detailing how Venus operates in the signs.

Your ideal mate will have a long range, multi-level plan when it comes to money and possessions, but may be overly conservative in some strange ways, or get involved in apparently sound progressive schemes involving friends which could take unexpected twists and turns. Your natural partner needs an ever-larger point of view, more innovative and willing to factor in new information. Often thinking they have things all figured out, they will be able to justify everything they think and say in some clever ways while overlooking the obvious. They are subtle communicators and will be aware of things in their environment that elude others, but may be overly sensitive to the vibes of those around them.

They may have had a very difficult childhood or early upbringing involving excessive strife, pressure, conflict, or a parent who was independent, always on the move, impulsive, or too impatient. They may suffer from peculiar ideas based in a parental attitude or rules of communication they learned in childhood. Your mate will seek comfortable and pleasant conditions when trying to be creative, find great stability in children and play, and are pretty traditional in their likes, dislikes, and recreational inclinations. If an artist, your mate's work will be naturally simple and straightforward, with the naturalness of the form revealing the beauty of the content.

Your partner has a natural aptitude for work involving speaking, writing, communications, or travel. As they will always need change and diversity in their work, they would do well in the media, but would be bothered by dramas involving people saying one thing when they really think something else. Your mate may have worked in communications or be working with someone in their family in some capacity, perhaps a sibling. Generally, though they can be very impersonal when doing a work for someone else, they'll always in some way be working for themselves and their own interests.

Because of their introverted tendencies, your sensitivity, sweetness, and nurturing instincts can be a big help to them. Because they suffered from some form of lack or deprivation when they were younger, at times you will be emotionally pulled to provide for their feelings, and attempt to take care of them in ways they've never known. The strength of your feelings, your tenderness, and your sense of closeness will enable you to penetrate the defensive shell they create when they're feeling insecure.

Their nobility will be the source and strength of their regenerative power. Your partner will try to do the right thing even when losses are inevitable, and find strength in social connections. How they deal with defeat will show you where their heart is really at. They can be empowered by shining a light on their desires, as well as how they dealt with old losses.

165

However, you both need to cultivate non-possessiveness and detachment, since you both share a fixed determination to hold on to what you value at all costs. You can help each other become the embodiment of "enlightened self-interest," with your power to gather and secure a base of supply complementing your mate's power of organized achievement through long term persistence.

Your natural partner will have a very particular and practical philosophy, a little too concerned with the details at the expense of the whole vision, but willing to be of service. At some point in life they may be called to work in a foreign land, or in an educational setting. Professionally, they seek positions that are stylish as well as substantial, and appearance will mean a lot in public affairs. Your mate will be quite a performer and always behave appropriately in public situations. Just make sure it's not a facade that vanishes behind closed doors. You may like to know what others don't, but in relationships, appearances don't mean much when things are unfair or out of balance. I'm sure your sensitivity and kindness doesn't like it when things are unjust for very long.

Your Beloved will have some very powerful and intense friends, people who are highly magnetic with probably more than one or two secrets. Your mate will be ambitious, but whether this is in worldly or spiritual things depends on who and what you attract through your own creative and playful self-expression. They will be motivated by great ambitions, probably always have more than one thing going at a time, and may run the risk of getting too spread out, or gamble on luck coming through just one more time, only to find unintended consequences. Any lack of a greater vision and future will be their sorrow or self-undoing, so assist them to see immediate possibilities, take a broader point of view, and get a greater sense of humor as they move from completion to ever greater fulfillment.

OTHER FACTORS

As could be inferred from earlier paragraphs, if you have a Sun in Cancer or a Cancer Ascendant, you will be attracted to certain sign energies more than others. Because you are a Water sign, you will be attracted to others with the Water element strong in their chart. You would do very well with someone with a Moon or Ascendant in Scorpio or Pisces, since these are the other two Water signs. You will also be very attracted to someone with Venus in Cancer, and they to you. You will naturally like each other, and could become very good friends fairly quickly.

You will almost always do well with any of the Earth signs, those being Taurus and Virgo, and as I said earlier, Capricorn. Here someone with a Moon or Ascendant in Taurus and Virgo would be very compatible for you, less so Moon in Capricorn if you have a Sun in Cancer. Someone with a Capricorn Ascendant would exert a very strong attraction on you. Even though your ruler, the Moon, doesn't do all that well with Saturn's no-nonsense coldness and rules, your Sun in Cancer is still very attracted to Capricorn's earthy, responsible, self-organizing authority. All the Earth signs will bring you a sense of grounded practical security and experiences stimulating your social tendencies, giving you much needed interaction and opportunities to express your kind and nurturing maternal influence.

People with strong Taurus energies bring growth to your solar energies, helping you broaden and gently stabilize your emotional power. Your ruler, the Moon, finds its "exaltation," or sign of greatest growth, in Taurus. Therefore, Taurus energies stabilize your restless feelings, and offer you a calm strength so you can be more secure, extroverted, confident, and caring in how you naturally express your light and power. Since this sign "sextiles" your Cancer energies, it will help you through productive opportunities to cultivate friendships, learn a larger social concern and involvement, and a much greater ability to enjoy yourself in social situations.

Someone with Aries or Libra energies may be more difficult because those signs "square" Cancer, indicating challenge, conflict, and the need to learn correct forms of diplomatic, fair, balanced, or direct and honest action or non-action. Also, your ruler, the Moon, doesn't do well with those sign energies, because they are usually too hot or cold, idealistic or hurried, and the Moon needs stability, security, and reassurance. Still, Libra grounds you and can satisfy your basic needs even if things get unsettled from time to time. They teach you balance as well as different perspectives.

Scorpio presents more of a mixed bag, since the Moon doesn't do well with the turbulence Scorpio brings, but understands and can be in harmony with its watery quality. You naturally do well with Leo energies, since there is harmony due to you both being ruled by the "lights," the Sun and Moon. You value what they are, and you seem to know their interior nature. Therefore you help them with their motivation, and assist them to close out old ways that have created them sorrow. You are naturally

168

comfortable with how aware, immediate, sensitive and childlike each other is, and can usually enjoy each other's company quite admirably.

You have a **SUN in LEO** (the following descriptions are also true if you have a Leo Ascendant)

If you've ever investigated astrology, you probably already know your ideal mate will have a heavy Aquarius influence, since that sign naturally complements your own highly energetic nature. Of course, this could mean an Aquarius Ascendant, Moon in Aquarius, or any number of other types of Aquarian influences, whether natal (birth chart) or progressed (how the natal evolves over time).

Your ideal mate will be good looking with fair features and have many unusual friends. They will hold progressive ideas, but some of them may prove to be too far out for your naturally conservative and diplomatic instincts. They will be idealistic, freedom-loving, pretty intelligent and inventive, but stubborn and strong-willed. Social progressives, they dream of a better world and are willing to do their unique part to make the future become real today. In many ways, your ideal mate will be more of a friend to you than most, but may lack warmth and the need for closeness that you want, whether you show it or not. You want to take pride in your mate, what they do and how they look and carry themselves. Try not to get too flustered when your mate does the unexpected, the unusual, or the daringly original, but be alert if things get too eccentric, weird, or bizarre.

Your Beloved will be ultra-social, probably have some form of artistic talent, and will usually be up for a good party. They will love many others in a very impersonal way because they'll genuinely love people for who they are and the better possibilities within them. Your natural partner will want to see the good in situations, even though they're smart enough never to overlook the downside of things. A great conversationalist, they will be open to exploring many different points of view without feeling like they have to decide on any one. Your ability to center on the light, what's relevant, and the inherent order and power in the moment will help your mate integrate things in a personal way. You are here to show them how to move their theories into life experience, assisting their decision-making process by your powerful positivity.

Your Saturn sign is very important in showing you the type of person you'll do best with, since Saturn traditionally rules Aquarius, your natural mate sign. The sign your Uranus occupies also symbolizes a higher, invisible aspect of your ideal mate's character. As you know from what you've read already, Venus also shows the mate you'll like the most, since Venus rules our ideal of beauty. You can find out a lot more about who and what attracts you in the next chapter detailing how Venus operates in the signs.

Your ideal mate could have peculiar circumstances surrounding their money, finances, and resources, and may be over-idealistic or confused in this area. No one will ever really know their financial situation, which may be the source of sorrow based in subconscious patterns or attitudes acquired in childhood. Their family will have had a lot of rules of conduct, some of which were too rigid. Money was always an issue in their childhood, whether too much or too little. Though capable of being Spartan, they will always seek more comfortable living conditions and will have friends who possess exceptionally fine homes.

Natural settings mean a lot to them, as they will be extraordinarily sensitive to their environment. Your mate will be very sharp and quick mentally, progressive and blunt in what and how they communicate, and have a pioneering vision. Very versatile, your Beloved will have fun playing with words and ideas, and have creative views about paradoxes which confound others. If artists, they will not be able to confine their creativity to one medium, or one instrument.

Your mate will learn to be careful of what they eat, as their stomach will be unusually sensitive, and being so naturally high strung, they should resist the urge to get by on nerves and endurance and consciously learn to relax. For their best physical and psychological well-being, they need a practical discipline that keeps them on a regular routine. Excessive criticism is a signal that something needs to be released. Whether directed at them, or received from them, nitpicking and excessive focus on all the little things that are wrong with someone or something is a sure sign that it's time to close an old agreement, habit pattern, or value system and begin a new dialogue.

More than many signs, your mate is highly susceptible to other people's emotional states, and should monitor unconscious urges and habit patterns to get to the roots of health problems. You can help them sort out what habits are natural to them, versus unnatural ones they've picked up from their friends just to be agreeable. They will be proud of their associations, and will love to see you shine, in a very impersonal way. They'll have a great sense of pride, if somewhat detached, but will debate with anyone in a second if they think they're being disrespected. They may not yield to your sense of order in their realm, but they'll be broadminded enough to allow you the order in your own realm.

They will worry too much about minor things, small losses and details that don't go as they would like, but will be more dismissive of what they've overlooked than willing to put themselves in a subordinate position. Paying attention to practical methodical steps will help them regenerate. They may be analytical or critical, and at times try to "fix" other people's values. Their higher learning may be a bit superficial or too idealistic in certain ways, but their philosophical and ethical view will always be humane, reasonable, well-rounded and balanced, since they're chasing a more beautiful vision of a more ideal future.

Though very sensitive of their public standing, they will nevertheless follow their desires regardless of the cost, even in the face of social disapproval. They will agree to no limitation placed on them by force, and will seem competitive in public situations, whether they mean to project that or not. They may be misunderstood due to the differences between their publicly held values and the values of the society they live in. At some point in their lives, they will have crashed and burned in a very public way, and shown their world the power of self-regeneration out of the ashes of the old.

They will have many friends from different cultures who live at a distance from them or even in foreign places. They will know quite a few people of a definitely spiritual or philosophical bent. To achieve their ultimate goals and ambitions they need to continue their education, and see the achievement of their goals as a long-range adventure, or a series of experimental quests for truth.

Your Beloved will be motivated by specific practical ambitions, and will always seek power, recognition, or greater effectiveness in their society. They may run the risk of being too conservative or pessimistic in their vision of what is possible for them. Binding conditions that are too restrictive will be their sorrow or self-undoing, as will excessively heavy responsibilities. Here you can help them to lighten up and be more playful and creative in organized and responsible ways. Then they'll mature by moving through completions and closing out old motives and inner ghosts keeping them stuck in obsolete self-images.

OTHER FACTORS

As could be inferred from earlier paragraphs, if you have a Sun in Leo or a Leo Ascendant, you will be attracted to certain sign energies more than others. Because you are a Fire sign, you will be attracted to others with the Fire element strong in their chart. You would do very well with someone with a Moon or Ascendant in Aries or Sagittarius, since these are the other two Fire signs. You will also be very attracted to someone with Venus in Leo, and they to you. You will naturally like each other, and could become very good friends fairly quickly.

You will almost always do well with any of the Air signs, those being Libra, Gemini, and as I said earlier, Aquarius. Here someone with a Moon or Ascendant in Libra or Gemini would be very compatible for you, less so Moon in Aquarius, if you have a Sun in Leo. Someone with an Aquarius Ascendant would exert a very strong attraction on you. Even though your ruler, the Sun, finds itself far from home in Libra and Aquarius, still all the Air signs will bring ideas and people stimulating your inspirational tendencies, and give you much needed interaction and opportunities to express your forever creative vitality.

People with strong Aries energies bring growth to your solar energies through understanding, fiery initiative, and showing you how to act quickly and directly in situations. Your ruler, the Sun, finds its "exaltation," or sign of greatest growth, in Aries. Therefore, Aries energies stimulate you to be more active, pioneering, and direct in how you naturally express your light and power. Since this sign "trines" your Leo energies, a mate with these energies strong in their chart will help you through a natural harmony and understanding to cultivate a pioneering vision, a powerful higher knowledge and truth, and a more self-reliant philosophy and spirituality.

Someone with Scorpio or Taurus energies may be challenging because those signs "square" Leo, indicating conflict through differing points of view with a need to learn correct forms of detached action or non-action. Your ruler, the Sun, doesn't do well with those sign energies, because they are usually too unmovable and into dramas of gain and loss, and the Sun needs the opportunity to shine and exert its authority on its own terms. Still, Scorpio grounds you and can satisfy your basic needs, even if things get unsettled from time to time. You naturally do well with Cancer energies, since there is harmony due to you both being ruled by the lights, the Moon and the Sun.

You are naturally comfortable with each other's sensitivity, and will usually be okay with the intimacy and genuine sympathetic caring and nurture that Cancer brings to your life.

You have a **SUN in VIRGO** (the following descriptions are also true if you have a Virgo Ascendant)

If you've ever investigated astrology, you probably already know your ideal mate will have a heavy Pisces influence, since that sign naturally complements your own highly durable nature. Of course, this could mean a Pisces Ascendant, Moon in Pisces, or any number of other types of Pisces influence, whether natal (birth chart) or progressed (how the natal evolves over time).

Your Beloved will be intuitive and have a subtle but powerful magnetism. Being more than a little mystical, they will be aware of things others only dream of, and able to know things by plucking hunches and visions out of the ether. Often "playing their cards close to the vest," you may feel they are keeping secrets, which may or may not be the case. They sometimes will procrastinate more than they should and take a judicial attitude if they think others have transgressed their moral code. If the moral sense is too narrow, they will be difficult to pin down because of how they justify their stance, and probably be contradictory as they retreat and submerge into their private world. You will know you have found your ideal mate when their moral sense is broad, forgiving, compassionate, and allows people to have their harmless human flaws without harsh judgments.

At their best, your beloved will be a wise visionary who clearly sees the future. They will join you in a relatively secluded life where they can be a kind of priest, priestess, or healer for others, able to help them see the long view and bless the passages in their lives. Your ideal mate will help you not to worry so much, or get lost in too narrow a focus through their elusive but profound sense of humor, and sensitivity to life's ironies. They will bring you a greater and deeper calm, as well as a fluid life in which you can achieve mutually satisfactory practical goals.

Your Jupiter sign is very important in showing you the type of person you'll do best with, since Jupiter rules Pisces, your natural mate sign. The sign your Neptune occupies also symbolizes a higher, invisible aspect of your ideal mate's character that will attract you. As you know from what you've read already, Venus also shows the mate you'll like the most, since Venus rules our ideal of beauty. You can find out a lot more about who and what attracts you in the next chapter detailing how Venus operates in the signs.

Your ideal mate will be impulsive, self-reliant, and willing to work hard and fast when it comes to money and possessions, but may make errors through haste, being too abrasive, or combative around how to use what they have. They may often think they have things all figured out, and though they will be by nature fairly flexible, they won't feel any great need to change their point of view or how it's communicated to others. They are comfortable with what they think, and don't change their attitude easily. This is where your ability to discern the practicalities of situations can be a big help to them.

They had a contradictory childhood or early upbringing, which may have involved two distinct types of family relations with inherent conflict. There was a lot of distractive activity in childhood, and at least one parent was absent, argumentative, or prone to ambivalence. Your mate needs security and a sense of their own space to be creative or really cut loose and have fun. They will have an unusual emotional connection to their eldest child, or be subject to moods and soul searching when trying to enjoy themselves, or dealing with those who are younger. Here your natural practicality and sense of how to order things to make them function better will assist the family dynamic.

They will want to be the boss in their work, and are a very heartfelt, loyal, clever subordinate when in service to someone. They will usually be found working at something where they can take the lead while laboring at a steady pace. Your beloved will send many peculiar signals to others in their lives that will make perfect sense over time. They will constantly be on the lookout for contradictions in others, and will naturally tend to focus on very specific things that they believe are right and wrong.

Your ideal mate will desire a more universal, deep and wide union with you, others, and even their own experiences, but may have a hard time putting it into words and actions. They will have a huge private world only they are aware of, and may be content to sit back and watch the movie of their life as a spectator. Here your sense of duty and order will help them (and the relationship) not to drift, since the two of you can provide complementary elements to the wholeness you are together. They will have a larger sense of things, and be abstractionists. You will focus on the practical details, and keep things on track.

Idealistic and philosophical about losses and defeats, your Beloved will be able to see the balance or karmic return in all issues of shared resources, both with you and others. Taking the long view, they know that a price must be paid between the individual and society. They may occasionally use this to justify doing things they shouldn't in order to get their "fair share." Just trust your natural discernment to know what needs to be accounted for, keeping it fair for everyone.

You both need to cultivate non-possessiveness and detachment in your ideologies and morals, since you share a fixed determination to hold on to your view at all costs. Your natural mate will need regenerative ideas, deeper attitudes, and more effective information to evolve to their spiritual potential. Debate helps them explore broader possibilities and wider points of view. You can help them enjoy the process more than they do. They definitely need to go back to school at some point to expand their higher potential.

Your mate will express open opinions which both conceal and reveal what they really think. A natural teacher, they have aptitude in the fields of media, writing, speaking, or anything promising adventure, freedom, greater worlds to explore, or just enjoyable travel possibilities. They do well working for themselves, as they need freedom to do as they want.

You can help them manage the details around their profession, since they tend not to pay attention to the small things that spell success or failure in most enterprises. They will also need good helpers and assistants in their profession so they don't get stressed trying to manage things they don't care about. They will claim the high and wide ground in public situations, and often be more the impersonal philosopher in the presence of others than the vulnerable and deep person you know them to be. They have the ability to gain a public following, but must not become grumpy or sarcastic when outsmarted.

Your natural mate will want their friendships to be practical, where things are accomplished or life is conducted on a very high level with a lot of social structure and perhaps formalities. Ambitious, they will seek to cultivate friends in positions of authority and power. You can help them be a lot more personal (and personable) by showing them the specific needs of the moment, and how to nurture and care for things. They will believe in the power of sheer persistence to accomplish their goals, and should be able to defer certain types of immediate gratification to focus on distant but more important prizes.

Their impersonality and sense that all of life is a strange movie may be a problem from time to time. Willfulness, eccentricity, and erratic behavior bring them sorrow or self-undoing. Here you can help them see a noble, heart-oriented view of things showing them the way to the consistent love they want more than anything else in this world. If they can just achieve a detached view of the greatest good for the greatest number, they'll be able to close out old movies and move into more angelic ones.

Your love will be motivated by forces seemingly beyond their control, with ideals which may not be able to be fulfilled in this world. If they're self-destructive, it's because they've pushed it to the edge and jumped over rather than anything you or anyone else said or did. If they can learn to let go of excessive independence, they'll clear out stagnant material from their subconscious mind and focus their magnetism to get the broad vision they want along with the freedom and opportunities to move into the future.

OTHER FACTORS

As could be inferred from earlier paragraphs, if you have a Sun in Virgo or a Virgo Ascendant, you will be attracted to certain sign energies more than others. Because you are an Earth sign, you will be attracted to others with the Earth element strong in their chart. You would do very well with someone with a Moon or Ascendant in Taurus or Capricorn, since these are the other two Earth signs. You will also be very attracted to someone with Venus in Virgo, and they to you. You will naturally like each other, and could become very good friends fairly quickly.

You will almost always do well with any of the Water signs, those being Cancer and Scorpio, and as I said earlier, Pisces. Here someone with a Moon or Ascendant in Cancer and Scorpio would be very compatible for you, less so Moon in Pisces if you have a Sun in Virgo. Someone with a Pisces Ascendant would exert a very strong attraction on you. All the Water signs will bring you deep feelings and experiences stimulating your social tendencies, giving you much needed interaction and opportunities to express your useful, practical influence.

People with Aquarius energies bring growth to your solar energies, as well as understandings and ways of being that are natural to you. Your ruler, Mercury, finds its "exaltation," or sign of greatest growth, in Aquarius. Therefore, Aquarian energies challenge your ability to synthesize your many ideas and points of view into a comprehensive, interconnected larger understanding. People with planets in Aquarius help you become more progressive, innovative, and unique in how you naturally express your light and power. Mercury doesn't do well with Leo energies, because they are usually too personal, combustive, and centered in their own powerful, natural self-expression. Mercury needs impersonality, reasoned understanding, and detachment, as well as innovative or unique rather than traditional points of view.

Someone with strong Gemini or Sagittarius energies may be more difficult because those signs "square" Virgo, indicating challenge, conflict, and the need to learn correct forms of practical, discerning and well-ordered action or non-action. Also, your ruler Mercury doesn't do well with Sagittarius energies, as it finds itself too hot and scattered over too much information, and Mercury needs ordering, structure, and prioritization to come to a consistent, integrated vision to do its best. Still, Sagittarius grounds your Virgo energies and can satisfy your basic needs, even if things get unsettled from time to time. Gemini, on the other hand, shows the way to your flowering and fulfillment in the world. Even though it squares your sign, you naturally do well with Gemini energies, since there is harmony due to you both being ruled by Mercury. You are naturally comfortable with each other's mental and analytical approach, curiosity, adaptability, and impersonality, and can usually keep up with one another admirably.

You have a **SUN in LIBRA** (the following descriptions are also true if you have a Libra Ascendant)

If you've ever investigated astrology, you probably already know your ideal mate will have a heavy Aries influence, since that sign naturally complements your own highly idealistic nature. Of course, this could mean an Aries Ascendant, Moon in Aries, or any number of other types of Aries influence, whether natal (birth chart) or progressed (how the natal evolves over time).

Your ideal mate will be intense, magnetic, strong, determined, and powerful. Your best partner would never be someone who is ambivalent, wishy-washy, glib or superficial, even though you might from time to time be attracted to someone with at least one of these qualities if there are strong planetary factors in your chart attracting you to these. Even then, your attraction is more due to you wanting to refine, balance out, and eliminate these qualities in your own nature rather than it being the most natural partner for you. Your ideal mate will be straightforward, probably somewhat impulsive, very dynamic, and highly self-sufficient. They will have the power to initiate any kind of activity quickly, and bring the fire or magic to any gathering or interaction. Highly self-reliant, they will quickly and definitely declare their intentions, and are the harbingers of new ideas, new ways of life, and new activities for people in their lives.

Your ideal mate will be naturally spontaneous, often quick to react (or overreact!) and will learn a lot about cooperation, moderation, and style from you. Always having 37 irons in the fire at any moment, they will often take things to the very edge, and then quickly dance away into other areas of action, thought, and feeling, which may confuse you and throw you off balance. You're here to teach them to play, be more romantic and explore the many shades of gray in life, perception, and experience by exploring various points of view. They teach you how to be sincere, direct, one-pointed, and self-referenced.

You also teach them how they can enjoy themselves a little more by slowing down and not being so confrontational or argumentative. They also teach you how to debate fairly, and not get distracted into theoretical points of view not really yours. You can help your mate take it easier, be kinder and lighten up, and show them how not to be so restless and jumpy. They can help you find, defend, and express something you really believe in.

Your Mars sign is very important in showing you the type of person you'll do best with, since Mars rules Aries, your natural mate sign. The sign your Pluto occupies also symbolizes a higher, invisible aspect of your ideal mate's character that will attract you. As you know from what you've read already, Venus also shows the mate you'll like the most, since Venus rules our ideal of beauty. It is also the planet that rules your Sun sign, giving your Venus an even more powerful influence. Being ruled by the planet of love itself, you are one of the most romantic signs of all! You can find out a lot more about who and what attracts you in the next chapter detailing how Venus operates in the signs.

Your ideal mate will go for security when it comes to money and possessions, but may be prone to inertia or be a little too comfort-loving. They may spend impulsively, but it's usually on something of real value. From time to time they will need to be less fixed about what they value and why, or how they view assets and their usefulness. They'll be clever, curious, very sure of themselves, and always in the know with an interesting (if contradictory) take on things. You can help them find the balance between their many points of view by offering them a more ideal picture of your sense of the object of their search. Sometimes they'll be impersonal in how they communicate, so try not to allow the bluntness or lack of polish to throw you off balance.

They'll be sensitive about their past, their family, or anything to do with home or their habits. Occasionally moody or defensive, you need to learn ways to help them feel secure before discussing these things with them. Innately creative and childlike, they will want to play and share and shine with you, as well as with all their friends. They will see the light at some point in their life because of a child. Hard workers, they will want to know the practical details of any plan of action, and the freedom to get it done in their own way as fast as they are able. They will be equally adept at taking the lead or following diligently.

Reasonable in relating to others, they will strive for fairness, balance, and justice in all their transactions in life, including you. They will definitely want everything 50-50, so that you will both share power and autonomy in the dance between the two of you. Take the initiative, and they will love you even more. Given your ideal mate's passion and intensity, your love life will never be boring. You want it light and free, perfectly complementing your ideal mate's depth and power regarding their likes and dislikes.

Your ideal partner will be a progressive philosopher who is up for an adventure, whether physical or psychological. They will be freedom loving, and encourage others in that direction. Though they may not seem open-minded due to the passion in how they state their attitude, if you make a good point, they will listen and eventually modify their point of view. They will have a legalistic approach to things, a natural teaching aptitude, and at some point in their lives will be long- distance travelers. They will be the boss in their profession, probably self-employed, and could attain to quite some influence, power, or fame. Though their situation will seem unstable from time to time, they will have the power of quick response and keeping things in motion will benefit them. You can show them the rhythm to things, or ways of refining their approach to make it more agreeable to others. They will be fairly ambitious, and their life lesson here is to serve others without dominating them, rule with a light hand, and be careful of the rationalizations for holding on to obsolete standards or wearing unnecessary chains.

Your mate will have some very unusual friends, very progressive and perhaps eccentric. They will have a natural love of people, and be willing to work and play in various group functions doing interesting things together. Thus you and your beloved should have quite a few satisfactory friendships and life experiences together. Somewhat intuitive, they will occasionally daydream more than they should, but it's a sign something in their lives is finishing, and new things are on the way. Though they would rather embrace new beginnings than hang around for endings, you can help them gracefully close out old ways of life and attitudes which only lead to suffering. Much of what they worry about is part of the generic human condition, and is teaching them compassion and forgiveness.

OTHER FACTORS

As could be inferred from earlier paragraphs, if you have a Sun in Libra or a Libra Ascendant, you will be attracted to certain sign energies more than others. Because you are an Air sign, you will be attracted to others with the Air element strong in their chart. You would do very well with someone with a Moon or Ascendant in Gemini or Aquarius, since these are the other two Air signs. You will also be very attracted to someone with Venus in Libra, and they to you. You will naturally like each other, and could become very good friends fairly quickly.

You will almost always do well with any of the Fire signs, those being Leo and Sagittarius, and as I said earlier, Aries. Here someone with a Moon or Ascendant in Leo or Sagittarius would be very compatible for you, less so Moon in Aries if you have a Sun in Libra. Someone with an Aries Ascendant would exert a very strong attraction on you. All the Fire signs will bring you exciting and warm feelings and experiences stimulating your social tendencies, giving you much needed interaction and opportunities to express your sweet, lovable, peacemaking influence.

Pisces energies bring growth to your Sun, helping you broaden and deepen your emotional expression. Your ruler, Venus, finds its "exaltation," or sign of greatest growth, in Pisces. Therefore, Pisces energies challenge your tendency to avoid or gloss over things, and lead you to be deeper, more compassionate, selfless, and empathetic in how you naturally express your light and power. They show you ways to complete things and see things from a vaster perspective. Since this sign "quincunxes" your

Libra energies, it assists you through combining productive opportunities with challenges to learn stability, nobility, and a deeper connectedness with the central order of things.

Pisces also helps you get outside your theoretical world and opinions, offering their own fluid, rhythmic, and intuitive approach to life showing you how to enjoy life to a greater degree. They move you through subtle, complex, and vast feelings, and force you to sacrifice certain attitudes and approaches so you can expand into your own greater ideal. Pisces brings adjustments in your tentative and balanced approach as well as vaster perspectives. Even though it may seem weird at times, it should be a productive learning experience for you when you're face to face with Pisces energies.

Someone with Cancer or Capricorn energies may be more difficult because those signs "square" Libra, indicating challenge, conflict, and the need to learn correct forms of nurturing or responsible efficient action or non-action. Still, your ruler Venus confronts mixed feelings with those sign energies, because it likes the soft watery sympathetic side of Cancer, and the earthy qualities of practicality and authority that Capricorn models. It is important to remember that Capricorn grounds you and can satisfy your basic needs, even if things get unsettled from time to time. Virgo is another mixed-bag sign for you. Your ruler, Venus, is naturally comfortable with Virgo's earth energies, but doesn't do well in that sign due to Venus needing compassion, forgiveness, and openness to a vast point of view, which are not Virgo's natural qualities. You naturally do well with Taurus energies, since there is harmony due to you both being ruled by Venus. You are naturally comfortable with how agreeable, moderate, and enjoyable each other are, and can usually enjoy each other's company quite admirably.

You have a **SUN in SCORPIO** (the following descriptions are also true if you have a Scorpio Ascendant)

If you've ever investigated astrology, you probably already know your ideal mate will have a heavy Taurus influence, since that sign naturally complements your own highly intense nature. Of course, this could mean a Taurus Ascendant, Moon in Taurus, or any number of other types of Taurus influence, whether natal (birth chart) or progressed (how the natal evolves over time).

This indicates that your natural mate will be good looking, firm but fair, and have some form of artistic talent. With classic features and probably a dimple in their cheeks, they will always try to live up to their ideal of a form of perfection, comfort, luxury, beauty, or well-polished grace and charm, and be affectionate, agreeable and pleasant (as long as you give them their way!)

Your Beloved will be a model of stability, someone you can rely on to be absolutely as good as their word. They will be dependable, generous, devoted, sympathetic, patient, reserved, and pretty secure. You'll never be able to push or pull them into or out of anything, and they'll show you how to enjoy life's simpler pleasures with more fulfillment and less discontent. Definitely into creature comforts and sensory pleasures, they don't understand why anyone else could ever live differently.

Being naturally harmonious and secure, they are able to bring a calm to you that other signs cannot. Many of your natural suspicions are alleviated by Taurus, since they are pretty much "what you see is what you get," consistent and usually pleasantly straightforward with no artifice. You'll certainly know where they stand, and they will have the strength to dance with you, resist you, persuade you, refuse you, and still love you deeply at the end of the drama. They will help you with certain practicalities, and you will help them to let go of what they need to with more ease and grace. They capture, and you transform. You also help to arouse a much deeper feeling intensity to their otherwise very comfortable lives. You are here to show them how to quicken the pace, assisting the decision-making process by "cutting to the chase."

Your Venus sign is very important in showing you the type of person you'll do best with, since Venus rules Taurus, your natural mate sign. As you know from what you've read already, Venus also shows the energies we'll like the most, since Venus rules our ideal of beauty. So in your case, Scorpio, this double Venusian influence gives your Venus sign attraction even more power, since the ruler of your natural mate is the planet of love itself! The sign your TransPluto occupies also symbolizes a higher, invisible aspect of your ideal mate's character which will attract you. Most people currently alive were born with this outer planet in Leo. You can find out a lot more about who and what attracts you in the next chapter detailing how Venus operates in the signs.

Your ideal mate will value mental training and discipline, and their communication skills and talent for mediation could bring them wealth, as will their resourcefulness and persistence. Clever and on the alert for the hidden value in objects and processes, they will be able to see multiple uses for things. They will be naturally studious, open to consider new information leading to any reasonable point of view, and sensitive to things in the environment which elude others. They will feel a strong need for a sense of family with their neighbors, and be very caring about their brothers and sisters, perhaps to the point of having to provide for them.

Your Beloved will come from a family with noble values, or a past that emphasized creativity and self-expression in a very natural way. They will want to be proud of their family and home, but can be too critical, nitpicky, or concerned with proprieties about small things, especially with their children. While they will want to be of service to their kids, they need to learn to lighten up, as do you. Your ideal mate won't do well with domestic disharmony. Note the snorting and stomping going on along with the smile, and learn how to disengage from pushing things too far.

They won't do very well with workplace conflicts either, and here is where your precision in getting to the core of any conflict can help them get oriented and back on their center. Your natural partner will have a very balanced approach to their work and strive to maintain harmonious and fair conditions in their work situation. They will expect their colleagues to be pleasant, well-mannered and reasonable. Their strong suit is their gift for mediation or peacemaking in the office. If your mate suffers from health problems, it's usually because of a lack of moderation, or some other imbalance between mind, body, and Spirit. They will definitely need lots of fresh air, human interaction, and romance to feel their best.

Your ideal partner will be as intense and possessive as you in their relationships, but conceal it beneath a very pleasant, even placid exterior. They will feel things as deeply as you do, but want to enjoy life more than explore all there is to probe. Though they will not like to lose anything or anyone, your mate will be philosophic about their losses and defeats, since they will instinctively know these open a new futures, distant horizons, and adventures that ultimately regenerate them. Their way to power is through some form of higher education, abstract mental development, or spiritual training, breaking free from old inertias. Here you help them tremendously through your skill at self-purification techniques to concentrate power and your ability to get beneath the superficialities of life.

Your natural partner will be a life-long learner, but slow and steady rather than flashy and quick. They will plug along until they reach the information they need that gives them the high ground of authority. If they travel, they could find themselves hanging out with some very powerful or influential people, or in a position of power or influence. That's when their true flowering can come forth, which is serving the greatest good for the greatest number in a very impersonal but idealistic way.

Your mate will be able to excel in media or anything involving group work or coordinating projects. They do well in any job where they can take many different components and weave them together in unique and specialized ways. They may also have an unusual profession or one of the ancient trades, such as working with plants or animals, bookbinding, candle making, metalworking, or taking unique products from one area and selling them in another.

They may also be involved in a profession of the future, working to bring forth innovations, inventions, and revolutionary breakthroughs in areas of human life.

Your natural partner will have some peculiar friends who may be contradictory, deceptive, or just strange. Their friends may also be mystics, very intuitive, or work behind the scenes or in an institution of some sort. Of course, your mate will have compassionate, humanitarian ideals, but may procrastinate more than they should about doing what it would take to fulfill them. Your love may even secretly hope that their friends will take care of the larger aspirations while they anchor the party. Their sorrow will come through impulsiveness, jumping to conclusions while delaying needed actions, or needless quarrels that quickly arise out of nowhere. You can help them turn quickly toward a new direction or action and stop being uselessly aggravated by the resistances of life. Your strength is in assisting them to focus on what needs to be cut out of the life to allow more movement and freedom so that they can find a new stability or enjoyment.

OTHER FACTORS

As could be inferred from earlier paragraphs, if you have a Sun in Scorpio or a Scorpio Ascendant, you will be attracted to certain sign energies more than others. Because you are a Water sign, you will be attracted to others with the Water element strong in their chart. You would do very well with someone with a Moon or Ascendant in Cancer or Pisces, since these are the other two Water signs. You will also be very attracted to someone with Venus in Scorpio, and they to you. You will naturally like each other, and could become very good friends fairly quickly.

You will almost always do well with any of the Earth signs, those being Virgo and Capricorn, and as I said earlier, Taurus. Here someone with a Moon or Ascendant in Virgo or Capricorn would be very compatible for you, less so Moon in Taurus if you have a Sun in Scorpio. Someone with a Taurus Ascendant would exert a very strong attraction on you. All the Earth signs will bring you a sense of grounded practical security and experiences stimulating your powerful magnetism, giving you much needed interaction and opportunities to express your intensely focused power of attraction and regeneration.

People with strong Capricorn energies bring growth to your solar energies, as your worldly ruler Mars finds its "exaltation," or sign of greatest growth, in Capricorn. Since this sign "sextiles" your Scorpio energies, Capricorns help provide you productive opportunities to learn practicality, maturity, and patient discipline. Capricorn energies challenge your ability to act responsibly over the long haul, and show you the way to be more deliberate, more efficient, and more organized in how you naturally express your light and power.

Someone with Cancer energies may harmonize with your Sun sign, but may be challenging because your ruler Mars doesn't do well with those sign energies. Cancer is usually too emotional, changeable, and subjective, and Mars needs practicality, discipline, and objectivity. You naturally do well with Aries energies, since there is harmony due to you both being ruled by Mars. You are naturally comfortable with each other's intensity, and can usually keep up with one another admirably.

Someone with Leo or Aquarius energies may be more difficult because those signs "square" Scorpio, indicating challenge, conflict, and the need to learn correct forms of gentle, noble, or impersonal action or non-action. They are as fixed and unmoving as you are, and show you the circumstances where force alone will not get you what you want. Still, Aquarius grounds you and can satisfy your basic needs, even if things get unsettled from time to time.

You have a **SUN IN SAGITTARIUS** (the following descriptions are also true if you have a Sagittarius Ascendant)

If you've ever investigated astrology, you probably already know your ideal mate will have a heavy Gemini influence, since that sign naturally complements your own highly energetic nature. Of course, this could mean a Gemini Ascendant, Moon in Gemini, or any number of other types of Gemini influence, whether natal (birth chart) or progressed (how the natal evolves over time).

Your natural mate will be curious, knowledgeable about many different things, clever, adaptable, and articulate. They will be able to argue many points of view, see things from several angles of investigation, and at times be highly impersonal. Very social, they'll know many different kinds of people, and have had very diverse experiences in their checkered lives. They will learn things easily, but may just as easily forget them and go on to other things. Specialists rather than generalists and theoretical with multiple practical skills, they may suffer from a lapse

194

of focus or getting distracted. If they don't learn to stand for something they'll fall for anything, and find themselves arguing complex mental abstractions that may lack an overview, or become traps of self-justification which create dilemmas.

Like you, your mate will think that there are always other possibilities just around the corner, and always have more than one thing going on. Because they will see many contradictory elements of things, they may be hard to pin down to any one point of view, and may lapse into cynicism. Your partner will be a great conversationalist with a vivid imagination going in many directions at once, and life with your mate will seem like you're with several people rolled into one. They will be attracted to the new and unusual, and will know some pretty far out things.

Your Mercury sign is very important in showing you the type of person you'll do best with, since Mercury rules Gemini, your natural mate sign. The sign your Uranus occupies also symbolizes a higher, invisible aspect of your ideal mate's character that will attract you. As you know from what you've read already, Venus also shows the mate you'll like the most, since Venus rules our ideal of beauty. You can find out a lot more about who and what attracts you in the next chapter detailing how Venus operates in the signs.

Your partner may be insecure financially, likely due more to the feelings they were raised with than any prediction of lack or want. In fact, your mate will be extraordinarily resilient financially through wanting to conserve what they have, and regardless of how much they complain, they'll have a fallback resource when all else fails. They will be involved in their family's finances somehow, or may inherit wealth. You can help them to be more generous, and not clutch emotionally when they have to let go of something.

Proud of what they know and learn, they will have a way of stating or declaring things rather than just saying them. Your natural mate will find light, clarity, and nobility from a sibling or a neighbor, and from learning how to communicate the central issue of a thing, rather than getting stuck in stubbornly defending marginal or tangential points of view that may be one-sided. They will claim power by asserting their ideas forcefully, and know so many details that they usually don't lose an argument. This is where your sense of humor and ability not to take things so seriously will assist their ability to learn some perspective, and your largeness of vision will help to expand their understanding in ways they do not know, no matter what they say.

Your mate will be very meticulous about their home, and learned to worry and fuss about a lot of little things when they were young. Not so precise and ordered in your home life as they will be, you can help them be a little looser, just as they help you get some order in your life. Health concerns were a big issue when they were young, and you can help them move beyond their fears and worries.

Your mate will learn fairness and balance concerning children, who affect their stability. To them, children represent an ideal, but they'll have to go deeper into their own values or pay a karmic debt because of a child, whether their own or another's. Your mate's vivid imagination almost effortlessly and spontaneously will create very agreeable forms of self-expression. They want to create beautiful forms, whether of play, art, or spontaneous expression. Their feelings about money and people, as well as their ability to regenerate, will directly affect their health. Their emotional state about health and work issues will show how degenerative or regenerative their magnetism actually is. They need to learn purification exercises and activities to change their health for the better.

Your Beloved is not exactly the model of consistency or responsibility, and so it will be up to you to honor the need for mutual freedom while they experience the textures that such freedom allows. Of course you both should be faithful as you move with the changing shapes in your relationship. As you express your natural openness to greater futures, they will have opportunities to stay fascinated with the different people you seem to be, and will naturally be excited to dance with the various facets of you.

Though always trying to figure you out, you will lead them on the adventure they crave in relationships. You have such an expansive personality, and are so generous and giving, you will lead your beloved out of their private mind-based world into a much broader way to live, give, and enjoy life. They may try to control your shared resources too much, and you can show them your persistence and ability to claim your own authority. Due to a legacy, or the social values they live within, they may feel chained or held back in some way. They have the ability to calculate a long-range plan to get what they desire, but what they ultimately wind up with may be more of a curse than a blessing if they don't use the right means to get to their ends.

Your mate will be able to see a progressive overview to life once they get beyond nervous bouncing around. Very intelligent but also willful, they will need an integrated higher education if they're to get the power and recognition they want. They will know some very unusual and far-out things, and have friends in distant places with unique personalities or who live differently from the mainstream culture. Your mate's friends will be pioneers in some way, or very self-reliant and action-oriented.

Your love may be insecure in their profession or public standing, and will try to cultivate a compassionate and caring image. There may be secrets or traveling connected with their profession, or they may have to do their thing within an institutional environment. They will make friends quickly, but may need to be less impulsive or abrasive or they will lose them just as fast. Your mate will find the edge of their future within a group situation, or because of a friend's power or need to do battle.

Your mate will have experienced sorrow or self-undoing due to vanity, stubbornness, or overindulgence in sensory pleasures. Money will be a big karmic determinant for them, how they use it or abuse it, and by how generous or selfish they are. They can clear out a lot of old inert subconscious material by changing their values or how they use what they have. Your love will want to capture some desires which may not fulfill them. If they're self-destructive, it's because they've refused to change their values rather than anything you or anyone else said or did. If they learn how to let go of being passive-aggressive, they'll transform a lot of stagnant personality tendencies and focus their power to bring them the rewards they want, along with the freedom and opportunities to move into the future.

OTHER FACTORS

As could be inferred from earlier paragraphs, if you have a Sun in Sagittarius or a Sagittarius Ascendant, you will be attracted to certain sign energies more than others. Because you are a Fire sign, you will be attracted to others with the Fire element strong in their chart. You would do very well with someone with a Moon or Ascendant in Aries or Leo, since these are the other two Fire signs. You will also be very attracted to someone with Venus in Sagittarius, and they to you. You will naturally like each other, and could become very good friends fairly quickly.

You will almost always do well with any of the Air signs, those being Libra, Aquarius, and as I said earlier, Gemini. Here someone with a Moon or Ascendant in Libra or Aquarius would be very compatible for you, less so Moon in Gemini if you have a Sun in Sagittarius. Someone with a Gemini Ascendant would exert a very strong attraction on you. However, your ruler Jupiter sometimes has a hard time with Gemini energies, since they tend to be too narrow for Jupiter's larger vision of distant adventures to live. Still, all the Air signs will bring ideas and people stimulating your inspirational tendencies, and give you much needed interaction and opportunities to express your forever expansive vision.

People with strong Cancer energies bring growth to your solar energies, helping you deepen your emotional expression and your caring, protective side. Your ruler, Jupiter, finds its "exaltation," or sign of greatest growth, in Cancer. Therefore, Cancers challenge your tendencies to run all over the place, scattering yourself too widely, and force you to be more tender, nurturing and focused in the present moment. They help you see what you really care about, offering you ways to teach others through giving generously of yourself in your natural expressions of light and power.

Since Cancer "quincunxes" your Sagittarius energies, it assists you through combining productive opportunities with challenges to learn detachment, friendliness, a vision of the greatest good for the greatest number, and a simple and gentle enjoyment of what you have and what you value. Cancer people and experiences help you to feel more in the moment, moving you through deeper, more complex and active feelings while you sacrifice certain attitues and expand into your greater ideal or enjoyment. Though it forces adjustments in your expansive approach, it is still a very productive learning experience for you any time you find yourself face to face with Cancer energies.

On the other hand, your ruler Jupiter doesn't do well with Capricorn energies, because they are usually too conservative and limiting, or too calculating and personal, for your naturally freedom-loving spontaneous nature. Virgo energies may also be difficult because that sign "squares" Sagittarius, indicating challenge, conflict, and the need to learn correct forms of compassionate, forgiving, freeing and adaptable action or non-action. Pisces, also a sign that squares you, is actually a very fortunate influence because it grounds you and can satisfy your basic needs, even if things get unsettled from time to time. You naturally understand Pisces energies, since there is harmony due to you both being ruled by Jupiter. You will be naturally comfortable with each other's movable, expansive, generous, and abundant styles, and usually have the ability to keep up with one another admirably.

You have a **SUN IN CAPRICORN** (the following descriptions are also true if you have a Capricorn Ascendant)

If you've ever investigated astrology, you probably already know your ideal mate will have a heavy Cancer influence, since that sign naturally complements your own highly sensitive nature. Of course, this could mean a Cancer Ascendant, Moon in Cancer, or any number of other types of Cancer influence, whether natal (birth chart) or progressed (how the natal evolves over time).

Your natural partner will be caring, sympathetic, romantic, tender, and kind, but may occasionally be too defensive because of feeling too vulnerable and easily hurt in the past. They will be sensitive and personal, sometimes too sensitive for comfort, whether theirs, yours, or anyone else who happens to be around. A natural homebody, your Beloved will be very focused on and involved with their home and family. Somewhat conservative and a little old-fashioned, they will naturally go out of their way to nurture and provide for those in need. Your mate will have a highly active imagination, may be moody, love their privacy, and occasionally brood or get stuck in the past. This is where your natural maturity and ability to calculate how to move the life experience forward into the Now can help them tremendously.

Your love will always be somewhat childlike, never miss anything going on, sometimes take things for granted or too personally, and probably resemble someone from your childhood. They will be natural mirrors and mimics, learn through imitation, and are very creative with an ability to read the feelings in the people around them once they learn objectivity and detachment. Your mate's naturally sensitive nature can help you decrease any hardness in your personality so you can feel more connected to everyday life. Being naturally protective, appreciative, and prudent, they will be able to care for you in ways that fulfill some of your primal needs. This will assist you with any deep feelings of being deprived when younger. They'll often play it safe, because they're focused on taking care of immediate needs to make the present situation as secure as possible.

Your Moon sign is very important in showing you the type of person you'll do best with, since the Moon rules Cancer, your natural mate sign. The sign that your Sun occupies also symbolizes a higher, invisible aspect of your ideal mate's character that will attract you. As you know from what you've read already, Venus also shows the mate you'll like the most, since Venus rules our ideal of beauty. You can find out a lot more about who and what attracts you in the next chapter detailing how Venus operates in the signs.

Your natural partner will have a strong pride of possession with a desire to be creative and playful even if conservative with money and resources. They could be overly traditional or sentimental in some inflexible ways, and their self-indulgences and vanities show you where you'll probably need to explore issues involving boundaries and responsibilities. They will do well by getting involved in creative projects or activities involving children bringing them money or things of value. Sports or art in some form could play a part in getting what they want in life. Your mate will shed light on why you want what you want and your path of self-regeneration.

They will be precise and detail-oriented in their communications, and worry about things in their environment they may not be able to do much about. They will do well when they find a mental discipline giving them a way to order and prioritize the usefulness of the information they are made aware of. Interested in all things concerning health and healing, they may seem ambivalent due to the skeptical nature of their mind which moves between its beliefs and doubts.

Though your love may be untidy, they will want a beautiful home, or an ideal living situation. You can help your partner learn balance or fairness in terms of the relative value of who does what. What you do and don't do related to their home, family, or past will be very important for you both in some public way. They felt pushed and pulled between many perspectives when they were young, and probably learned how to go along to get along, even if it meant being insincere. Their parents probably tried to project or uphold an ideal of some sort, and they had to go along with their assigned role, regardless of how insecure they felt.

They experienced some intense power struggles around their self-expression or children in some way, and their losses in life will be the source of their power of regeneration through play and creativity, or stuck feelings that don't help them or anyone else. They will be very critical of their self-expression. They will want freedom in their work, and may travel as a result of their profession, so you may have to move when you're with your love! They are natural teachers, offering expansive ideas to help others fix things or make them work better.

In their relationships they'll often feel like they have things all figured out, and will justify everything they think and say from a personal angle. However, because they can be too subjective in their perspective, they could take some things for granted, and here you can introduce some balance and perspective. Be mature, and willing to find ways to work things out using time as your ally.

Your mate may have a lot of rules about relationships learned in childhood from a parent who was too old-fashioned or rigid. In this case you need to honor your own wisdom and maturity based in your own life experience. These will help to structure the dance between you in a manner appropriate to who you both are right now, not who either of you were when younger.

Your mate's uniqueness or genius will come out as a result of their losses, or they will suffer losses as a result of a friend. You can help them learn more impersonality and detachment through pointing out a bigger long-range picture. They will want absolute power over their finances, and are capable of doing some strange and innovative things to get what they want. They will have some very intuitive flashes of the future, but may not take many people into their confidence about what they see. They are capable of having a deep and wide visionary and compassionate spiritual philosophy, once they work out inner confusion and ambivalence.

In their profession they will usually be straightforward, hardworking, intense, dynamic, efficient, and to the point. Your partner will know how to take the initiative and want to be the boss, but may also provoke challenges or quarrels by their blunt outspoken style. They will want to take on tasks where they can work in short bursts of energy at their own pace, but may find themselves overwhelmed with all they've committed to do. They may even pioneer at something, or be the first to do something in their area. Finding stability in their friendships, they like to share the pleasures of the world with their friends. However, their excessive nature may attract hedonists, and here your self-discipline can be of great help to them. They can anchor the resources in any group and be the cohesive force holding things together and keeping things on track.

They will have fairly simple and natural ambitions, but can get too spread out or split between too many things going on, and as a result create unnecessary dilemmas and conflict. Your mate will need to learn mental and verbal reserve, and not try to talk circles around things. Your ability to help them not get distracted will be of great use to them. You can also help them organize their priorities so they don't get confused trying to fit too much into any given picture.

OTHER FACTORS

As could be inferred from earlier paragraphs, if you have a Sun in Capricorn or a Capricorn Ascendant, you will be attracted to certain sign energies more than others. Because you are an Earth sign, you will be attracted to others with the Earth element strong in their chart. You would do very well with someone with a Moon or Ascendant in Taurus or Virgo, since these are the other two Earth signs. You will also be very attracted to someone with Venus in Capricorn, and they to you. You will naturally like each

205

other, and could become very good friends fairly quickly.

You will almost always do well with any of the Water signs, those being Scorpio and Pisces, and as I said earlier, Cancer. Here someone with a Moon or Ascendant in Scorpio and Pisces would be very compatible for you, less so Moon in Cancer if you have a Sun in Capricorn. Someone with a Cancer Ascendant would exert a very strong attraction on you. However, your worldly ruler Saturn gets conflicted with Cancer energies, as they are usually too personal, sensitive, and introverted in their own self-sustaining natural self-expression, and Saturn does its best when reminded of fairness, moderation, thoughtfulness, beauty, and idealism. Still, all the Water signs will bring you deep feelings and experiences stimulating your social tendencies and give you much needed interaction and opportunities to express your practical, mature, and responsible influence.

People with strong Libra energies bring growth to your solar energies, helping you balance and refine your personal power and authority. Your ruler, Saturn, finds its "exaltation," or sign of greatest growth, in Libra. Therefore, Libra energies round out your self-sufficient ambition, and offer you beautiful and easy interactions so you can be more mature, refined, stylish, and even-handed in how you naturally express your light and power. However, since this sign "squares" your Capricorn energies, Libra often brings some difficulty or conflict through differing points of view with a need to learn correct forms of sensitive, honest, and direct action or non-action.

Someone with Aries energy may be difficult because that sign "squares" Capricorn, with the same effect as above. Also, your ruler Saturn doesn't do well with Aries energy, because it is usually too impulsive, self-centered, and lack diplomacy, and Saturn needs thoughtfulness, consideration, and balance. Still, Aries grounds you and can satisfy your basic needs, even if things get unsettled from time to time. You naturally do well with Aquarius energies, since there is harmony due to you both being ruled by Saturn. You are naturally comfortable with each other's thoughtfulness, and can usually keep up with one another admirably.

You have a **SUN IN AQUARIUS** (the following descriptions are also true if you have an Aquarius Ascendant)

If you've ever investigated astrology, you probably already know your ideal mate will have a heavy Leo influence, since that sign naturally complements your own highly energetic nature. Of course, this could mean a Leo Ascendant, Moon in Leo, or any number of other types of Leo influences, whether natal (birth chart) or progressed (how the natal evolves over time).

Your natural mate will be highly magnetic, powerful and good looking with fair features, a radiant smile, a mane of hair, and be the ruler and law of their realm. They will be quite the actor or actress, and hold a view that expects everyone to join the royal play with them at the center of activity. Playful, noble, creative, dramatic, and ultra-social, they'll usually be up for a good party. They'll probably possess some form of artistic talent, which may come out in their lifestyle as well as their personal style. Though always striving to be gracious and put on the best show they can, they will also be stubborn and strong-willed. Your mate will love what and who they love in a very personal, heartfelt, spontaneous way, and never lack ego strength or opinions. They will definitely be part of some sort of social elite, and willing to do their dramatic part to make a more enlightened world become real.

Your ideal mate will take a personal pride in being with you, but may be a bit hot to handle and sometimes expect you to show more personal loyalty and attachment than you feel. Your mate will want you to take pride in them and in yourself and your accomplishments. Just try to pay attention and not get an attitude when your mate is roaring at you because you've done something too unexpected, unusual, eccentric, or bizarre. Your beloved will hold traditional ideas, and occasionally may prove to be too conservative or rigid for your naturally progressive and freedom-loving instincts. Your ability to center on the big picture, integrating all the pieces into a coherent overview of the whole of things will help your mate to find their place in the larger scheme of things. You are here to show them how to move their enthusiasms and convictions into life experience, assisting their sense of passionate social service through your detached visionary forms of social progress.

Your Sun sign is very important in showing you the type of person you'll do best with, since the Sun traditionally rules Leo, your natural mate sign. The sign the Moon occupies also symbolizes a higher, invisible aspect of your ideal mate's character. As you know from what you've read already, Venus also shows the mate you'll like the most, since Venus rules our ideal of beauty. You can find out a lot more about who and what attracts you in the next chapter detailing how Venus operates in the signs.

Your natural mate will be concerned about their money and resources, and always be seeking ways to make their assets work more effectively. They will value the resources of the natural world more than most, but must not underestimate their ability to set their own course when it comes to the most efficient use of their energies to earn their keep. They will come to value deeply those who work on their behalf. Their sense of discernment will be their most valuable resource once they develop it. Trying always to be fair and balanced in their view of things, your mate will weigh many different points of view before pronouncing their judgment of things. They will need beauty, peace, and harmony in their environment, and seek their siblings' evaluation of important things. In many ways, they will see you more as a brother or sister, someone to play with, than a mate.

Your natural partner will come from a past with many power struggles and losses, and will have had to turn their back on many desires and toxic emotions in this life. The roots of their discontent will run very deep, and there isn't much you can do except remember you're here to show them a vision of a more ideal future. You can teach them how to detach from stuck feelings so they can purify the foundations of their life. Your mate will believe children should be free to explore what they need to, and be willing to give them the widest future they are capable of seeing. Your mate will expect that children should achieve the best education possible, even if it means going some distance to get it. They will definitely glimpse a higher truth and vision because of a child. At some point in their life they will work for someone with great power or authority, or find themselves in a position of power and authority where they are working in service to those in subordinate positions.

Your Beloved will have a liberal policy when it comes to their relationships, but expect major loyalty nonetheless. They will want the relationship to be perpetually fresh and unique, a special creation they share with their significant other on the royal throne, i.e., you. They will follow a higher law and ideal in all their relationships, and always put on their best face, even when ordering others "off the list." And in their mind they probably will keep lists, of who and what pleases them, who and what does not, and what they have yet to decide on.

They will have conflicted feelings about their desires, and occasionally be subject to peculiar impulses and magnetic or psychic disturbances. These come because of over-receptivity to either the collective unconscious or the subconscious desires or inner conflicts of someone else. Your partner will be prone to losses due to the deception of others, which they will try to take philosophically. However, your mate will run the risk of having their compassion, which they value deeply, taken for weakness by those who don't really care for or about them. The ones who do this may lose your mate's companionship forever.

Your beloved will have a progressive philosophy, but may be a bit argumentative when it comes to spiritual matters. Still, their pursuit of truth will be genuine, spontaneous, and the source of their own connectedness with life. They definitely pursue new ideas and want to be the first to know things. Always looking for new fields to explore and master, they have a self-sufficient philosophy, believing each must do their best in the moment. Your mate will try to present a very pleasant picture to the world, displaying the best they have so all can feel a more secure enjoyment in the shared associations.

Your ideal partner will have a wide variety of friends and acquaintances, many of whom will be regarded as brothers or sisters. Their friends will usually be articulate, intelligent, and very interesting, if somewhat inconsistent. Your love will have a multiplicity of ambitions, and be the source of much information in any group situation they're in. Their sorrow will come from taking things too personally, or something related to their family of origin which will show them a facet of the universal human condition with its common and basic needs. Their habits may also be part of their self-undoing, and you can help them to close out old life conditions by focusing on what they really need in the here and now.

OTHER FACTORS

As could be inferred from earlier paragraphs, if you have a Sun in Aquarius or an Aquarius Ascendant, you will be attracted to certain sign energies more than others. Because you are an Air sign, you will be attracted to others with the Air element strong in their chart. You would do very well with someone with a Moon or Ascendant in Gemini or Libra, since these are the other two Air signs. You will also be very attracted to someone with Venus in Aquarius, and they to you. You will naturally like each other, and could become very good friends fairly quickly.

You will almost always do well with any of the Fire signs, those being Aries, Sagittarius, and as I said earlier, Leo. Here someone with a Moon or Ascendant in Aries or Sagittarius would be very compatible for you, less so Moon in Leo, if you have a Sun in Aquarius. Someone with a Leo Ascendant would exert a very strong attraction on you. All the Fire signs will bring energy, inspiration, and people who will stimulate your natural openness and curiosity, and give you much needed vitality and light to express your forever progressive imagination. However, your worldly ruler Saturn gets conflicted with Aries energies, as well as Cancer. Cancer energies are usually too personal, sensitive, and introverted in their own self-sustaining natural self-expression, and Aries is too impulsive and pays too little attention to form. Saturn does its best when reminded of fairness, moderation, thoughtfulness, beauty, and idealism.

People with strong Libra energies bring growth to your solar energies through Libra's sense of balance, fairness, reasonableness, and sociability. Your ruler, Saturn, finds its "exaltation," or sign of greatest growth, in Libra. Also, since your co-ruler Uranus is exalted in Virgo, both these signs stimulate you to be more balanced and practical in how you naturally express your light and power. Since Libra "trines" your Aquarius energies, a mate with these energies strong in their chart will help you through a natural harmony and understanding to cultivate a greater vision of social service, a more progressive and balanced social ideal, and could introduce you to co-workers you need to proceed with your goals and ambitions.

Someone with Scorpio or Taurus energies may be challenging because those sign "square" Aquarius, indicating conflict through differing points of view with a need to learn correct forms of creative or playful action or non-action. Your rulers, Saturn and Uranus, don't do well with those sign energies, because they are often too unmovable or inflexible in matters of gain and loss, and your rulers need opportunities to organize and innovate, exerting authority on their own terms. Still, Taurus grounds you and can satisfy your basic needs, even if things get unsettled from time to time. You naturally do well with Capricorn energies, since there is harmony due to you both being ruled by Saturn. You are naturally comfortable with each other's sense of responsibility, and usually are okay with the organization and connections to people of power and authority that Capricorn brings to your life.

You have a **SUN IN PISCES** (the following descriptions are also true if you have a Pisces Ascendant)

If you've ever investigated astrology, you probably already know your ideal mate will have a heavy Virgo influence, since that sign naturally complements your own highly durable nature. Of course, this could mean a Virgo Ascendant, Moon in Virgo, or any number of other types of Virgo influence, whether natal (birth chart) or progressed (how the natal evolves over time).

Your ideal partner will believe in the virtue of working at making a better world. They will aspire to personal excellence in many details of self-improvement, complementing your own mysticism and intuitive awareness enabling you to know things others don't. Your mate will be very rational, organized, and want things to work more perfectly.

That is why they will be practical and detail-oriented, and probably focused on health issues as an important part of their self-maintenance. Naturally willing to be of service, they will always be aware of more efficient ways to make things happen, but may nitpick and get too focused on minor things, ignoring the bigger picture. This is where your sense of the larger general situation will help balance their focus on many smaller issues and details.

Your mate will worry about things in ways that create nervous tension, so your ability to demonstrate gentle detachment can assist you both to a more fluid dance. Your mate will have the virtues of discernment and ability to put everything in its proper place so the larger whole or operation functions more efficiently. Your power is in the imaging, theirs is in how to make it work. They will teach you how to mobilize yourself in a practical way while you will teach them detachment and doing the work for its own sake, not with an eye to a specific outcome. You can teach them how to play while they work, while they can teach you how to work while you play. They will show you ways to get the job accomplished, while you will teach them emotional depth and adaptability.

Your Mercury sign is very important in showing you the type of person you'll do best with, since Mercury rules Virgo, your natural mate sign. The sign your Uranus occupies also symbolizes a higher, invisible aspect of your ideal mate's character that will attract you. As you know from what you've read already, Venus also shows the mate you'll like the most, since Venus rules our ideal of beauty. You can find out a lot more about who and what attracts you in the next chapter detailing how Venus operates in the signs.

Your ideal mate will always be learning a more balanced approach to wealth, what they value, and how they use it. Partnership will be important in your mate's resources, and they will value you and all their past partnerships, personal and professional, as part of what they draw on to sustain their self-image. Very moderate in their approach to capturing and possessing whatever they feel is aesthetically pleasing to them, they will also have a very penetrating view of things, always analyzing and probing deeper and deeper into their understanding of what they desire to learn.

They will be aware of small details that others overlook, and as such are natural detectives. Ultra-sensitive to their environment, they must learn to detach from counterproductive or emotionally stuck thoughts and opinions. Due to their habit of seeing what's wrong or needs correcting in situations, you can antidote any tendency they have to criticize or be a malcontent by practicing detachment, discernment, and generating positivity and good will.

They will have been taught to value learning across a very broad range of knowledge from a very early age, and probably traveled extensively when young. At some point, you both will have more than one residence at the same time, such as a summer home and a winter home. Your natural mate eventually will want to make their home in a place far from where they were born, either to find you, or if later, to fulfill your mutual need for adventure in your lives. They may also have lived on or near a college campus, a spiritual center, or a transportation center in their early days, or want to do that when they are older.

Occasionally tending to be a bit of a taskmaster on themselves and others, you help them to forgive and lighten up. A lot was expected of them as children, and they may in turn expect a lot from their own children. Try to help them to be realistic in their rules, and moderate and fair in their spontaneous expressions. Their art or creative expression will show them their bondage to harsh perceptions and forms of perfectionism. Your mate will be extraordinarily inventive in their work, able to see a bigger picture while taking care of the details needed to carry the work through to its ideal state. They will be happiest when working with friends, or working within a group dedicated to a larger vision of an ideal.

They will have a very strong subconscious connection with all their partners, but may not always be clear about the signals they are sending or receiving. Through their ability to be truly an equal with others, and neither subservient to nor dominant over them, they will learn not to be so critical and forgive much without comment. They will be prone to peculiar dreams and vague notions regarding people, and may be too blunt or impulsive in trying to get what they want. They will become very combative when subject to losses, and their regenerative strength comes when they turn quickly toward a better future and act on it.

Your Beloved will have a pretty simple and straightforward philosophy, believing any true spiritual living involves a certain degree of creature comforts. When confronted with a philosophical challenge, they are instinctively stubborn and unwilling to change their moral outlook, and may dig in their heels while insisting on wanting everything pleasant. You can capture your mate's imagination using honey rather than vinegar, so keep the ideas flowing and communications open, showing them the other side of the coin, or other parts of the picture. Your mate will present two distinct facets to their world, and will probably have a profession involving reading, writing, or some other form of communication. They definitely will have two distinct professions in their lifetime, or two specialized functions within a larger field of activity.

They will treat their friends like family, and at some point in life, may open your home to a group function, such as a place where an organization can meet. Since some of their friends may be a bit self-indulgent, watch the habit patterns. Your mate will be proud of your home, but may be too fussy in some way. Any vanity, arrogance, stubbornness or selfishness will be their source of self-undoing or sorrow. Transcending pride about lesser things, they need to come to an enlightened motive, and act honorably and magnanimously when bringing their various business affairs to completion. More than most, your beloved will do very well in all meditation practices that awaken the heart, so encourage them in this direction to bring forth their dignity and courageous nobility

OTHER FACTORS

As could be inferred from earlier paragraphs, if you have a Sun in Pisces or a Pisces Ascendant, you will be attracted to certain sign energies more than others. Because you are a Water sign, you will be attracted to others with the Water element strong in their chart. You would do very well with someone with a Moon or Ascendant in Cancer or Scorpio, since these are the other two Water signs. You will also be very attracted to someone with Venus in Pisces, and they to you. You will naturally like each other, and could become very good friends fairly quickly.

You will almost always do well with any of the Earth signs, those being Taurus and Capricorn, and as I said earlier, Virgo. Here someone with a Moon or Ascendant in Taurus or Capricorn would be very compatible for you, less so Moon in Virgo if you have a Sun in Pisces. Someone with a Virgo Ascendant would exert a very strong attraction on you. All the Earth signs will bring you a sense of grounded practical security and experiences stimulating your powerful imagination and universal wisdom, giving you much needed interaction and opportunities to express your ability to forgive and bring an end to old patterns and cycles.

People with strong Cancer energies bring growth to your solar energies, helping you deepen your emotional expression and your caring, protective side. Your ruler, Jupiter, finds its "exaltation," or sign of greatest growth, in Cancer. Therefore, Cancer energies challenge your tendencies to scatter your emotions too widely or let yourself be imposed on, and force you to be more tender and nurturing to yourself in the here and now. This sign helps you to see what you really care about, offering you ways to take care of yourself and others in compassionate, forgiving, and wise emotional actions which naturally express your light and power.

Since Cancer "trines" your Pisces energies, a mate with these energies strong in their chart will help you through a natural harmony and understanding to learn to feel more in the moment, moving you through deeper, more complex and active feelings. Though it forces emotional movement despite your ambivalence, it is still a very productive learning experience for you any time you find yourself face to face with Cancer energies.

On the other hand, your ruler Jupiter doesn't do well with Capricorn energies, because they are often too conservative and limiting, or too calculating and personal, for your naturally expansive, forgiving and compassionate nature. Someone with Gemini energies may also be difficult because that sign "squares" Pisces, indicating challenge, conflict, and the need to learn correct forms of discerning, practical, optimistic, freeing or adaptable action or non-action. Also, your ruler Jupiter doesn't do well with Gemini energies, because they are usually too restless and scattered among a thousand contradictions, and Jupiter needs a focused, personal experience of nurturing within a big picture to do its best. Sagittarius, also a sign that squares you, is actually a very fortunate influence because it grounds you and can satisfy your basic needs, even if things get unsettled from time to time. You naturally understand Sagittarius energies, since there is harmony due to you both being ruled by Jupiter. You will be naturally comfortable with each other's movable, expansive, generous, and abundant styles, and usually have the ability to keep up with one another admirably.

CHAPTER EIGHT

VENUS, WHO WE LIKE AND WHY WE LIKE THEM

Because Venus is the part of us which likes things and enjoys being liked, as well as what we appreciate and value, the sign our Venus is in shows us the quality of who we like and why we like them. All signs have something likeable about them, and our Venus naturally shows who we are attracted to. In this chapter, we'll explore some of the many qualities of Venus in each of the 12 signs. This will give you hints about the type of perfect mate you'll be naturally attracted to!

VENUS IN THE SIGNS

Venus in Aries

You instinctively like people who are direct, simple, innocent, forceful, and spontaneous. Naturally attracted to those who are straightforward and relate their values to their self-image, you're quick to commit to a relationship, sometimes too quickly. You are not attracted to manipulators or people who whine and make excuses.

Be more aware of why you like what you like, and be more objective and less impulsive in what you value. You and the people you're attracted to may have rushed into relationships in the past only to crash out again when they realized others didn't have the clear and strong feelings they did.

Because you're on a lifelong romance of constant activity, you and your mate will always be on the move! You want a lot of non-stop experiences with your mate, and expect them to be as straightforward and honest in their likes and dislikes as you are.

You will believe what you want to believe about others, whether it is accurate, realistic, or even useful, so beware of jumping to conclusions and justifying them after the fact. Once someone has your loyalty, your mind and heart are made up, and it would take a bomb blast to shake either of you loose from your commitment.

However, if another betrays you, then your Venus quickly leads you to feel and know the old dream is over, never to return. Because you're on a lifelong romance of experiencing as much as you can, if a relationship ends for whatever reason, you are fairly good at turning to a new future, rapidly leaving the past behind. With the emotional frankness and spontaneity of this position, there is some need for caution so that you or those you're attracted to don't get aggravated on slight provocation.

You have no problem confronting others on their relational inconsistencies; just beware of getting into relationships where you or others are drawn into unnecessary arguments and conflicts because of impatience, internal pressures, or lack of self-control. Though not naturally attracted to these qualities, you need someone who can teach you to have more patience and long-term follow-through. Another thing your Beloved will do is help you learn to like those things and people which expose you to new experiences and values, whether you instinctively think you will like them or not.

The worldly expression of your Venus is affected by the sign position of your Mars, which may involve oppositions and conflicts, since Venus is in "exile" in Aries, the sign opposite Libra, which it rules. The spiritual expression of your Venus is affected by the sign position of Pluto.

Venus in Aries is in its own 12th sign. The interactive instincts express value as active harvests in each moment. There can be issues of impatience creating sorrow and unexpected endings. This position shares a phase relationship with Venus in Virgo.

Venus in Aries is in its own 7th sign. The interactive instincts express a sense of perspective/proportion as initiatives in relationships. There can be issues of frankness feeling like pushiness. This position shares a phase relationship with Venus in Scorpio.

Venus in Taurus

You like people who are affectionate, genial, simple, and agreeable. Your ideal mate will join you in the pursuit of enjoying the finest life has to offer in the pleasures of the senses, whether food, drink, clothes, adornments, or any other thing which makes life enjoyable. All your relationships are geared toward pleasant, stable, and straightforward interactions, and because you are so naturally inclined to pursue the pleasures of this world, either you or your mate or both run the risk of overindulgence.

When you find your beloved, you will both have to learn a healthy moderation and open to new likes from time to time to expand your comfort zone. Regardless of differences in social positions or financial situations, your relationships help you experience the value in all things, and increase your capacity for appreciation.

You probably have an artistic gift, may be a patron of the arts, and really enjoy easy social interactions. You may be stubborn, but you also are reliable and consistent, probably good-looking, fun to be around, and enjoy love's peaceful silences and tenderness as well as its more boisterous demonstrations. You love to touch and be touched in every way which delights your senses.

Because you're on a life-long romance of enjoying all life has to offer, you naturally live by the knowledge that "pleasure shared is pleasure doubled." You and your mate will want to provide others a greater sense of enjoyment. Always up for a good party, you both will know how to entertain in a stylish way so all will enjoy the fullness of the experience.

As a result of the fixity and directness of your affections, once you hit a comfortable groove with your partner, things will just go and go and go. Even when things are rocky, this position will endure, as you and your mate will value stability. When there is discontent, it is usually balanced by the many things you enjoy.

Your values are very fixed, for better or worse, and your mutual determination to share pleasurable experiences will be so strong that you'll move from discomfort to comfort with a steadiness of purpose that nothing can shake. This life you and your Beloved will learn more from detaching from lesser pleasures and expanding with moderation into greater enjoyments and more refined forms of sensory experience than from denial of your pleasure principle.

Because it is in the sign it rules, the worldly expression of your Venus is determined by itself; the spiritual expression of your Venus is affected by the sign position of Venus' "higher octave" Neptune and TransPluto.

Venus in Taurus is in its own 1st sign. The interactive instincts express value in its own natural terms, making relationships pleasant. There can be issues of inertia and stubbornness keeping things stuck in a rut. This position shares a phase relationship with Venus in Libra.

Venus in Taurus is in its own 8th sign. The interactive instincts express a sense of perspective/proportion through attracting all it thinks will bring pleasure. There can be issues of overindulgence leading to losses. This position shares a phase relationship with Venus in Sagittarius.

Venus in Gemini

You are the ultimate people pleaser, knowing how to say the right thing at the right time, and really like the process of exploring all the points of view which open your imagination. You're witty, clever, and adaptable in relationships, but sometimes too restless due to a lack of mental focus. You will present many faces to your beloved, just as they will with you, and each of you has lots of acquaintances. You don't do well with jealous people.

You and your ideal mate would be bored by anything less than lots of variety in how you relate to others, as you will find you're both chameleons who change with the "psychic weather," continually examining and reorienting relative to your environment. You and your mate will like changing your environment in small ways. You are multifaceted, clever, curious, adaptable, and probably somewhat contradictory at times. You are so open to a wide range of experiences that occasionally you may have too much on your plate, and will only be able to "share" your experiences after you've already had time to think about them.

Because you're on a life-long romance with ideas, you both will love good discussions, exchanging ideas which help each of you discover new perspectives which lead to new questions and further discoveries. You love to experiment, think out loud, explore and talk yourself and others into and out of many different ideas. You have a pleasant voice and communication style, and many insights into social values and interactions, even if some of these seem not to be very well thought out.

Though this position occasionally seems to be fickle or shallow in their affections, it's actually an innate curiosity discovering different ways you like interacting with others. You and your mate will want to have many different types of relationships, and both of you need a lot of freedom to be "different." That in no way makes your commitment superficial.

Because there are many things to like, your need for variety will naturally lead you to express many different values and ways of relating to others. Just remember a stable relationship may feel better in the long run than the uncertainty of constantly changing affections based in internal arguments or indecisiveness. You both will be more intent on discovering and sharing your feelings and values than in making sense of them.

The worldly expression of your Venus is affected by the sign position of your Mercury. The spiritual expression of your Venus is affected by the sign position of your Uranus, Mercury's "higher octave."

Venus in Gemini is in its own 2nd sign. The interactive instincts express value in thoughts and conversations to secure their worth. There can be issues of getting scattered through too many attractions. This position shares a phase relationship with Venus in Scorpio.

Venus in Gemini is in its own 9th sign. The interactive instincts express a sense of perspective/proportion in an infinite exploration of all there is to like to find the right view. There can be issues of believing "the grass is always greener elsewhere." This position shares a phase relationship with Venus in Capricorn.

Venus in Cancer

You like those who are sensitive, warm, cuddly, nurturing and maternal in their values and interactions. You or those you're attracted to may be somewhat sensitive and have many private or subjective concerns and feelings which are related to your early home lives and how you saw values and affections expressed there. Thus this position often involves loving a partner who resembles a family member, or someone from your past who cared for you, even as far back as childhood.

You're naturally attracted to those who can help you feel more secure, even though this Venus position can also indicate an attraction to someone who is insecure. Be careful that you're not attracted to someone who is defensive, suspicious, or moody, as these will create needless turmoil disrupting whatever emotional security you've both managed to achieve.

Because you're on a life-long romance with intimate feelings, you are attracted to those who will always be youthful or child-like in how they express affection, and both of you will hold definite traditional values. Your ideal mate will be caring, kind, and nurture you and others, and both of you will help each other to forgive and move on rather than brood over the past.

Often feeling vulnerable (for all kinds of reasons), you have a strong need to feel completely safe, protected, and at ease in your intimate moments with your mate. However, because of insecurities natural to this position, one or both of you may lack confidence, or not know how to give the other emotional nurturance so both of you can feel secure. Be reasonable in your expectations and don't take things too personally or one or both of you will wind up frustrated.

Your ideal mate will be protective, caring, and sympathetic, willing to nurture and enjoy the intimacy of feeling a sense of family ties in your mutual friendships and interactions. There's a lot of sentimentality in this position. You'll both be on the lookout for what you can capture or appreciate with no risk to any previously held value. This caution tends to exclude more than it includes, so teach each other how to be more proactive in life, and take a genuine interest in caring for those in need. Ideally, your mate will know how to nurture others through a very personal sensitivity to what most needs to be provided in the moment, and have an enormous sympathy for others' insecurities.

The worldly expression of your Venus is affected by the sign position of your Moon. The spiritual expression of your Venus is affected by the sign position of your Sun.

Venus in Cancer is in its own 3rd sign. The interactive instincts express value through caring about everyone and everything in the immediate environment. There can be issues of overprotectiveness and sensitivity to perceived slights. This position shares a phase relationship with Venus in Sagittarius.

Venus in Cancer is in its own 10th sign. The interactive instincts express a sense of perspective/proportion through sensitivity to how one is perceived in public. There can be issues of becoming too subjective in professional settings. This position shares a phase relationship with Venus in Aquarius.

Venus in Leo

You are the most loyal of friends, creative and shining, a dynamic socialite who will find and hold center stage in every interaction or social gathering lucky enough to have you there. You are attracted to those who present a dramatic image to the world, and will "shine it on," doing their best in any situation, whether either of you feel very competent and powerful or not. Despite some insecurity from the intensely personal nature of this position, your Beloved will share your attitude that "the show must go on," and your mutual love of life's dramas will make your relationship the stuff of which legends and myths are made.

With Venus in this position, you are naturally attracted to those who are great actors or actresses, regardless of how large or small their part on life's stage. They may be "drama kings" or "drama queens," and even project feelings that are exaggerated, so beware of grandiosity, as well as sulking and petty jealousies, whether yours or theirs. Vanity runs high with this position, so you both should cultivate some detachment and not take things personally. You both want to take pride in your associations, and will naturally attract others who shine, have noble values, or are refined culturally.

Because you're on a lifelong romance of inspired self-expression, you and your mate will be very creative, and both of you will be attracted to creative or powerful people. Your mate will want to take pride in you, and you in them. Together you can create the parties that become legendary, and both of you will prefer associating with dramatic, powerful, beautiful, dynamic people with whom you can play and express yourselves spontaneously, making your social interactions an art form. Neither you nor your Beloved will have any patience with crude, rude, or coarse people, and though your Majesties will probably be gracious enough not to say anything to embarrass others publicly, they will be off your "A" list, never to return.

You have tremendous ego strength, and you're naturally attracted to others with ego strength. If someone challenges what you or your mate like or value, you both will become lions, rising up to defend and maybe attack, always with the grandest of styles. You both will value genuineness, respect, straightforwardness in affections, and loyal support from your friends and admirers, which you will reflect back to them, playfully or artfully packaged in a beautifully expressed form. You and your mate will like children and all that expresses the playful, creative, spontaneous side of human nature.

The worldly expression of your Venus is affected by the sign position of your Sun. The spiritual expression of your Venus is affected by the sign position of your Moon.

Venus in Leo is in its own 4th sign. The interactive instincts express value through creativity and playfulness with intimates. There can be issues of taking too much pride in one's background rather than a creative grounding in the present. This position shares a phase relationship with Venus in Capricorn.

Venus in Leo is in its own 11th sign. The interactive instincts express a sense of perspective/proportion through heartfelt expression of its goals and ambitions. There can be issues of taking things too personally when it may have been nothing personal. This position shares a phase relationship with Venus in Pisces.

Venus in Virgo

You are precise, methodical, and practical in how you bestow your affections, and have a checklist when it comes to what's acceptable in your relationships. You, like those you are naturally attracted to, are not spontaneous in your likes and dislikes, and so you run the risk of letting your expectations interfere with attracting someone who is human, with all their faults. The more you are locked into expectations, the more likely it will be that you will find yourself with someone who is fussy, critical, or overly concerned with what's proper. Be practical, since many things can be worked out over time.

You tend to worry a lot about small things in relationships, so your ideal mate will help you to focus on a broader point of view or a plan to work through any issue. They will also help you become more pragmatically optimistic in your emotional responses and help you let go of the need to control or manipulate outcomes. The more you enlarge your ability to enjoy your interactive world by widening the focus and definition of your feelings, the more you'll enjoy life.

You like people who are into plants and animals as well as their work, which will incorporate beauty as well as practicality. They will help you learn not to worry about the minor annoyances in life that only you notice, and you can help each other be less rigid in how you express affections and more realistic in your expectations of others.

Because you're on a life-long romance of perfecting your appreciation of beauty, you and your mate need to learn to be more spontaneous in expressing your feelings, and not worry so much about being proper. Your mate will help you to be less rigid or compartmentalized regarding who and what you like, and both of you will assist each other to keep a sense of proportion. Together you will learn to explore why you criticize what you do in your relationships, and let go of the need to overanalyze things while understanding how everything fits into the bigger picture.

You are attracted to extraordinarily capable people who are able to solve problems and accomplish tasks that would be overwhelming to others. When you're with your ideal mate, many will turn to one or both of you in times of trouble because of your common sense, practicality, and willingness to be of genuine service. You and your partner will be the voice of sanity to others, helping them to ground themselves in some thing or action of functional value.

The worldly expression of your Venus is affected by the sign position of your Mercury. The spiritual expression of your Venus is affected by the sign position of your Uranus, Mercury's "higher octave."

Venus in Virgo is in its own 5th sign. The interactive instincts express value through precise planning to capture what it wants. This position gives a precise creativity. There can be issues of the potential for nit-picking to become a game. This position shares a phase relationship with Venus in Aquarius.

Venus in Virgo is in its own 12th sign. The interactive instincts express a sense of perspective/proportion through precision and order at the harvest time in relationships. There can be issues of not seeing the forest for the trees. This position shares a phase relationship with Venus in Aries.

Venus in Libra

Your Venus makes you a very beautiful person and a true romantic in every sense of the word. You are attracted to beauty in countless forms, so it's safe to say both you and your mate will be easy to look at, easy to be around, naturally diplomatic, refined in manner, and very well-liked by one and all. You'll both have an extraordinary social sense, and know how to make others feel at ease with grace, charm, and sensitivity.

233

In some way you want your partnerships to be the perfect picture of an ideal, but perhaps a little too focused on the beauty of your self-generated self-image. You are attracted to what is called "classic beauty," and love the finest in cultural enjoyments. You (and they) will also have an artistic gift of some sort. There is some indecisiveness in this position, so learn to value those who appreciate the many shades of gray in commitments, as well as a well-rounded view of things.

Because you are on a life-long romance with beauty itself, you do not get along well with those who are too hard in their affections, prone to argument or conflict, or extremists. You are attracted to those who know how to compromise and negotiate, diplomats who are always willing to go part of the way, but wary when it comes to committing to absolutes.

The caution in this position is to overcome ambivalence in affectional matters because there are quite a few beautiful people to choose from in this forever-changing world. You're learning from each other not to be swayed, first one way and then another, in your loyalties. You're learning to grow beyond your need not to disappoint anyone, and to go deeper into the inner nature of those you're attracted to before you take them into your confidence.

Your ideal mate may share your vision, but remember that not everyone holds the high standards you do. You both will pursue an ever-more perfect picture of life, relationships, living and working environments, and sense of self. You and your mate will help each other to understand that to be perfect, one must be perfectly human, which may not look anything like what you think it should. In any case, slow your feelings down a little so you don't run past the beautiful mate waiting for you while you're chasing your ideals over the rainbow of your wildest imagination.

Because it is in the sign it "rules," the worldly expression of your Venus is determined by itself; the spiritual expression of your Venus is affected by the sign position of Venus' "higher octave" Neptune and TransPluto.

Venus in Libra is in its own 6th sign. The interactive instincts express value through the many small adaptations needed to prepare for public view. There can be issues of imbalances due to over-receptivity to others' old business. This position shares a phase relationship with Venus in Pisces.

Venus in Libra is in its own 1st sign. The interactive instincts express a sense of perspective/proportion on its own terms and of its own initiative. There can be issues around constructing a house of mirrors, seeing only what is pleasant. This position shares a phase relationship with Venus in Taurus.

Venus in Scorpio

You like your relationships intense, and so you'll be attracted to a mate who may be too intense for others' comfort zones. You are attracted to explorers, researchers, and detectives, and definitely do not like superficial people. You often attract those who feel misunderstood, but that's due more to their own intensity than anything else.

Your Beloved will be very deep and complex emotionally with a need not to take things so personally. You will help each other to lighten up even as you enjoy going deeper into the connectedness you will share. This need for an ever-deeper union may be overwhelming from time to time so you'll need to figure out ways to get the space you each need while maintaining intimacy. This is a very intense and physical position, and so you or your mate may run the risk of being frustrated when one of you needs to be more light and open in your expression of your feelings.

Because you're on a life-long romance of ever-greater intensity, you're both learning detachment in how you express what you express. You and your Beloved may always remain somewhat of a mystery to each other, with your relationship a dance on the edge of the deep and occasionally dark side of intense feelings.

This life you're letting go of jealousy and possessiveness and getting a grip on your considerable magnetism so that others are fascinated by the magic and not turned off by sarcasm or the extreme intensity. You and your mate may make others uncomfortable by easily getting behind their facades, and you both are here to learn to value and appreciate the forms of what you capture as much as the quest for what is underneath or behind them.

They will help you release your inner pressures and tensions, and show you how to let go of old feelings more graciously. You'll teach each other the importance of being as intensely FOR things and people as you can be against them, and help each other to release stagnant feelings and negative emotional states so you both can master your magnetism and attract what you want.

The worldly expression of your Venus is affected by the sign position of your Mars, which may involve oppositions and conflicts, since Venus is in "exile" in Scorpio, the sign opposite Taurus, which it rules. The spiritual expression of your Venus is affected by the sign position of your Pluto.

Venus in Scorpio is in its own 7th sign. The interactive instincts express value through what is given or denied in relationship, constantly seeking the value in relationship. There can be issues of attractions which are too intense This position shares a phase relationship with Venus in Aries.

Venus in Scorpio is in its own 2nd sign. The interactive instincts express a sense of perspective/proportion through capturing what is needed to feel more valued. There can be issues around nothing being good enough to find self-worth. This position shares a phase relationship with Venus in Gemini.

Venus in Sagittarius

You are no doubt well-traveled, well-read, well-educated, or well-opinionated, with freedom your guiding light. When you find your ideal mate, you will begin an adventure which will take both of you places you've never been before, physical or psychological, in both outer and inner space. When you attract a person you love, new horizons and new possibilities will open in you. You like people with an acute sense of humor, irony, and life's absurdities.

This position often indicates attraction to someone who likes sports or animals (especially horses), someone from a different culture or country, or someone with a definite spiritual inclination. You will encourage your mate's good humor and willingness to consider broader options. You'll both have active imaginations, probably not be very jealous (unless there are other indicators), and not open to either of you being emotionally confining or confined.

Because you're on a life-long romance of opening to wider horizons, neither of you will want anyone interfering with your mutual freedom to do exactly what you want when you want. No one will ever tie either of you down, as you both have a wanderlust. You need a lot of freedom to explore the many different value systems the world has to offer, without needing to make logical or orderly sense of any of it. Due to the changeability of this position with its ever-expanding sense of more things to like, from time to time you may get confused, or give confusing signals about what you think you like at any given moment.

You and your mate may need more steadiness in your affections through exercising a simple, gentle self-control. You can really help each other with any lack of clarity in your affections as a result of constantly changing feelings and values, since you're both striving for greater knowledge, understanding, and freedom in your relationships and emotional expression.

You'll both be open to new ways of appreciating life, and won't like anything or anyone cramping your style. As you meet many varied people from equally varied backgrounds, you will be exposed to diverse, strange, and wonderful interactions and values as a result of the mental and physical adventures promised by this position. Attracted to distant cultures in space and time as well as educated people, people with this position are more prone to find a mate among people associated with academia, travel, foreign lands, law, media, philosophy, spirituality, or anyone who represents freedom and newness.

The worldly expression of your Venus is affected by the sign position of your Jupiter. The spiritual expression of your Venus is affected by the sign position of your Neptune.

Venus in Sagittarius is in its own 8th sign. The interactive instincts express value through optimism in regenerating a vision of worth to be achieved. There can be issues of seeing too many paths which drain rather than establish. This position shares a phase relationship with Venus in Taurus.

Venus in Sagittarius is in its own 3rd sign. The interactive instincts express a sense of perspective/proportion through valuing information which relates the immediate situation to the bigger picture. There can be issues of seeing too many possibilities and running past the ideal. This position shares a phase relationship with Venus in Cancer.

Venus in Capricorn

You are refined, cultivated in your tastes and affections, and always proper when in company. Your ideal mate will mirror the refined set of emotional values you've both studiously cultivated your whole lives. You had to act older than your age since childhood, and are totally controlled in how you conduct yourself in any social gathering.

As such you will be attracted to someone who is fairly conservative, responsible, and take the safe position in any judgment call. Beware of too many social calculations that stifle your enjoyment. This position is naturally conservative and cautious, and those with Venus in this sign are attracted to mature or older people, or people in positions of authority or responsibility.

You are naturally attracted to people with an organized approach to life, relationships, and experiences. Just beware of being too diplomatic or always expressing the safe or appropriate position. When you're with the mate natural for you, from time to time professional responsibilities will interfere in your time together. Since your beloved will feel that a certain amount of sacrifice, duty, and discipline are associated with relationships, both of you should try to cultivate opportunities to express your more romantic, warm, and playful tendencies.

Open to new likes from time to time to expand the range of your aesthetic possibilities, and learn how to enjoy life with more gusto. Your mate will be traditional in their likes, with an admiration for discipline and reverence for established standards of excellence. Your mate will help you claim your personal power in the world, and be more positive in your emotional expression.

Because you're on a life-long romance with mature affections, both of you should assist each other to use your power of perseverance to learn to express tenderness, spontaneity, and creativity as a part of your daily discipline. This will help to lighten up your relationship so your natural caution and pragmatism don't starve your shared need for affection.

At some point in life you will be attracted to someone of power and/or wealth, or they to you. If this is the case, your positions may keep you apart, unless one of you can break free of the need to be bound to proprieties, rules, and codes of conduct created in another age for people in a different world than the one we presently live in.

The worldly expression of your Venus is affected by the sign position of your Saturn. The spiritual expression of your Venus is affected by the sign position of your Uranus.

Venus in Capricorn is in its own 9th sign. The interactive instincts express value through its own truth of being appropriate and useful. There can be issues of too much control or pessimism restricting the future. This position shares a phase relationship with Venus in Gemini.

Venus in Capricorn is in its own 4th sign. The interactive instincts express a sense of perspective/proportion through self-discipline at the root of relationship. There can be issues of hardness denying the ability to enjoy life. This position shares a phase relationship with Venus in Leo.

Venus in Aquarius

You are attracted to strange and unusual people and values, and you and your Beloved will have unique progressive qualities. Your romance will seem like it's a highly specialized yet universal form of the human ideal, and you may feel like the romance has its roots in another time period, either two hundred years ago or two hundred years in the future.

You are detached in your affections, idealistic and noble, humanitarian and very friendly, and you'll be attracted to someone with these traits as well. Your mate will be your friend, complex yet simple, an angel with a vision of greater things. With your ideal mate, you will attract dynamic and electrifying people and experiences during your varied and exciting relational journey.

In a very impersonal way, you genuinely like people in general, and have a lot of varied types of friends. Your ideal mate will be open-minded and freedom loving, idealistic, innovative with some very abstract ideas about romance and human relationships. Though ultra-progressive there will also be something strangely traditional about who you attract. Being idealistic, you see beauty where everyone else sees jagged edges, and you try to keep the angelic ideal of the best in human relationships in view amidst the swampy lowlands of most normal human interactions.

Because you are on a life-long romance with an ideal of friendship, you are attracted to anyone who is future-oriented, intelligent, and unique. At some point in your life you will be attracted to the avant-garde, the bohemian, the bizarre, or the outrageous. Remember the big picture and be cautious when approaching your outer edge of experience.

Your mate will be very strong, have an extraordinarily wide range of self-expression and values, with a sense of the larger or wider values and goals of humanity. They will be loyal in a curiously detached way. Since both of you can be phenomenally removed and neutral in your affections, find someone who can help you achieve an ever-greater warmth of feeling, deepening your affection for one and all. Together you can get more grounded in your values, likes and dislikes, with an ability to interact with others on their terms as well as yours.

Your mate will support your visionary ideals, and ideally foster your natural charisma, artistic talent, or genius. Your partnership will honor the uniqueness in each other, and you'll probably find yourself associating with friends who also possess their own unusual, phenomenal, or fantastic talents.

The worldly expression of your Venus is affected by the sign position of your Saturn. The spiritual expression of your Venus is affected by the sign position of your Uranus.

Venus in Aquarius is in its own 10th sign. The interactive instincts express value in the culmination of friendships and public activities. There can be issues of focusing too much on appearance and not enough warmth in public settings. This position shares a phase relationship with Venus in Cancer.

Venus in Aquarius is in its own 5th sign. The interactive instincts express a sense of perspective/proportion through children and creative self-expression. There can be issues with being too impersonal to make lasting commitments. This position shares a phase relationship with Venus in Virgo.

Venus in Pisces

Your most ideal loving relationship will be based in universality, compassion, and forgiveness. You bring these to your relationships, and your beloved will embrace these values as well. Some of your relationships have a very surrealistic quality, and at times seem like a fantastic movie or a dream.

Your Beloved may be somewhat of a mystery to you, and you to them, with your relationship at times seeming to be a universal dance on the edge of timelessness. Learn to spot the subtleties, and be wise in your silences without being fooled. You're attracted to those who are empathic, intuitive, and visionary but may at times be a little too obscure. You or they may feel misunderstood, due to the deep and vast complex feelings you're both tuned in on.

Because you're on a life-long romance of vast feelings of unity, empathy, and the universal human experience, both of you will learn not to take things so personally, and will help each other to lighten up even as you enjoy going deeper into the connectedness you will share. Your ideal mate will assist the fluidity in how you express yourselves, and help you overcome any problems you have with self-pity, ancient sorrows, reclusiveness, or daydreaming.

Your Beloved will bring a larger view and feeling-experience to all interactions, but may have problems wanting it all ways at once without having to make up their mind one way or another. Your ideal relationship will teach you both not to preprogram any suspicion or distrust which leads either of you to try to trap others in dualistic morality systems. You and your mate will have a natural ability to put yourself in another's place, and instinctively know how to relate to others as though you were reading their mind and able to anticipate what they are about to express. You both may make others uncomfortable by easily getting behind their facades without them knowing how you do it.

Because both of you are unusually susceptible to other's psychic states, you and your mate will know each other in a deep feeling way, and will send subtle signals when something's strange. You can help each other release anything inappropriate picked up from someone else's subconscious mind. There will be a natural compassionate protectiveness in all your relationships, but without separateness. Your relationship will help you both realize when it's time to end old values or ways of relating to yourself or your life, or when others are creating needless frustration or suffering, or making you feel trapped. Together you will learn to forgive yourself and them and it and let it all be washed clean in a greater Divine Compassion and Love.

The worldly expression of your Venus is affected by the sign position of your Jupiter. The spiritual expression of your Venus is affected by the sign position of your Neptune.

Venus in Pisces is in its own 11th sign. The interactive instincts express value in empathic and compassionate friendships or in groups. There can be issues of picking up on others' sorrows and getting overwhelmed emotionally in public situations. This position shares a phase relationship with Venus in Leo.

Venus in Pisces is in its own 6th sign. The interactive instincts express a sense of perspective/proportion through service to others, seeing the value of holding back before making adjustments. There can be issues of too much sympathy creating constant self-adjustments leading to confusion. This position shares a phase relationship with Venus in Libra.

CHAPTER NINE

VENUS RETROGRADE

We now turn to an important factor of what it means when Venus is retrograde in a chart, or when it's retrograde in the sky. It's normal to find one or more planets retrograde in a chart, because all planets from Mercury out to Pluto go retrograde at regular intervals. Mercury is retrograde 3 or 4 times a year, Venus every 18-19 months, and Mars every 26 months, more or less. The outers all go retrograde once a year for several months. Because Venus is retrograde for several weeks every year and a half, these recurring periods are obviously an important recurring factor in our lives.

Let's begin with what "retrograde" actually means. All planets go retrograde as a function of their orbits except the Sun and Moon. All planets speed up and then slow down in their orbital speed relative to the Sun and Earth. This is also true for the Moon, but we don't call it retrogradation. The Sun seems to speed up or slow down a little based in what sign it's in relative to the Earth, which is actually the Earth speeding up or slowing down in its orbit, based in whether it's at perihelion (closest to) or aphelion (farthest away from) the Sun.

Because a retrograde is a time when a planet seems to be going backward, these are periods of retracing a degree span already covered once by that planet. It is actually a time when the planet's speed is slowed relative to when it's direct in motion. All retrogrades give us a three step process in our response to the planetary retrograde; when it is moving forward and slowing to go retrograde, when it is retrograde and we're getting a different sense of that span of prior experience, and when it's direct in motion again and we now understand that span.

First, the planet transits a span of degrees in one or two signs as it moves forward through that span of the zodiac. Then when the planet retrogrades, it seems to move back across that span again, retracing those degrees. That gives us a different view of that planetary sign experience.

It is a time of reflection, review, re-evaluation, and reconsideration of our associations of that planetary sign expression in our charts. Then when a retrograde is done and the planet begins to speed up and finally goes direct in motion, it again moves across that span of degrees. That span becomes an important area in our lives, since we get 3 experiences of that planetary lesson in that part of the zodiacal reality.

All retrogrades help us integrate what we learn as we move forward in our lives and affairs. Some parts of our evolution move forward quickly as the planets move forward in motion through the signs. But then at some point, each planet slows down, goes retrograde, and we get a new look at ground already covered. When any planet goes retrograde, there is an inward turning, a greater receptivity to unconscious factors, and a retracing of steps already traversed. Then when the planet resumes forward motion, it symbolizes a time when we can take what we learned, then re-learned, or viewed and reviewed, and apply those lessons in new ways.

What Is Venus Retrograde

Let's begin looking at Venus retrograde by examining what we know about the qualities of Venus. As we know, Venus symbolizes what we like, what we value, what we appreciate, and our overall aesthetic inclinations. When Venus is direct in motion we get Venusian "information." When it slows down and goes retrograde we get a new view of what we just learned about those energies and can find a new appreciation and admiration for whatever that transit is related to in our lives. It could be a time of finding new value in old interactions and things, or an internal check on what we've been valuing up to that point.

When transiting Venus goes retrograde, it definitely affects everyone's values, pleasures, love life and other close relationships. It is a perfect time to reflect on these things, or for memories of real world "echoes" of these past experiences to come forth. These periods may bring back old value systems for new evaluation, or a return of old memories of things we valued and appreciated in the past. These periods are good for recalibrating our view of money, wealth, and things in general, as well as why we value what we do in our relationships, and whether we're working off of old tapes, old hurts, old attachments, and old aversions in relationships that bear no resemblance to what the life we're living today.

Because Venus is associated with Narcissus, we can get a different look at direct and indirect forms of narcissistic behaviors, or how people in our past exhibited these. We can see if we adopted mannerisms in the past which distorted our expression, as well as our subconscious vanities and superficialities which enable us to be seduced by the passing fancies of our world.

Because of the inward and/or review qualities of the retrograde, we can explore different ways to relate to others or different ways to image what we like and how we like it. It can bring back old relationships, old memories of relationships, or old relationship patterns updated for the present. During Venus retrograde periods, we can review, revalue, reevaluate, and re-image what we appreciate and how we express our appreciation. They are particularly good times for seeing ourselves through the eyes of others, and/or from the perspective of how we used to relate juxtaposed with how we're relating now.

Venus is our inner romantic picture of things, people, and ideas, mirrored out to our world. Its glyph, resembling a hand mirror, shows that it symbolizes our vanities and our self-reflected images of beauty. None of these are a bad thing, but we must revise them from time to time lest we be pursuing images that will no longer satisfy our evolved self and life.

How Does Venus Retrograde Affect Us?

As with all retrogrades, Venus retrograde takes us on a journey back. Not merely "back" through the shadow span of the retrograde, but sometimes literally "back" to previous Venus retrograde periods, or even to "echoes" of past lives. As retrogrades often bring us to circumstances where we have to go back to "pick up the threads of the past" in order to move those planetary affairs forward, Venus retrograde has its own internal cycles of its various stations which show us how the larger cycles of Venus in our chart affect us over time.

The signs Venus occupies when retrograde show us the qualities of what we're reviewing or revaluing, while the house(s) in which the retrograde occurs in our charts shows us where we're "going back," "going within," reviewing and reflecting, reconsidering and recalibrating. Venus retrograde gives us a look through the mirror at the recent past, the distant past, and maybe even "through the past darkly," so we may remember our difficult Venusian experiences in the past and see how they shaped our responses so we may heal those wounds.

A Venus retrograde period may bring memories of old painful hurts and misunderstandings, but in re-experiencing old wounds we are given opportunities to free ourselves of subconscious patterns which leave us frustrated or unresolved. These are perfect times to reclaim or appreciate our mature values to eliminate the echoes of memories of perceptions based in prior ignorance or victimization. That some people hurt others is a reality in this impermanent world. Still, we do not have to suffer needlessly based in old emotional habits that do not serve our need for love, wisdom, veneration, compassion, and self-respect. A Venus retrograde gives us a new angle on our likes, affections, values, and anything in the subconscious mind which could seduce us into illusions or false values.

As I offered you in Saturn: Spiritual Master, Spiritual Friend, Venus' duality is Wisdom/Folly. It shows how our subconscious mind responds to our self-conscious mind, creating our "mental offspring." Venus shows us our vanities, selfishness, and narcissistic ways of relating so we may come to know how to capture more beautiful forms of our inner picture of a higher, refined, elegant life and relationships in the perfect ways, places, and times. All of these things can be seen from a different angle when Venus is retrograde. We can see how our subconscious mind works when liking or not liking someone or something, and can get a new approach to the value of the traits of whatever sign it's retrograde in.

As you know by now, Venus in general symbolizes our likes and dislikes, our pleasure principle and social emotions, attitudes, and behaviors. Because it rules the signs of Taurus and Libra, it measures our values, how we use what we have, what we wish to capture that we can possess, and all our equal relationships, including both personal and business partnerships.

A Venus retrograde throws the ongoing transiting experience of our Venusian filters into reverse in the house it is transiting, and also gives us a "look back" at the affairs of the houses with Taurus and Libra on the cusp. If we have a planet in Taurus or Libra, we get an inward look at that planetary function and how it was shaped in the past. That gives us an objective angle to correct that planetary function.

So if we have Sun in Taurus or Libra, a Venus retrograde will give us a look back at how our light has expressed itself in various ways throughout our lives. If we have a Moon in Taurus or Libra, the retrograde will give us a look back on old habits and ways of feeling and experiencing our lives. It is the same for any other personal planet in those signs, with new value or appreciation possible with ideas (Mercury), values and relationships (Venus) or ways of doing things (Mars) during Venus retrograde periods. As with Mercury retrograde people doing well during Mercury retrograde periods, I have found people with Venus retrograde in their natal charts make a lot of progress during transiting Venus retrograde periods.

Obviously, this also leads us to see that certain generations and subgenerations are more affected by Venus retrograde periods than others. For example, there are many people on Earth with Neptune in Libra, Uranus in Libra, and Uranus in Taurus. Each of these groups will have their outer planet patterns reviewed during each Venus retrograde and can come to a new way of valuing or appreciating those spiritual functions in their lives.

Those with Saturn in Taurus or Libra can come to a new value or appreciation of their duties and responsibilities, or get insights into what they need to value if they want to fulfill their purpose. Those with Jupiter in those signs can come to a new value or appreciation of their vision, truth, or future-in-the-making, or why certainly relationships had to end and we were protected during the process.

Using Venus Retrograde Wisely

Often when we get what we believe we want, we are forced to deal with unanticipated consequences. People do not turn out to be as we hoped, relationships take strange turns that have little or nothing to do with what we thought, and we often take things too personally when it really is another's issue. When we dance with others, it triggers them to make internal choices, just as it does with us.

Often we are not fully conscious of these changes until down the road we find we do not like certain things about them as much as we did before that. Then we go through awkward disengagements, or reposition ourselves by asserting values (Venus) that we didn't express before. Obviously this can create emotional misunderstandings, problems, tensions, and wounds. The value of Venus retrograde is the ability to find a new way of appreciating what happened, or a new perspective about what was given and what was denied, retracing certain steps to come to a balanced view (Venus) of the past, present, and future.

Our inner Venus represents balance, fairness, justice, right proportion, beauty, harmony, cooperation, and rhythmic grace. If we are not living these qualities the best we are able, Venus retrograde periods assist us in finding a new perspective on these qualities distinct from who we were, or who we thought others to be.

When old wounds and other old memories of difficult relationships re-surface during Venus retrograde, we are given an opportunity to heal them the best we're able through re-examining what we valued and why we went through those wounding experiences. By going back to the source of the wound, we can find courage and power in re-claiming our appreciation for who we are in the moment. Old hurts can be seen for their value in liberating us from frustrating interactions and possessions we no longer valued. Venus retrograde is good for reconnecting with those we once loved (whether in the body or memory), or finding a new appreciation for people in our past who allowed us to express ourselves without feeling shamed or devalued.

Venus Retrograde in the Elements

Venus retrograde affects all of us differently depending on where our natal Venus is and what sign the transiting Venus occupies when retrograde. Generally speaking, transiting Venus retrograde in an Earth sign is in harmony with its Taurus side, and offers us opportunities to be pragmatic and practical in updating our likes and dislikes to current values and conditions freed from old subconscious tapes that are not useful in our present day to day relationships to people and things. Transiting Venus retrograde in an Air sign is in harmony with its Libra side, and offers us opportunities to be idealistic, fair, just and balanced in updating our likes and dislikes to our current values and conditions.

Transiting Venus retrograde in a Water sign is favorable to its exaltation qualities in Pisces, but can be too intense, or sensitive, or over-receptive to the feeling currents of others. Transiting Venus retrograde in a Fire sign is not as favorable as the other elements, since Fire is excitable, hot, and is always on the move, unlike balanced and cool Libra and comfortably immovable Taurus.

Natal Venus Retrograde

When we have natal Venus retrograde, while the Venusian sign experience will be the same as if Venus were direct, the retrograde indicates that a) the Venusian function will be turned inward, seeking within the self what may only be known through external interactions, or b) the affectional nature will be constantly comparing what it likes and what it captures against what it did or didn't like in the past or what it could or couldn't capture in the way of a perceived ideal relationship.

Venus retrograde may lead a person to try to find love and affection in ways which resemble the past, even if that past isn't consciously or correctly imaged due to it being a past life pattern. In these cases, this life becomes a challenge to review why that person likes what they do, or why they have doubts about what they like and why they like it.

A natal Venus retrograde may also indicate a love or like which was formed in early life when the person was there and then they suddenly disappeared or left without explanation. And because of the delay factor in all retrogrades, a person with natal Venus retrograde may want something which they don't get until long after they wanted it, setting up inner questions about if not then, why now?

This brings us to a crucial factor in natal retrogrades, which is when they go direct by progression. In astrology, there are only four possible ways to have a planet retrograde, those being

1) The planet was retrograde when we were born and it will stay retrograde through our lives;

2) The planet was retrograde when we were born and it will go direct at some point in our lives;

3) The planet was direct when we were born and it will go retrograde at some point in our lives and stay retrograde for the rest of our lives;

4) The planet was direct when we were born and it will go retrograde at some point in our lives and then go direct at a later point in time.

The majority of us have planets which fit at least one of these possibilities. Only progressed Mercury or Venus can be direct at birth, go retrograde by progression, and eventually go stationary direct after a number of years.

For most people with Venus retrograde at birth, eventually it will progress and go direct in motion, marking a time in life when many things which were directed inward or to the past will turn outward and be more current in its expression. These people are given a great blessing, since the Venus-ruled areas of life which were slow, confused, or introverted in relationships will begin to feel easier to navigate due to Venus making a pass over a familiar span of degrees.

If natal Venus is direct at birth and goes retrograde by progression, it's also indicative of a two-step process, where the person experiences the direct impressions of Venus before needing to reflect, go inward, or see how those Venusian experiences are related to the past. If it happens early enough in life and the person lives long enough, it will at some point go stationary direct much later in life. The two stations (retrograde and direct) mark threshold states, with the retrograde station showing the beginning of an inward journey after reaching a limit in outer experience, and the direct station showing the beginning of taking the retrograde reflections into the world in new forms.

Venus Inferior Conjunction with the Sun

Because they both stay relatively close to the Sun (from the perspective of Earth), the retrograde periods of Mercury and Venus give us important points when they conjunct the Sun in what's known as "the Inferior Conjunction." Any time a planet conjuncts the Sun, it represents a fusion and illumination of that planetary principle with the Sun. When a planet is retrograde, it represents a fusion of Life (the Sun) with the "backward oriented" movement of the planet.

While Life (the Sun) moves steadily forward, Mercury and Venus are constantly speeding up and slowing down, moving at changing speeds. At times they race ahead of Life and see distant horizons of Mercurial and Venusian interest. Then they slow, go retrograde, and "bring the news back" to the Life at the Inferior conjunctions. They continue to move slower than normal until they go stationary direct, and begin to chase the new experiences indicated by the span the Sun has traversed since the Inferior conjunction.

Then they race forward, accelerating until they make what is called a "Superior Conjunction" with the Sun, also representing a "fusion of Life and Likes" (in the case of Venus) which we then carry into the future Venus direct period. Both types of conjunctions represent Light illuminating Relatedness, with the Inferior showing the illumination of inward and/or backward turned values and likes, and the Superior showing the illumination of outward and forward turned values and likes.

Whereas when direct both Mercury and Venus race forward ahead of the Sun (as our mind and attractions often do!), when retrograde they internalize, or become receptive to inner energies we may not have paid attention to before then. In the case of Venus, it may lead to a realization of how we are impacted by Venusian energies from "the outside" that influence what we like or don't, why we like what we like, why we believe we're getting what we want from others or not, and a host of other Venus retrograde possibilities.

The period after an Inferior conjunction and before Venus goes direct is a time when ways of relating and liking things and people are absorbed by Life, or Life takes on the results of subconscious or collective interpersonal feelings returning to source. Eventually Life (the Sun) gets as far from Venus as it can, Venus goes stationary direct, and begins to speed up preparing for the next Superior conjunction.

A chart done for the exact Inferior Conjunction offers us elements of things related to "Venus fused with the Sun" energy which impacts the following weeks until the next Venus Superior conjunction, which gives us a new and different take on "Likes fused with Life" until the following Inferior Conjunction. The degree of the Inferior conjunctions and Superior conjunctions are important, since they indicate how our Life will merge with our values and relationships to bring forth a "liking of our light." These conjunction degrees give clues as to the themes and lessons related to how our relationships and values will be internally explored from the Inferior to the Superior, and how our relationships and values will be externally expressed from the Superior to the next Inferior during the 19 months between the Inferior conjunctions.

That's why it's useful to examine the different stationary retrograde and direct points Venus has made in our charts, as well as the various Inferior and Superior conjunction points as well. Each of these marked points at which our Venusian experience of life changed in some way, or accented a specific area of our chart. Each of these were major points of

Venusian "pulses" which affected our lives for many months after they happened.

Venus Retrograde in the Signs

I've found people with Venus retrograde, whether natally or by progression, need more time to explore what they feel and why they feel it. Because of the retrograde, the Venus function works at a slower pace. While this can be good for reflection and review, unfortunately this can also lead to endless distractions by passing Venusian people and things.

The sign of a natal Venus retrograde gives us clues about what is being internally reviewed. This is where taking a look at the progressed Venus is valuable, since it tells us where the retrograde process ends and where the direct movement begins. Usually when the progressed Venus goes direct it's in the same sign as when it went retrograde. However, if it retrogrades back into the previous sign and then goes stationary direct at the end of that sign, then the Venus retrograde and direct experience will be two fold. The dominant issues are found in the sign Venus occupies the longest, while the platform for forward motion is found at the stationary direct sign and degree.

This section offers a few hints about how to use Venus retrograde in the signs to good advantage. While not specifically describing qualities of Venus retrograde in the birth chart, I will state that if you have Venus retrograde at birth, you have nothing to fear! You're merely re-tracing steps you already did in a past life so you can review what you are attracted to and why.

The sign Venus is in shows where you're working out these internalized reflections, like, and dislikes, and what you need to learn to express in a more direct way. If there are questions about why you are or aren't getting what you want, detach and take a new look at your Venus sign position with an eye to externalizing those qualities the best you're able, or see their value in helping you get behind your own or others' Venusian misdirected expressions.

Venus retrograde in Aries: This is a "cut to the chase" Venus retrograde, where we can reflect on why we were so quick to jump into and out of relationships in the past. This position helps us understand why it's better to show caution in our affections, balancing desire to act with a bit of restraint. With Venus retrograde in Aries, there may be difficulty in absorbing the meaning of relationships until later on, after time and experience remind us of what we liked "back then." This position is good for getting insights into our own and others' genuineness.

Venus retrograde in Taurus: This is a position which believes that which brought pleasure in the past can bring it in the future, but because the future never exactly mirrors the past, there can be clinging to old things and likes long after they no longer satisfy. This position can get stuck in past relationship imbalances related to money or things, and has to learn to trust that if they disperse as they accumulate, they will enjoy what they have in the here and now more than what they used to hold on to. This position is good for getting insights into our own and others' ways of enjoying life.

Venus retrograde in Gemini: This is a position which constantly looks back at old ideas to see if they have any value or application in the present, and is constantly wondering if there are new ways to understand what people said and if they really meant what they said. There is a tendency to pre-program responses to what people might say, resulting in questioning whether something different should have been said or if something different should be said now to correct what was said or unsaid in the past. This position is good for getting insights into our own and others' flexibility in understanding.

Venus retrograde in Cancer: This can show us how our internal signals either create suspicion or intimacy in our close relationships, and whether we're working off of childhood needs or our current needs. This creates an internalized sentimental longing for close relationships we may never have known, or a desire to recreate relationships from childhood which gave us a sense of protection and belonging. There is a need to dispel internalized suspicions or defensiveness against attacks which may never come. This position is good for getting insights into our own and others' security needs.

Venus retrograde in Leo: This position questions the value of play and spontaneity, and either internalizes creative expression or finds creative inspiration and expression through roundabout means or via the subconscious mind. There may be a need to see ways to express the heart freed of the value systems of the past, or find a joy in expressing things which trigger other people's creativity. Finding a naturally playful way to appreciate life and self is the solution to many inhibitions. This position is good for getting insights into our own and others' ego assumptions.

Venus retrograde in Virgo: This position is over analytical of love's changes and imperfections, and runs the risk of being too perfectionistic to like anything or anyone as they are. Since there are many "check lists" to fulfill, try to look above the details and detach from too much criticism. Though there will be many doubts about the ability to give and receive love in natural ways, this position can help us understand that if we let ourselves be led into a balanced view we'll find more harmony than worry. This position is good for getting insights into our own and others' understanding of how the parts relate to the whole.

Venus retrograde in Libra: Beware of being too idealistic in what you believe things should have looked like "back then," and be fair in your assessments of what's important and what's not important in love's constant changes. This brings endless comparisons of the many shades of interactions in your social life, as well as reflections of previous relationships and their interactive dynamics. Get a new perspective on your expectations of how others do or don't hold up their end of the deal. This position is good for getting insights into our own and others' imbalances.

Venus retrograde in Scorpio: This helps us get to internalized antagonisms, and open perspectives and insights into how our values synch with others or don't. This position can be intensely dissatisfied with what it feels as it looks externally for what it can only find internally, and vice versa. Periods of solitude are excellent for getting to the core of likes and dislikes and eliminating old emotional heaviness, with a need to "break free of the cocoon" from time to time and enjoy the freedom each new relationship brings us. This position is good for getting insights into our own and others' attachment to stuck feelings.

Venus retrograde in Sagittarius: No one can inhibit our freedom but ourselves, and it's on us to enjoy the adventure. This is excellent for taking a look inward to see how old values and relationships freed us to get where we are, and reconnecting to what we value about our freedom and ability to move forward into more expansive relationships. This helps us see old impulsive relationships in our past we tired of quickly, or how our changing philosophy created inhibitions or misunderstandings in past relationships. This position is good for getting insights into our own and others' willingness to commit.

Venus retrograde in Capricorn: This creates internal calculations about expressions of affections, and offers insights about why we chose to leave unhealthy relationships behind which were bad investments of time, energy, and/or money. This can show us how we internalized hardness when we didn't need to, or how barren relationships in the past set up barriers to trusting our primal innocence. This position is in "reflective group oriented" mode, where past relationships can be seen in a pragmatic light. This position is good for getting insights into our own and others' investments in relationships.

Venus retrograde in Aquarius: This position is highly idealistic, and compares all relationships with its internalized ideal of what it should look and feel like. This is a very detached position, and tends to attract unique, progressive, and unusual relationships with people who will be friends more than intimates. Current relationships lead back to past ideals, and sometimes friendships develop into closer connections leading to a wish that the relationship could go back to what it once was. This position is good for getting insights into our own and others' vision of the relationship ideal.

Venus retrograde in Pisces: This position is highly receptive to collective feeling impressions, so there will be a sense that life is a movie where anything could show up at any time ranging from the distant past to the unknown future. There may be a tendency to dwell too long on old hurts or disappointments, or a pattern of too many complicated feelings ever to get to a clear expression of likes and dislikes. Sorrow can result from too much hesitancy, or getting lost in the subtleties in mixed signals. This position is good for getting insights into our own and others' willingness to forgive and let it be.

Venus Retrograde Cycles Across Time

An important long wave factor is that Venus repeats its retrograde and direct pattern every 8 years. This means that wherever Venus goes retrograde in our charts, it's near the same place relative to where it was 8 years ago, as well as16 years ago and 24 years ago. These recurring periods of reflection, returns, regression, and looking inward via the Venus function are important in showing how our Venus response has changed over the years.

By noting the retrograde Venus function in the various houses in our charts where these retrogrades happened, we can get a better sense of how we have evolved in those areas, using 8 year "steps" to see our evolving Venusian awareness in our lives. Have fun reflecting on these "action beats" in various parts of your life, and especially whatever Venusian insights, rehearsals, reflections, and revelations happened during and after these periods.

While I cannot offer a thorough interpretation of how these might have manifested for each sign, by taking a look at where they happened you can track your changing Venus expression across the years, and why you stopped liking certain things in certain parts of your life while also beginning to like other things.

Venus Retrograde in Scorpio and Libra

Venus was retrograde in Oct/Nov 2002, moving from 16 Scorpio back to 1 Scorpio. That was echoed in Oct/Nov 2010, when Venus retrograded from 14 Scorpio back to 28 Libra. This sequence was echoed yet again in Oct/Nov 2018 when the retrograde span was between 11 Scorpio and 26 Libra. In Oct/Nov 2026 the span is between 9 Scorpio and 23 Libra, in Oct/Nov 2034 the span will be between 7 Scorpio and 21 Libra, and in Oct/Nov 2042 the span will be between 4 Scorpio and 19 Libra.

Venus Retrograde in Gemini

After 2002, the next one in May/Jun 2004 was from 27 Gemini back to 10 Gemini. That was echoed in May/Jun 2012 when Venus retrograded from 24 Gemini back to 8 Gemini. It was echoed yet again in May/June 2020 when the retrograde span was between 22 Gemini and 6 Gemini. In May/June 2028 the span is between 20 Gemini and 4 Gemini, in May/June 2036 the span will be between 18 Gemini and 2 Gemini, and in May/June 2044 the span will be between 16 Gemini and 29 Taurus.

Venus Retrograde in Capricorn

After the 2004 Venus retrograde, the next Venus retrograde in Dec 2005/Jan 2006 was between 2 Aquarius and 17 Capricorn. That was echoed in Dec 2013/Jan 2014 when Venus retrograded from 29 Capricorn back to 14 Capricorn. The next in the series was the Dec 2021/Jan 2022 retrograde span between 27 Capricorn and 12 Capricorn. The next in this series will be in Dec 2029/Jan 2030 when the span is between 25 Capricorn and 9 Capricorn, followed by the Dec 2037/Jan 2038 retrograde between 22 Capricorn and 7 Capricorn, and the Dec 2045/Jan 2046 retrograde between 20 Capricorn and 4 Capricorn.

Venus Retrograde in Virgo and Leo

After the previous retrograde in 2005/2006, the next Venus retrograde was in Jul/Aug 2007 when the span was between 3 Virgo and 17 Leo. That was echoed between late July and early September 2015 when Venus retrograded from 1 Virgo back to 15 Leo. This will be echoed between late July and early September 2023 when the retrograde span is between 29 Leo and 13 Leo. This is followed in July/Aug 2031 when the retrograde span is between 27 Leo and 11 Leo, in July/Aug 2039 when the span is between 25 Leo and 8 Leo, and in July/Aug 2047 when the span is between 23 Leo and 6 Leo.

Venus Retrograde in Aries and Pisces

After the July/Aug 2007 retrograde, the next Venus retrograde was in in Mar/Apr 2009 when it moved from 16 Aries back to 30 Pisces. That echoed the Mar/Apr 2001 retrograde between 18 Aries and 2 Aries, and was echoed in Mar/April 2017 when Venus retrograded from 14 Aries back to 27 Pisces. The next in this series will be in March/April 2025, when Venus will retrograde from 11 Aries to 25 Pisces. This is followed when Venus retrogrades from 9 Aries to 23 Pisces between late February and early April 2033, and again between February and April 2041 when the span is from 7 Aries to 21 Pisces. The retrograde span between February and April 2049 is from 4 Aries to 18 Pisces.

CHAPTER TEN

THE PROGRESSED MOON, SATURN CYCLES, AND CRITICAL CHOICES IN RELATIONSHIPS

Our progressed Moon is extremely important in marking points of emotional change as our needs lead us from old ways of living to new ones. The progressed Moon cycles begin at birth, and it transits all the signs in our chart until it returns to its natal position when we're 27 years old. As the Moon transits each sign we get a "feel" for those types of energies. Even if we don't have a planet in a given sign, when our progressed Moon is in that sign we get a firsthand experience of that energy.

Because our Moon symbolizes our primal instincts, the progressed Moon shows how our evolving instincts process our outer world experiences. This is where we have to take into consideration that our first 21 years are entirely shaped by our family and cultural matrix, so a lot of what we believe we want or need, if it's related to our childhood experiences and hierarchy of needs, was shaped by forces beyond our control.

As we grow into our 20s and beyond, our progressed Moon helps us replace childhood needs and reactive or unconscious feeling states with more appropriate and mature responses. There's also another crucial planetary factor in how and when we mature. While the progressed Moon symbolizes our inner emotional development, because of our dance with "real world" factors limiting and shaping us, we find understanding and competency through transiting

Saturn. While our inner Saturn shows us how to throw off attitudes which make us feel victimized by circumstances, transiting Saturn challenges (and confirms or denies) our belief in how developed we think we are by bringing us times when we have to demonstrate our maturity and effectiveness.

The progressed Moon and transiting Saturn represent two factors in our development, the first emotional and the second practical. These two energies work together to help us create our personality which will protect and nurture us while allowing our sense of purpose to fulfill itself. The dance of these two planets allow us to understand our progressed feelings shaping our choices at critical points as we come to ever-deeper realizations of which parts of our lives work for us and which don't.

The Progressed Lunar Cycle

As we've discussed, finding our perfect partner takes time and our willingness to dance with all kinds of people so we know what works for us. However, "what works for us" changes as we age and come to know who we really are and what we really want and don't want. It's why who we thought would be a perfect partner during one part of our life suddenly isn't the partner we thought we wanted. Then we have to re-frame our search. The trick is to understand how we have changed, and a key to understanding this is found in our progressed Moon cycles.

As I offered earlier, the progressed Moon symbolizes how we experience life on a month to month level, and shows our general "feeling atmosphere" in progressed areas of our lives related to what sign it's in. Progressions (secondary directions) are calculated by counting each day after birth to symbolize an entire progressed year. So if we count 10 days after birth, we'll see the progressed positions for our planets when we were 10 years old.

Because the Moon takes about 27.3 days to orbit the Earth, it shows our progressed Moon will return to its birth position when we are 27+ years old. This is called a progressed Lunar return, which is an extraordinarily important time when we re-set our emotional defaults. We get clear about how we feel about life and our future potential, because we have felt, "up close and personal," all of the sign energies in the zodiac. We have experienced feelings associated with all the signs and houses in our chart, and at 27 have an initial sense of completing one emotional journey as we prepare for the next one lasting through our mid-50s.

During its 27 year journey in our chart the progressed Moon interacts with all our other planets, activating echoes, memories, and past things related to those planets. Over the span of 27 years, the progressed Moon opens us to feel every possible character trait of the signs. As we become aware of our ever-changing feelings, our sense of what we need and how we want to express ourselves evolves, which changes who we attract.

When our progressed Moon conjuncts our other planets, we begin new ways of experiencing and expressing those parts of our personality. When it touches our Sun, we "feel our Light." When it touches our Venus, we "feel what we like." When it touches our Jupiter, we "feel a new vision." We all hit a crucial point in our sense of what we want, as well as what we can't live with, when our progressed Moon conjuncts our natal Saturn. These are when we get a "feel for our responsibility to ourselves," because these periods require that we get clear about our duties, obligations, and perceived deficiencies so we can drop what we no longer need. These are times to get rid of whatever makes us feel weighted down, stifled, incompetent or inadequate.

As our progressed Moon dances with our natal Saturn throughout our lives, we get to examine how we feel about the burdens of our life, and change those things which oppress us. All contacts with our Saturn are opportunities to claim our power to throw off our heaviness and embrace the joys of life. Even hard times become blessings which allow us to get clear about what to do to take care of ourselves.

As our needs change, so will our choices in relationship. While healthy relationships will continue and become richer, others disappear and new people show up. Everyone we dance with contributes to our emotional self-awareness and helps us learn what and who we can and cannot live with.

The progressed Moon shows us our changing needs over time, and puts the focus on specific areas of our lives as it travels through our houses. A very important time in our lives is when the progressed Moon conjuncts our Ascendant, as we get a new feel for our self-image and a new experience of what we've become as a result of all we've been through since we formed the old self-image now ending. We get a new sense of what we care about, what we feel is or isn't necessary, and find a "new identity" after a period of examining and reflecting on the types of people we want to be around and how we want to feel about things in the future.

In this 27+ year cycle, there are significant shifts about every seven years depending on how fast or slow our progressed Moon is moving. It's one reason why we all confront dramatic changes in our lives every seven years. Our progressed Moon's dance with transiting Saturn marks shifts at key points in life showing when our needs have changed, allowing us to reorient and take advantage of our emotional awakening.

These periods when our internal responses change forever allow us to take a new look at how we feel about daily life, habits, and how we want to live. At 27 we realize we no longer care about some things, and don't want to continue certain personality traits. We've completed a whole cycle of emotional experience, and 27 is the time when we begin anew.

SEVEN YEAR SHIFTS

Moving From Childhood to Adulthood

The relationship of our progressed Moon with transiting Saturn shows how our emotions relate to our sense of being obligated to someone or something. As I explain in my book Saturn: Spiritual Master, Spiritual Friend, Saturn is what binds and limits us, but it also shows us our path to self-mastery and the ability to shape a better future. The Moon shows our internal reaction to things, while transiting Saturn represents worldly circumstances forcing us to look at what we will and won't be a part of.

At birth, we begin all of our life cycles, and are absorbed into our subjective feeling-experiences. Around age 7 we hit a major turning point in our day to day life around the time we begin elementary school when we realize the adult world has rhythms which don't revolve around us. We instinctively adapt our self-expression, and begin new relationships with people who are different than our nuclear family. Around this time, we also have to deal with adult authorities who are not our family and must do as they say. As Saturn also makes a shift in our lives during age 7, we begin to learn different rules which serve us until they don't.

About 12-14 years old, we experience another major emotional shift as we begin adolescence. Because the progressed Moon opposes its birth position around then, many feelings surface, especially in the realm of relationships. This awakening and reorientation leads us to re-shape our personality in how we relate to others because we've become more sensitive to other people in our peer group. During our early teen years we begin to explore our power to oppose people and things we don't like. We are happy when others approve of us, and are unhappy when they disapprove. We struggle to establish our "equalness" with others, though of course we lack the emotional maturity and life experience which are the foundations of our ability to be an equal on our own terms. Still, our adolescent "self" creates patterns which will attract future relationships, many of which will be abandoned as we mature.

The period after 12-14 is difficult, because it seems others have all the power, and we're struggling to "fit in," often with people and situations where we don't. By our middle and late teen years, we have certain expectations and try to conform to roles determined by our family, but are also rebelling against the parts of our lives which feel too rigid or oppressive. That's often why as teens we become (to

274

whatever degree) non-conformist and oppositional to people and assumptions of "who we should be."

Around 19-20 we have another emotional shift related to our public self, reputation, or how we feel about the direction of our life, We also become more sensitive about how others are viewing us as seen through our feeling filters. Our early to mid-20s is somewhat of an emotional harvest period, finishing at the Lunar return at 27 when we realize we've finished an entire feeling cycle, and now care about many different things than we did when we were young. By 29, we know what parts of our life and which relationships no longer work for us. We know which rules no longer apply to us, and renew our quest to find people and experiences we believe will fulfill our needs..

LUNAR RETURNS AND SATURN RETURNS

During the progressed Lunar returns at 27 and 54-55, we go through a fundamental transformation. At each of these critical junctures we are able to be more objective about what we need for a sense of well-being. As we replace emotional responses creating strife with those leading to peace, our relationships change because we attract new people who are perfect for who we are at that point in our life.

At each Lunar return we realize we've completed an entire cycle of all the sign experiences, and feel we're more complete yet different than before. Those emotional "re-set" periods bring new awakened feeling-awareness, giving us a sense of how to experience life differently with deeper emotional connections because of all we've been through up to then.

At age 27, we are at a peak in our biological cycle. Our hormones are at a peak, our energies are at a peak, but because of metabolic changes between 27 and 29 associated with transiting Saturn, we realize we cannot sustain previous levels of activity. Saturn also brings us the realization that we just don't care about some things anymore and our needs have changed. In our late 20s we know we are moving into unknown emotional realms. While we want to feel emotionally comfortable, whether this ultimately leads to freedom or bondage (or both) is determined by what we've accepted or rejected up to then.

The changes in our feelings shown by the progressed Moon support some of the subsequent choices associated with transiting Saturn, while also showing us our inner sense of lack or need. The relationship of our inner nature to outer events shapes who we meet and when. That's why we have radically different needs in all our relationships after age 30 than we did before then.

The First Whole Cycle
Progressed Moon and Transiting Saturn

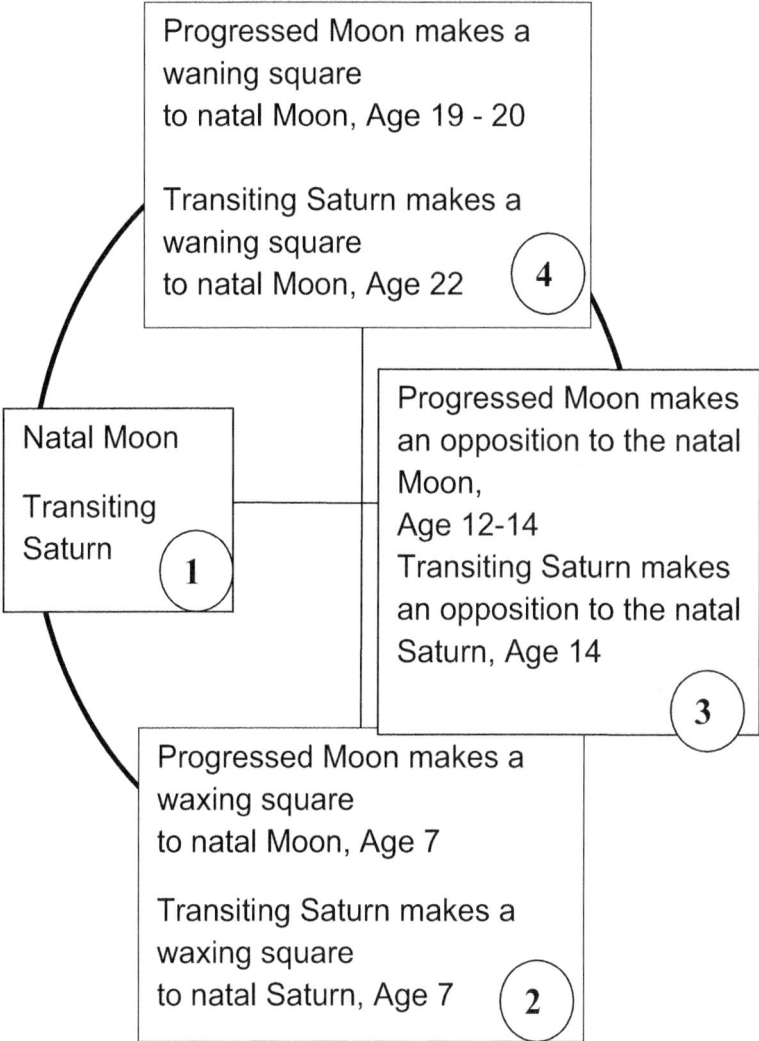

Progressed Moon makes a
waning square
to natal Moon, Age 19 - 20

Transiting Saturn makes a
waning square
to natal Moon, Age 22   **4**

Natal Moon

Transiting
Saturn   **1**

Progressed Moon makes
an opposition to the natal
Moon,
Age 12-14
Transiting Saturn makes
an opposition to the natal
Saturn, Age 14

3

Progressed Moon makes a
waxing square
to natal Moon, Age 7

Transiting Saturn makes a
waxing square
to natal Saturn, Age 7   **2**

Subsequent Whole Cycles
Progressed Moon and Transiting Saturn

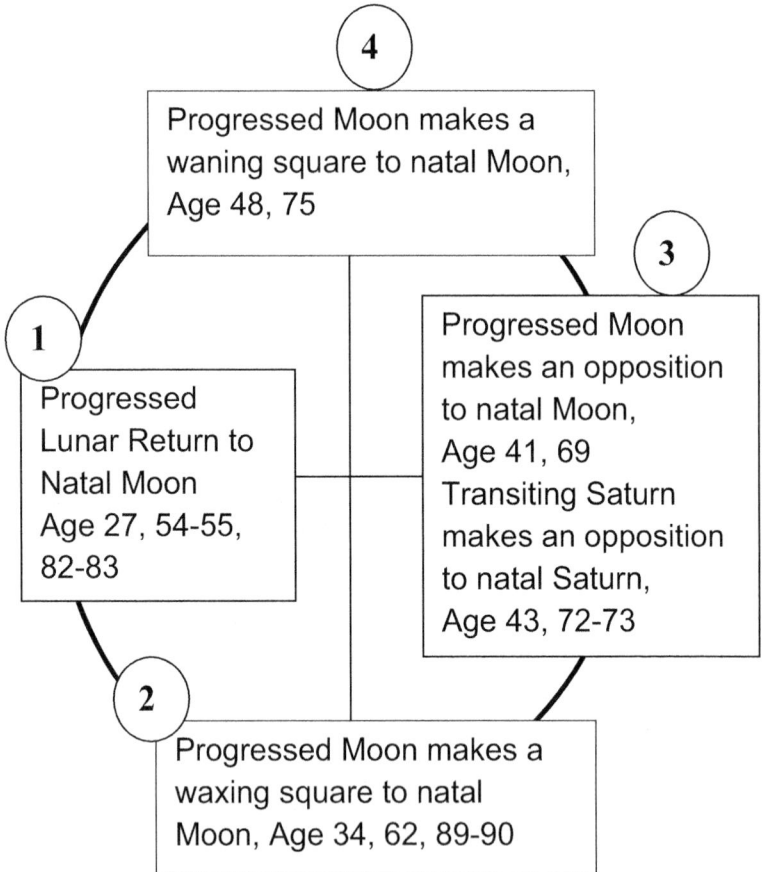

(4)

Progressed Moon makes a waning square to natal Moon, Age 48, 75

(1)

Progressed Lunar Return to Natal Moon Age 27, 54-55, 82-83

(3)

Progressed Moon makes an opposition to natal Moon, Age 41, 69 Transiting Saturn makes an opposition to natal Saturn, Age 43, 72-73

(2)

Progressed Moon makes a waxing square to natal Moon, Age 34, 62, 89-90

Down the Road

The choices, major decisions, endings and beginnings around the time of our first progressed Lunar and transiting Saturn return between 27-29 shape subsequent emotional and life shifts about 34-36. The next big shift in our early 40s brings us to a point of mid-course adjustments. By then we know who we are and whether we're emotionally fulfilled, and have to adapt to find what and who we believe will nurture us in the future.

At 54-55 we have our second Lunar return and at 57-59 the second Saturn return, both indicative of momentous changes. This period is one when we primarily set aside many things in our past we no longer care about and are free to use our understanding and wisdom in more fulfilling relationships. This completes two cycles of emotional experience, yielding peace and clarity about what life has given us, what we might receive in the future, and what we'll probably never get. By then we know what we care about, and no longer want what will not nurture us.

* * * * * * * * *

Throughout life, we learn to let go of behaviors which keep us feeling oppressed or pulled off our center. As we mature we learn not to give power to things and people which distract us from our spiritual equipoise. Even when life's rough patches throw us off balance, we always feel better when we consciously choose productive responses rather than fall into fear, clutching, pessimism, or illusions.

Major life changes give us opportunities to learn, adapt, grow, and see our power to choose wise and productive responses and relationships, renouncing feelings of weakness or neediness. Our lives are a journey from ignorance into mastery. As we grow, we let go of unhelpful attitudes and by our willingness to be the best person we can be, our striving, adaptability, perseverance, and a sense of humor guarantees us an every-more fulfilling life rich in healthy relationships. While the way to healthy relationships continually reminds us not to make assumptions or take anything or anyone for granted, eventually we can find partners who are perfect for us, whether in business, pleasure, or life.

CHAPTER ELEVEN

Help Mates, Soul Mates, and Your Twin Flame

In our wild and crazy world, millions are "looking for love, in all the wrong places." As we explored earlier, we're all conditioned to a greater or lesser degree by our family and cultural matrix. Some of these responses are obvious and some aren't. We're all trying to understand how to get what we believe we want, and wind up frustrated whether we get them or don't. That's because until we see things from the eyes of our Higher Self rather than our lower self, we're always going to wonder whether the love we've found will last a lifetime.

As we travel life's paths, everyone we meet teaches us something about ourselves and our responses to life. Those we feel some sort of affection for fall into two groups; help mates and Soul mates. Each and all of these will strengthen our heart in some way. In this chapter we'll explore the qualities of help mates and Soul mates to draw a contrast to the Twin Flame, who will always be your friend and Beloved.

Help Mates

While there are similarities between help mates and Soul Mates and the Twin Flame, a help mate or Soul Mate is completely different than our Twin Flame. There is a vast difference between those who help us, those who travel with us across space and time awakening the potential for us to experience and demonstrate unconditional Love, and our Divine Other.

Throughout life, it's a great thing to have help mates. A help mate is someone who is a genuine help to us. We have many help mates throughout our lives who assist us as genuine allies and friends, whether for an hour or a lifetime. I've found help mates are open to meeting our other help mates, since "pleasure shared is pleasure doubled." and truly, we're all more capable and aware and knowledgeable together than we are separately.

Welcoming true friends who are help mates assisting us to greater friendships and connectedness opens the door to other happy relationships. Our true friends inspire our love and ability to be loved, and bring knowledge of what makes us happy. Our help mates and true friends assist us to see what is in our best interests, as well as the greatest good for the greatest number. Our friends and help mates call forth our heart's response in genuine love, affection, a healthy self-respect and mature strength of character so we can dance in the relationship without going into spaces that are in no one's best interests. A true friend is a godsend, whether for a day or a lifetime.

Soul Mates

Anyone who brings out your capacity to expand your lesser love to a greater love is a Soul mate. A Soul mate is one who brings out our Soul, for better and/or for worse. A Soul mate is someone who takes us on a timeless adventure. They show up in both genders. They will take you to the heights, and often to the depths, They may or may not be your friend, but they change your life forever.

Our Soul Mates are many. We will dance with many people who are our best friends and lovers across time, and hopefully we learn all we need to about conditional and unconditional love from all of them. We can always find the greater love we seek, but we also must have a plan and patience as we move through the various changes and lessons resulting from the impermanence of all bonds except the Twin Flame.

When you find a Soul Mate, you always feel like you've known them before, in some other space and time. We feel a timeless bond, and usually decide to make a relationship in some way which works for both of us. We find things we like in common, and discover things we never knew before. We have our work and they have theirs. We have our baggage and they have theirs, but Soul Mates don't care, since they're on a path to destiny, for better or worse. Bonnie and Clyde were as much Soul Mates as Paul Newman and Joanne Woodward or Eleanor and Franklin Roosevelt.

Soul Mates appear in many ways, but they all share a bond which brings them together to do their "Soul work." Soul Mates strengthen our hearts, often through challenging life circumstances. That is why they're called Soul Mates. They put you in touch with your Soul. If they didn't they wouldn't be your Soul Mate.

That's why a Soul mate may or may not be the best material for a lifelong partner. Soul Mates can even break your heart so you know what unconditional love can feel like if you or they choose to end the relationship for whatever reason.

Our love grows through being tested, and there's no greater test than to know the object of one's love is gone. Even though we no longer see them, touch them, hear them, or feel their presence, because we shared a greater love, we have to hold our love we experience without having that person there. That is transforming conditional love to unconditional love.

Anyone who helps our hearts grow stronger is a Soul Mate. We have many throughout our lives. Some we laugh with, some we cry with, and some we do both with. They can be our best friend or worst enemy, family or strangers. They always test our heart, since the heart is the seat of our knowledge. The mind compares and contrasts, but ultimately cannot "know" in the deepest sense, since that is found in our heart's "direct knowing."

Our Soul Mates test us to the limit. While there's always an element of destiny in a Soul Mate relationship, remember each is a personality with flaws. Usually it's not our Soul which does the relationship in, but rather our personality flaws. These types of "Soul invoking" relationships help us to a greater compassion, since to be "perfect" in this world means to be perfectly human, with flaws and imperfections and wounds and all the other difficulties accompanying being a human.

A Soul Mate may or may not break your heart, but they will leave an indelible memory and change your life forever. Soul Mates bring you the lessons of a lifetime, in both your inner and outer reality. They may or may not be your lover, and usually show up as friendly Spirits, but you always come together for as long as it takes for you two to change each other's lives forever. Remember you have been a Soul Mate to them just as they were to you. Because you have stirred and transformed each other's Souls and know

284

what a Soul love feels like, at some point you'll be ready to meet or re-connect with your Twin Flame. So what's the difference between a Soul Mate and a Twin Flame?

The Twin Flame

While friends, help mates, and Soul Mates are many, there is only one Twin Flame. The Twin Flame is our true other half, the "Divine Other" we were separated from at the beginning of the human race millions of years ago. I read long ago from venerable sources that the reason the split occurred was because there were not enough Souls to populate the early species. We needed a certain number of Soul-infused humans to ensure the survival of the race. That required Souls to split and inhabit separate bodies.

It is safe to say that our Twin Flame is someone who will show up initially as a friend, help mate, and definitely a Soul Mate, but over time it will develop into a loving relationship phenomenally greater than any of these. It may be intense, it may be mellow, it may burst forth in a moment, or take 20 years to fulfill itself, but when we meet our Twin Flame, they will become unforgettable to us. Again, they always appear initially as a help mate or Soul mate, but they never feel like "random strangers" since this is you on an eternal level.

While a Soul mate will open us to many things we've never known before, and help us grow as human beings, we and they can still have significant differences which ultimately show us they are not our Twin Flame. In the presence of our Twin Flame, there will be a natural compatibility and easy harmony between you. Even when the personalities are not agreeing on something, there's still an essential harmony in the important areas.

Our Twin Flame will be a genuine help to us, a friend who we will spontaneously love and whose company we will enjoy. This is a useful signpost. Basically, if they're not our friend, if there isn't a healthy affection, kindness, and respect so we can dance separately and together over time and through various experiences, then they're not our Twin Flame.

How Personality is related to the Twin Flame

We are Soul/Spirits having human experiences. In becoming our Highest Self, we have to feel all the feelings there are to feel so we can become emotionally strong, aware, and wise. Because we're humans, we and our Twin Flame still have ego stuff to contend with, since we're all in a body with feelings, ideas, and memories that condition our behavior. We've all developed personality habits which may obscure our ability to recognize our Twin Flame, and why we need patience, maturity, and good will toward others even if they initially don't seem to be a "perfect fit."

As a result of our childhood and various experiences in our adult lives, we all learned unhelpful habits of perception. We all have preconceptions and ego limitations. These naturally result in misconceptions and assumptions about our Twin Flame. I have known countless people who projected their desired image of "the Beloved" into their world, and attracted forms of that image. They love intensely and then they disagree, and eventually part for good, feeling badly because their mind thinks they have lost their Twin Flame. That's why we should never put that kind of baggage on anyone we meet. While we all make assumptions and have hopes and dreams, in the initial stages of the relationship I've found it better to allow it time to develop organically.

That's why marriage is not necessarily a marker that someone is a Twin Flame, since many who fall in love believe they've found their Twin Flame until the breakup! That's a human problem of having feelings and ideas which may be unclear. The tragedy of life is sometimes we find ourselves unable to take advantage of our best chances due to circumstances set into motion before then. But the blessing of life is that if we are determined to grow into our Highest Self, allowing nothing and no one to block our intention, eventually we'll find ourselves in a relatively enlightened state surrounded by loving, wise, intelligent friends and group workers.

Many wonder if they will ever find their Twin Flame. While of course there are never any guarantees, due to that being in the realm of the Lords of Karma, the good news is that with so many billions of Souls alive on Earth, our Twin Flame could very well be somewhere we could find them. With instant communications and extraordinary mobility unlike any other time in history, there's a great chance we could find our Twin Flame if we cultivate personality traits which could attract them to us or us to them.

This raises an important fact. You cannot "break up" with your Twin Flame. If you could break up, then s/he is not your Twin Flame and it's best to cut cleanly so you can move on without toxic emotional residue getting in the way of you finding your perfect mate in the future. We all have a lot of karma to work through. It's why we go through so many relationships with people who are not our Twin Flame, and why we should take a positive view even when we break up with someone. Better to bless them for opening our heart, and know we are again free to find the Beloved. Once we find our Twin Flame, it is inconceivable that you could break up, since it would be like "breaking up" with your kidneys or liver. You cannot do it.

Even during times of chaos when people are at odds with each other, the one heart you and your Twin Flame share would never yield to useless antagonism or invite any tension into your lives and relationship. Remember: You're not identical people with identical perspectives; you simply love each other beyond time and know in your heart of hearts you are both good to and for each other.

Even when you and your Twin Flame disagree or are at odds about something, you would never consider breaking up with them if they were in fact your Twin Flame. One breaks up with random strangers, friends who are no longer friends, and Soul Mates, but not the Twin Flame, as it would be unimaginable to have met them and then not go through life with them. In the presence of the Beloved, there will be no desire to destroy what you feel for each other once you recognize each other and resolve that old personality habits won't mess up your dance.

If you've broken up with someone who touched you deeply, or even broke your heart, they were more likely a Soul Mate who gave you the opportunity for your love to grow more unconditional. As we learn the difference between conditional love and unconditional Love, we develop the "inner vision" which will help us recognize our Twin Flame.

What To Look For

The Twin Flame is a complement to our life energy. That doesn't mean they're the same, or a mirror, of who we are. They are, however, the most natural relationship we'll ever have, and over time the differences will merge into the pure shared love of two Soul-Spirits experiencing no separation. Finding and recognizing the Twin Flame has nothing to do with our beliefs, expectations, passing experiences, or the images we have in our subconscious mind or desire mind.

Your Twin Flame will inspire the best in you, and your relationship will never lead to an unhealthy dependency or manipulation. Your Twin Flame will never put you down in ways that make you feel slimed or unworthy. As you can see, a Soul Mate could teach you through both fortunate and unfortunate experiences, but your Twin Flame will always be a true friend. No one wants to hurt one of their dearest friends. Hurting them is like hurting yourself.

Your Twin Flame will inspire a spontaneous joy and anticipation of joys to come, but not in ways that make you feel anxious, unfulfilled, or on the wrong track. We may experience these to the degree we're trapped in ego assumptions and desires, but our Twin Flame will never try to make us feel these ways. Your true love would never want you to feel anything other than the power of your shared loving hearts.

Regardless of how demonstrative you are or aren't, there's always a sense of a timeless love which puts your heart at peace. At times it will feel like an indescribable love, overwhelming in its intensity as it leads us into unknown dimensions of an all-consuming experience. However, this sort of love is empowering, and never leads us to give away our power in unhealthy ways.

We never have to give away our power in an equal relationship because we share it with others in healthy ways, because we are loving equals. With friends and Soul Mates, sometimes we have more power, and sometimes they do. Imagine these sorts of power sharing relationships taken to the highest level of intuitive cooperation!

No one EVER "settles for their Twin Flame." A Twin Flame IS your other half, across space and time, forever and ever. If you ever met, you could never imagine anyone else under any circumstances, since your Twin Flame is your absolute complement. They are everything you've ever wanted, imagined, or dreamed of, and you are the same thing for them. You are different, but perfectly complementary. I mean perfectly.

A Soul Mate may even have some qualities of your Twin Flame. However, even the karmic or "fated" relationships do not necessarily indicate one of them is our Twin Flame. Because we were separated from our Self at the beginning of the human race, and since then we've had countless karmic encounters with others who are not our Twin Flame, we have generated countless types of karma to be worked through.

If they are truly your Twin Flame, you'll be of one heart instantaneously (even if the anticipation stuns your personality!) They could not have resisted what they would have picked up in you, and the attraction would grow over time and experience rather than diminish. The cup is always filled to the brim. So take a look back at the many Soul Mates you've danced with to see elements of your Twin Flame, since those who awakened your Highest Self were teaching you a greater love. They all showed you facets of your heart's desire.

Because of personality differences, we cannot expect to agree with our Beloved or them agree with us all the time. In healthy relationships there is an ease of give-and-take in how power is shared so that neither feels weakened or diminished by being with the other. I've never surrendered my power in a relationship, nor have I accepted anyone else surrendering their power in a relationship.

There could never be any lasting friction between our belief system and the belief system of our Twin Flame. Even if we are involved in different life works, we and they still will "pray at the same altar," so to speak. You will value the Love you share more than any worldly thing.

Remember, the Twin Flame is our Divine complement. We and they will both be striving for inner fulfillment, and our Twin Flame will also want to be liberated from fear and all unworthy feelings and thoughts. We all want to experience "the memory of the Divine Light that I am," since even in our Wholeness we will want union with God. And of course, because God loves gratitude, appreciation of what we've been given and being given and will be given guarantees us more to be grateful for.

If we are not whole and complete as we are, we will never know the greater wholeness of being "At One" with another. It's a dance, not a contest. The dance with our Twin Flame is a reunion of the self with the Self, where both become more loving and wise. We each take turns demonstrating our power to love, and it generates something more than either of us knew before then.

The Reunion of the Self with the Self

Our relationship with our eternal Self is the most important relationship we'll ever have. We discover that dance between our lower self and our Higher Self through our interactions with random strangers, help mates, and Soul Mates.

While all our relationships mirror this to some degree, the dance we experience with the Eternal is beyond our ego. As we learn to be our eternally loving Self, we are led through many intense desires and experiences into a limitless higher Love unlike any we ever knew. Embracing our ability to be the love we seek ensures at some point we'll find others who also are living their higher love.

Finding our Twin Flame (not who we assume is a Twin Flame) is best described as the reunion of the Self with the self, the Sacred Conjunctio, where both are more than they were. It's like a homecoming between true friends who have known each other since the beginning of time. Our Twin Flame gives us a sense of a truly settled heart we share together, where we are as in love with that person at age 70 as we are at 25.

When your heart is settled and the mutual love is growing, there shouldn't be any sense of urgency in the relationship, and not much doubt as to "should I or shouldn't I?" You will both feel strengthened and whole, individually and together, as you allow your ever-growing love to conquer all your ego limitations.

I have heard some offer that they believe the Twin Flame describes "the same soul" concept, where there is a "rhythm of "attraction and repulsion" that lessens over time until both ultimately come together and stay together as an integrated Being. Remember our Soul is inherently non-dual, since it exists beyond the mind and all which is termed "impermanent." We split "Our Eternal Self" at the beginning of time. There could be no split subsequent to that initial thing, as it would further fragment our eternal Self experiencing Oneness to no good purpose, because that purpose already happened millions of years ago.

We need no "time" to integrate with our Twin Flame, other than working through personality quirks. We couldn't not love them for all the tea in India! Again, it's like finding our oldest best friend in the world. They naturally will accept who we are and the work we do, and we will do the same for them.

What Happens If Circumstances Prevent A Relationship With Our TF?

Once you meet your Twin Flame, even if you are kept apart by outer circumstances, you'll forever have love and affection for that person. It would be painful if one or both of you were already married, but even in that circumstance your Twin Flame would be a "friend for life" even if you never had contact after the initial interaction. It would be difficult to meet one's Twin Flame if one were single and the other married, since it makes for uncomfortable timing on expressing our hearts. It would certainly seem that life is playing a trick on the both of you if one is available when the other is not.

The attraction could be so intense that one or both of you might withdraw or keep at a distance because of the impossibility of feeling such a strong connection without the ability to fulfill the relationship. However, there would be an attraction forever which would never leave the consciousness. Once united, we can never part. We may wind up friends, co-workers, colleagues, and even lovers, but once we find them and they find us, neither wants to be apart and always welcomes the presence of the other. Of course, you could meet when you and/or they are married, and then later on find each other again if you and they are divorced.

Once you meet your Twin Flame, even if you have to part in this world, at some point in time you will again come together, on whatever plane. Because magnetic resonance works as it does, we would reincarnate together, find each other again, and probably live our entire lives in relatively fulfilled happiness in the company of the other. This is a coming together that, even though tested severely, could never come apart.

If one of the two Twin Flames is married, it can be difficult, but if the Other is truly our Twin Flame, then love and friendship will prevail. Even when this life is done, we will reincarnate in the future so that one or both can fulfill karma, get free of unions that need severing, and find each other at some point. From then on, you will never be apart on Earth.

As long as we're here, we could be misunderstanding the signs and signals. But once we're on track, they're our best friends, even if one is married. There would never be anything inappropriate between the two of you because highest respects would govern the relationship.

Romance Above, Romance Below

Some who are searching for their Twin Flame believe the Twin Flame has nothing to do with romance, or physical things, and is seldom if ever a romantic love partner. I'll turn that around and ask why wouldn't there be a romantic attraction between two who have been together yet separate since the beginning of humankind?

I believe "romantic" is in the eye of the beholder, and "romance" is something naturally cultivated as part of any courtship between Souls. In any relationship with someone we're attracted to, of course there are romantic elements, whether physical or more ethereal. That's because in the eternal romance of the self with the Self, as we dance with others we learn to enjoy the closeness, the thrill, and the warmth that loving relationships bring us.

When we are with our Twin Flame, we are with a part of ourself we separated from millions of years ago. When we find our Twin Flame, we have reunited with a part of our eternal Self. If we are young, of course there will be an irresistible "urge to merge." This would be normal and natural between any two beings who love each other. However, "the romance of the Soul" between us and another is an entirely different dimension of Love.

That's why earlier I offered you the value of courtship, since we are on a lifelong courtship with the Beloved. Courtship always has a romantic component, since our Soul is communing with the Soul of another. Both courtship and romance will probably have expression as a sexual attraction when we are younger. And it's equally true that as we age and enter the season of the Grey Hair, the physical element in romance is less important than the courtship we maintain with the Beloved. Courtship at any age is very romantic! And while looking at the face of our young Beloved is always exciting to our heart, it's equally exciting to see that beautiful face as it ages. Wrinkles and grey hair can be very beautiful!

Most romantic relationships get pretty intense when they begin. These open us to experiencing a greater love than we knew before. They bring out deep feelings, strong attachments, and sincere hope that they will last. Most of these should be considered Soul mates, since they're bringing us to a state of greater awareness and experience of our Soul's love for another.

However, some Soul mates will break your heart. These are challenges forcing our love to grow from conditional love to a greater unconditional Love. If we can break up with someone, and one or both have no desire to resume the relationship, it's a clear signal they are a Soul mate and not the Twin Flame. We would never break up with our Twin Flame once we found each other. It would be like splitting yourself in two, since your Twin Flame is the other part of your Soul-Spirit you've been searching for since the beginning of time.

Can Our Twin Flame Be Seen in the Synastry Between Two Charts?

The chart of the Twin Flame can be seen; the thing is, any chart could be the Twin Flame. The desire mind can't see clearly what is in its eternal best interest. There are many charts which could be the Twin Flame. And we have to experience plenty of Soul Mates before we can recognize the possibility that person could be our Twin Flame. That said, our Twin Flame is in our chart; but our awareness determines who we attract.

While there will always be elements of harmony as well as potential friction between two charts, I have never seen consistent astrological markers which accurately predict two people are Twin Flames using synastry. While it's easy to see compatibility between charts, so far there are no case histories of actual Twin Flames letting us know which astrological factors could be important. Ultimately, I believe we cannot verify that someone is our Twin Flame using synastry, since birth charts are conditioned by time, and our Twin Flame exists "out of time.

The chart reveals emotional baggage and ego issues which most people bring with them into relationships, but over time these resolve and don't become dysfunctional to the point we become frustrated and we end the relationship. I do believe Twin Flames have already danced through many experiences across lifetimes to adjust their karma, becoming more loving and wise to demonstrate their best Self when their "other half" shows up. That way when a person meets their Twin Flame they are instantly harmonious with each other, and able to give and receive in healthy ways.

Because they've been on Earth for as long as we have, they too would have emotional baggage and ego issues, just as we do as a result of living our lives. This comes with being human. Our Twin Flame is not the same as us, even if they're our "other half." On meeting our Twin Flame, we may or may not have to confront their past karma, or they confront ours, but we would always be mutually supportive and never undermining our Twin Flame's ability to deal with their karma.

Because true love is beyond any ego limitation we might have, over time we and our Twin Flame can grow beyond our old limitations in an ever-expanding wisdom. If we strive for the Highest, we will eventually see the manifestation of a form of the Beloved.

There will obviously be harmony between our chart and the chart of our Twin Flame, but that's also true for Soul mates and help mates. Since we're here to help each other overcome our human deficiencies and embrace a Soulful life, getting hung up on whether someone is or isn't our Twin Flame is not as helpful as becoming the best friend we can be to all who come into our lives.

When you first meet your Twin Flame there will be a strong attraction, whether one or both of you chooses to act on that attraction or not. As your relationship develops, you'll see them as a Soul Mate. This is the first step in recognizing your Twin Flame. Let the love, let the experience, let the knowledge of each other develop organically, naturally, easily over time. There's no need to rush, push, or get impatient. It will be intense, gentle, easy, thrilling, and feel like a timeless adventure you've never had and always had. It is your dance with your Beloved.

While our Twin Flame is indicated in our chart, in fact our Twin Flame will have their own chart. Who knows what astrological chart is best for you, and shows you the reunion with your Self? That's why any chart could be that of your Twin Flame. They will have had their destiny, their trials, their sorrows, their weaknesses, and their "dark night of the Soul." They will also have had their strengths, wisdom, intelligence, and determination to be their best Self.

Remember each of you is fully human, with all your imperfections. But each of you are also recognizing, to the core of your Being, a love beyond description, one you would never abandon for anything. Each day will feel like a new adventure in renewing your life and love.

Like you, your Twin Flame will want to find their Beloved, while being true to themselves and their hearts. Just like you. When two hearts who were originally at One Together finally find each other, then no matter the trials, the ups and downs, it takes to find each other and finally connect with each other, you will know peace. And excitement. And joy. And renewal like you've never known before, since you have found your Beloved. You will know your self as both individual and complete.

Having done many thousands of charts in my life, and seen thousands of couples' charts. I have only met a handful of couples I believe are Twin Flames, as it played out in their lives over many decades. I have seen many charts for Soul mates, who it's clear they are in that relationship to bring a greater love to each other, and fulfill certain pre-existing karmas between them. They seem to help each other's Souls come forth through all kinds of experiences, offering each opportunities to learn to turn lesser forms of love to a greater Love. But even these don't seem to have anything to do with whether two Beings are Twin Flames.

Even though we can suspect someone is our Twin Flame and relate to them as our eternal Other, we will never know for certain if they are our Twin Flame until after we're no longer in a body. It cannot be seen in a chart, since it is beyond the chart, and could be just about any chart. That's why we want to cultivate friends who are our Soul Mates. Then we are with people who share our Soul bond AND are our friend.

This is where there will obviously be astrological compatibility, but even with very harmonious chart placements, we cannot know the timeless by any known technique of chart analysis. I have seen the most harmonious charts split, and the most frictional stay together. Usually there's just enough harmony to show our affinity, and just enough friction to show our individuality. That's why we cannot know if someone is our Twin Flame until we've had a life together with miles of troubles and triumphs in our rear view, and even then, they may be a Soul Mate rather than a Twin Flame.

It is entirely possible we cannot know who our Twin Flame is until we're no longer in the body. How can the eternal be known by our finite perceptions and feelings? Because our Twin Flame is beyond our speculations and assumptions, it's better to cultivate friendships, since a sincere friendship will always open the door to ever-greater loving relationships. Unless there is a friendship beyond the centuries that grows ever deeper and more loving by the year, then that person is not one's Twin Flame.

Our Divine Other is Us and Not Us

When we are in the presence of our Twin Flame, there is an instant recognition of "the other" quickening everything in us. We may or may not finish each other's sentences, but we may dream the same dream at the same time, or remember "other lives" at the same time. Because we are complements, we probably developed differently, in different areas of Self-realization.

Also, we may or may not be "at the same level" of awareness, since we're speaking of complementary energies, not identical. In any relationship, each of us is more aware of some things and less aware of other things. Even if one is spiritually oriented and the other isn't, there will come a time when the more evolved of you would realize it wasn't working, usually because the less evolved is reverting to ego limitations. Still, if both are willing to accept the need for growth, love will absolutely move both closer together, with the less evolved willing to rise to the occasion of a greater love than they had ever experienced before.

The Twin Flame will bring forth feelings on a different level than all the other lovers, spouses, and everyone else you've ever known. That's why it's important to prepare to meet our Beloved as our highest, best, most loving Self. We want to greet "the Beloved" in our highest spiritual expression. The interesting thing is they will naturally bring that forth in us, and we'll bring that forth in them, without manipulation or demands.

That's why striving to be the best spiritual human we can is paramount if we want to attract our Divine Other. We originally split on Earth, and that's where we'll come back together. Relationships which become more loving over time, encouraging our Soul-Spirit to express itself naturally and organically, are great opportunities to learn how to recognize the eternally loving relationships we've cultivated across time "in Heaven and on Earth." One of these is our Twin Flame.

Being with your Twin Flame is an ongoing, real time, "here and now" experience, a timeless love beyond your wildest dreams. You will feel that eternal love you have for each other every moment of your existence, whether you speak it or show it or not. You are each unique and a light unto yourselves; and yet you are one together. Your hearts are at peace.

Finding Happiness

There are many ways to find happiness, and many ways not to find it. By opening our imagination to ways to find happiness, we can BE that happiness as we live our lives.

We are told that all humans seek happiness and an end to suffering. We can definitely achieve these two aims. First and foremost, ending our suffering requires mental self-discipline, focus, and a willingness to change our attitudes which contribute to our suffering, but that's not what we're discussing here.

Since the best way to fight evil is to promote what is good, finding happiness is a must if we in fact want to lead a happy life. Finding happiness requires two things. One is recognizing what will truly make us happy here and now. The other is in learning to cultivate an attitude which welcomes the experience of being happy, and recognizing when it's time to BE happy. Since all humans seek happiness, one of the main issues is where will we find happiness, and why do we believe that we will find happiness in those ways?

Regardless of where we find happiness for any length of time, ultimately because life moves on and we move on, what makes us truly happy changes with time and maturity, That's why we must have a degree of detachment from what made us happy in the past, so we can see if those things still bring us happiness. While some things will make us happy for our whole lives, other things must be released so new things can enter to expand our sense of what will make us happy.

Cultivating an attitude which welcomes happiness involves releasing tendencies to be pessimistic or unhappy. The mind can be very rigid in its beliefs and attitudes, and is usually more focused on "knowing" what is "right and wrong," or "good and bad." This is where we must ask ourselves the classic question from time to time: "Would you rather be right or would you rather be happy?" While occasionally we can be both at the same time, more often our need to be "right" gets in the way of our being "happy." (Everybody does this to some degree. I found asking this question to myself and others usually finishes any argument, if only for me.)

Even when we've cultivated an attitude that welcomes being happy, we have to learn to recognize when we have the opportunity to BE happy. I have known many who yearned for happiness but didn't take the opportunity to experience it because their minds were busy elsewhere. This is where we have to learn to be in the present moment, and if there's an opportunity to feel something fulfilling, meaningful, joyous, or just simply be happy, embrace that experience in the here and now.

Happiness is a state of mind which must be cultivated. If our happiness is attached to anything in the outer world, it will be transitory, since all forms pass away. We may find great happiness in things, but ultimately those things leave, to be replaced with other things. To be truly happy we must learn to know when and how to let go, and at the right time choose something better which will bring us renewed happiness. It's useful to remember great happiness is often found in giving away something of value to another who will also value it, since as we consciously learn to let go in the right way and time we create space for better things to come. As we release, we are freed from old inertias and can claim our happiness on new terms.

A lot of life's happiness comes as we let go of inhibitions, including those which make us feel separate from ourselves or others, or disconnected from life as it unfolds each minute. A feeling of inner freedom is the nature of our eternal Soul/Spirit. The more we remember we are the joy of being a loving, wise, intelligent consciousness, the more we'll experience happiness, since our minds will be attuning to the greater Love we are. The mind perceiving a greater Love can lead it to happy thoughts, since we know at our core we are a beautiful, loving Being.

In our quest to be happy, from time to time we have to examine our bondage to our "craving for happiness" we feel, since that prohibits any true happiness from taking root. We've all known people trying too hard to find happiness who often miss it when it's happening. Again, this is where the ability to detach from listening to the scratchy mental grooves we've recorded in our minds is important. We all have unhelpful thoughts from time to time which we have to counter with more positive thoughts which will lead us back to our natural happiness when we're not distracted by unhelpful thoughts and feelings.

Remember, we are not separate from the One Life we all are together. That means we all pick up on thoughts and feelings in the collective atmosphere. When I was younger, this confused me because I was thinking thoughts and feeling feelings which made no sense to me. That troubled me until I learned astrology and understood that though we may feel isolated, we are as surrounded by life and love as a fish in water.

Because we're all One Life together, anyone who cultivates an expanded feeling-awareness is bound to feel more of All-That-Is. We do feel what others are feeling, we feel what others have felt in the physical space we occupy, and we also feel what others have felt who are not in our physical space. It's why our feeling experiences are often difficult. Because all of us are learning how to navigate feeling all there is to feel, the general level of confusion and suffering will be experienced by anyone with an expanded feeling-awareness.

That's why learning to spot when our thoughts and feelings are taking us to a negative state or attitude allows us to move our view into a more positive state of mind. We cannot avoid what we need to learn. We are here to learn certain things and become the best human Being we can be. While life is a series of challenges across the 12 frequencies of human existence, as we learn positive responses we come out of fear and confusion.

Cultivating an attitude of happiness, positivity, good will and the "will to good" is an invincible tool we all have which helps us create a happy life. This is entirely within our own power, and nothing can take it away.

As the old proverb tells us, "We cannot prevent the birds of worry from flying overhead, but we can prevent them from making a nest in our hair." Being happy is always right here, right now. There is no other time to be happy. So the next time your mind wants to take you into an unhappy space, you have the power to decide to focus it elsewhere to find a more fulfilling, more joyous, more empowering happiness.

Finale

You are one with life. You are one with the world Soul, and are an expression of its life and love. Thought the ordeal of Self-perfection is long and difficult, it is possible to find our heart at peace with another, and all the troubles and uncertainties of youth seen as events helping us recognize and find the Beloved.

While the road to the Beloved is often difficult, and we must kiss many toads along the way, eventually, if we pay attention, we shall see the eyes of the Beloved. After we have chased all our projections, then we can see clearly. Even when a relationship seems to fail, it still leads us into unknown possibilities.

We do not want to greet the Beloved with a bad attitude, or when we are less than our best. And yet the Beloved will gladly welcome us in our brokenness and our wholeness, our human-ness and the eternal Love we are. Finding the Beloved is like coming home. It will seem like the sanest, best thing you ever could have done. A peace will come over your heart which will make it clear that all of your life trials have led you to be able to recognize the love you are reflected in the eyes of your Beloved. Then all your thoughts and hopes and fears and dreams will merge into the light of clear realization that you ARE the Love you were seeking before and you are at one with your Beloved. You will each be the reflection of the love you are, individually and together. This is your Divine Birthright.

CHAPTER TWELVE

The Art of Attraction For All Signs

We determine who and what we attract by our own energies, both consciously and unconsciously. Our desire mind has its set of what it wants to attract, as does our subconscious mind. This is why it's a good thing to examine our behavior patterns to make sure we're acting, feeling, thinking, and speaking in ways that will bring us together with our ideal mate. If we can grow beyond old habits that only bring frustration in relationships, we can attract someone we really could love, and who can love us for who we are, because we are becoming more loveable ourselves.

If we're not attracting the mate we want (including better qualities in a partner we already have), then perhaps we need to get a better picture of what we want and need, or change something inside us that is blocking our ability to get our heart's desire. If a behavior or attitude needs to be changed so that we can receive our heart's desire, we must examine why we expect what we expect. If we really look within and honestly decide to change, we will eventually receive what is right for us.

Many of our attitudes were shaped by people who challenged or distracted us. Everyone has been hurt in relationships, and copped an attitude or two. Those probably won't bring us the mate who we hope to find.

If we don't let our hearts get hardened by our hurt, we can learn both what we want as well as what we don't want in our relationships. Then we can focus on getting the love we really want here and now, and do better than we've done before. Our willingness to grow beyond old desires can bring us a better partner than we've known, but only if we open our imagination and understand what could be true, good, and beautiful for us in the future.

If we're trying to be our best self, then we will eventually attract someone else who is also trying to be their best self. Those are the people who could over time become good friends. If we are attracting friends, we avoid being hurt by being attracted to someone who is not our friend and aren't trying to be their best self.

Here appearances and old patterns of liking and disliking often distract us. If we would attract our Beloved, we must understand what that means to our heart. We are not bound to old patterns; they only exist to show us where and how we need to grow in our faith and trust that we can attract our Beloved at the right time, once we are clear about who is best for us. By using our imagination to dream, we actively attract those who could be true friends, those we could have fun with and talk to and go places with. As our friends would never deliberately hurt us, that has to be the primary focus of who we would attract for a mate.

As we discussed earlier, Leo (the sign of the heart) and Aquarius (the sign of friendship) are natural mate signs for each other. Leo is the sign of personal love, Aquarius is the sign of impersonal love and friendship. If we're with someone who loves us, even though it may become strained, they'll stay our friends. They may or may not agree with us, but a friend will never do anything to undermine us, or make us feel less than our best.

Our friends may challenge us, but they will always love us. Where the heart is steady, love will endure through all kinds of challenges. May you go forth courageously and with a good heart, and attract your ideal partner with the knowledge you now have about yourself and what your beloved just might look like!

AFFIRMATIONS FOR ALL SUN-VENUS SIGN COMBINATIONS

Sun in Aries

Sun in Aries Venus in Aquarius
I affirm that I am willing to attract someone who is fair, romantic, idealistic, balanced, cooperative, creative, harmonious, adaptable, and considerate. My partner will be brilliant, unique, an idealist and a true friend. My mate will be the perfect one for me to learn how to become my highest self.

Sun in Aries Venus in Pisces
I affirm that I am willing to attract someone who is fair, romantic, idealistic, balanced, cooperative, creative, harmonious, adaptable, and considerate. My partner will be compassionate, intuitive, humble, adaptable, patient and unselfish. My mate will be the perfect one for me to learn how to become my highest self.

Sun in Aries Venus in Aries
I affirm that I am willing to attract someone who is fair, romantic, idealistic, balanced, cooperative, creative, harmonious, adaptable, and considerate. My partner will be assertive, demonstrative, energetic,

confident, inspiring, quick-witted, and enthusiastic. My mate will be the perfect one for me to learn how to become my highest self.

Sun in Aries Venus in Taurus
I affirm that I am willing to attract someone who is fair, romantic, idealistic, balanced, cooperative, creative, harmonious, adaptable, and considerate. My partner will be dependable, affectionate, creative, durable, patient, devoted, and stable. My mate will be the perfect one for me to learn how to become my highest self.

Sun in Aries Venus in Gemini
I affirm that I am willing to attract someone who is fair, romantic, idealistic, balanced, cooperative, creative, harmonious, adaptable, and considerate. My partner will be creative, versatile, humane, expressive, and open minded. My mate will be the perfect one for me to learn how to become my highest self.

Sun in Taurus

Sun in Taurus Venus in Pisces
I affirm that I am willing to attract someone who is expressive, trustworthy, determined, courageous, inspiring, magnetic, and tenacious. My partner will be compassionate, intuitive, humble, adaptable, patient and unselfish. My mate will be the perfect one for me to learn how to become my highest self.

Sun in Taurus Venus in Aries

I affirm that I am willing to attract someone who is expressive, trustworthy, determined, courageous, inspiring, magnetic, and tenacious. My partner will be assertive, demonstrative, energetic, confident, fearless, quick-witted, and enthusiastic. My mate will be the perfect one for me to learn how to become my highest self.

Sun in Taurus Venus in Taurus

I affirm that I am willing to attract someone who is expressive, trustworthy, determined, courageous, inspiring, magnetic, and tenacious. My partner will be dependable, affectionate, creative, durable, patient, devoted, and stable. My mate will be the perfect one for me to learn how to become my highest self.

Sun in Taurus Venus in Gemini

I affirm that I am willing to attract someone who is expressive, trustworthy, determined, courageous, inspiring, magnetic, and tenacious. My partner will be creative, versatile, humane, expressive, and open minded. My mate will be the perfect one for me to learn how to become my highest self.

Sun in Taurus Venus in Cancer

I affirm that I am willing to attract someone who is expressive, trustworthy, determined, courageous, inspiring, magnetic, and tenacious. My partner will be caring, kind, sensitive, mature and nurturing. My mate will be the perfect one for me to learn how to become my highest self.

Sun in Gemini

Sun in Gemini Venus in Aries
I affirm that I am willing to attract someone who is idealistic, generous, open-minded, cheerful, tolerant, and honest. My partner will be assertive, demonstrative, energetic, confident, fearless, quick-witted, and enthusiastic. My mate will be the perfect one for me to learn how to become my highest self.

Sun in Gemini Venus in Taurus
I affirm that I am willing to attract someone who is idealistic, generous, open-minded, cheerful, tolerant, and honest. My partner will be dependable, affectionate, creative, durable, patient, devoted, and stable. My mate will be the perfect one for me to learn how to become my highest self.

Sun in Gemini Venus in Gemini
I affirm that I am willing to attract someone who is idealistic, generous, open-minded, cheerful, tolerant, and honest. My partner will be creative, versatile, humane, expressive, and open minded. My mate will be the perfect one for me to learn how to become my highest self.

Sun in Gemini Venus in Cancer
I affirm that I am willing to attract someone who is idealistic, generous, open-minded, cheerful, tolerant, and honest. My partner will be caring, kind, sensitive, mature and nurturing. My mate will be the perfect one for me to learn how to become my highest self.

Sun in Gemini Venus in Leo

I affirm that I am willing to attract someone who is idealistic, generous, open-minded, cheerful, tolerant, and honest. My partner will be loving, creative, playful, noble, fearless, devoted, and honorable. My mate will be the perfect one for me to learn how to become my highest self.

Sun in Cancer

Sun in Cancer Venus in Taurus

I affirm that I am willing to attract someone who is mature, organized, honorable, trustworthy and faithful. My partner will be dependable, affectionate, creative, durable, patient, devoted, and stable. My mate will be the perfect one for me to learn how to become my highest self.

Sun in Cancer Venus in Gemini

I affirm that I am willing to attract someone who is mature, organized, honorable, trustworthy and faithful. My partner will be creative, versatile, humane, expressive, and open minded. My mate will be the perfect one for me to learn how to become my highest self.

Sun in Cancer Venus in Cancer

I affirm that I am willing to attract someone who is mature, organized, honorable, trustworthy and faithful. My partner will be caring, kind, sensitive, mature and nurturing. My mate will be the perfect one for me to learn how to become my highest self.

Sun in Cancer Venus in Leo

I affirm that I am willing to attract someone who is mature, organized, honorable, trustworthy and faithful. My partner will be loving, creative, playful, noble, fearless, devoted, and honorable. My mate will be the perfect one for me to learn how to become my highest self.

Sun in Cancer Venus in Virgo

I affirm that I am willing to attract someone who is mature, organized, honorable, trustworthy and faithful. My partner will be practical, dependable, unselfish, meticulous, and discerning. My mate will be the perfect one for me to learn how to become my highest self.

Sun in Leo

Sun in Leo Venus in Gemini

I affirm that I am willing to attract someone who is progressive, smart, friendly, altruistic, inventive, and self-sufficient. My partner will be creative, versatile, humane, expressive, and open minded. My mate will be the perfect one for me to learn how to become my highest self.

Sun in Leo Venus in Cancer

I affirm that I am willing to attract someone who is progressive, smart, friendly, altruistic, inventive, and self-sufficient. My partner will be caring, kind, sensitive, mature and nurturing. My mate will be the perfect one for me to learn how to become my highest self.

Sun in Leo Venus in Leo

I affirm that I am willing to attract someone who is progressive, smart, friendly, altruistic, inventive, and self-sufficient. My partner will be loving, creative, playful, noble, fearless, devoted, and honorable. My mate will be the perfect one for me to learn how to become my highest self.

Sun in Leo Venus in Virgo

I affirm that I am willing to attract someone who is progressive, smart, friendly, altruistic, inventive, and self-sufficient. My partner will be practical, dependable, unselfish, meticulous, and discerning. My mate will be the perfect one for me to learn how to become my highest self.

Sun in Leo Venus in Libra

I affirm that I am willing to attract someone who is progressive, smart, friendly, altruistic, inventive, and self-sufficient. My partner will be cooperative, creative, considerate, adaptable, and romantic, someone I can share ideals with. My mate will be the perfect one for me to learn how to become my highest self.

Sun in Virgo

Sun in Virgo Venus in Cancer

I affirm that I am willing to attract someone who is compassionate, intuitive, imaginative and spiritual. My partner will be caring, kind, sensitive, and nurturing. My mate will be the perfect one for me to learn how to become my highest self.

Sun in Virgo Venus in Leo

I affirm that I am willing to attract someone who is compassionate, intuitive, imaginative and spiritual. My partner will be loving, creative, playful, noble, fearless, devoted, and honorable. My mate will be the perfect one for me to learn how to become my highest self.

Sun in Virgo Venus in Virgo

I affirm that I am willing to attract someone who is compassionate, intuitive, imaginative and spiritual. My partner will be practical, dependable, unselfish, meticulous, and discerning. My mate will be the perfect one for me to learn how to become my highest self.

Sun in Virgo Venus in Libra

I affirm that I am willing to attract someone who is compassionate, intuitive, imaginative and spiritual. My partner will be cooperative, creative, considerate, adaptable, and romantic, someone I can share ideals with. My mate will be the perfect one for me to learn how to become my highest self.

Sun in Virgo Venus in Scorpio

I affirm that I am willing to attract someone who is compassionate, intuitive, imaginative and spiritual. My partner will be deep, intelligent and magnetic, someone I can merge with deeply. My mate will be the perfect one for me to learn how to become my highest self.

Sun in Libra

Sun in Libra Venus in Leo
I affirm that I am willing to attract someone who is forthright, honest, energetic, and can help me be true to myself. My partner will be loving, creative, playful, noble, fearless, devoted, and honorable. My mate will be the perfect one for me to learn how to become my highest self.

Sun in Libra Venus in Virgo
I affirm that I am willing to attract someone who is forthright, honest, energetic, dynamic, and can help me be true to myself. My partner will be practical, dependable, unselfish, meticulous, and discerning. My mate will be the perfect one for me to learn how to become my highest self.

Sun in Libra Venus in Libra
I affirm that I am willing to attract someone who is forthright, honest, energetic, and can help me be true to myself. My partner will be cooperative, creative, considerate, adaptable, and romantic, someone I can share ideals with. My mate will be the perfect one for me to learn how to become my highest self.

Sun in Libra Venus in Scorpio
I affirm that I am willing to attract someone who is forthright, honest, energetic, and can help me be true to myself. My partner will be deep, intelligent and magnetic, someone I can merge with deeply. My mate will be the perfect one for me to learn how to become my highest self.

Sun in Libra Venus in Sagittarius
I affirm that I am willing to attract someone who is forthright, honest, energetic, dynamic, and can help me be true to myself. My partner will be adventurous, generous, magnanimous, tolerant, and optimistic. My mate will be the perfect one for me to learn how to become my highest self.

Sun in Scorpio

Sun in Scorpio Venus in Virgo
I affirm that I am willing to attract someone who is gentle, reliable, straightforward, harmonious, affectionate, patient and devoted. My partner will be practical, dependable, unselfish, meticulous, and discerning. My mate will be the perfect one for me to learn how to become my highest self.

Sun in Scorpio Venus in Libra
I affirm that I am willing to attract someone who is gentle, reliable, straightforward, harmonious, affectionate, patient and devoted. My partner will be cooperative, creative, considerate, adaptable, and romantic, someone I can share ideals with. My mate will be the perfect one for me to learn how to become my highest self.

Sun in Scorpio Venus in Scorpio
I affirm that I am willing to attract someone who is gentle, reliable, straightforward, harmonious, affectionate, patient and devoted. My partner will be deep, intelligent and magnetic, someone I can merge

with deeply. My mate will be the perfect one for me to learn how to become my highest self.

Sun in Scorpio Venus in Sagittarius
I affirm that I am willing to attract someone who is gentle, reliable, straightforward, harmonious, affectionate, patient and devoted. My partner will be adventurous, generous, magnanimous, tolerant, and optimistic. My mate will be the perfect one for me to learn how to become my highest self.

Sun in Scorpio Venus in Capricorn
I affirm that I am willing to attract someone who is gentle, reliable, straightforward, harmonious, affectionate, patient and devoted. My partner will be mature, organized, honorable, trustworthy and faithful. My mate will be the perfect one for me to learn how to become my highest self.

Sun in Sagittarius

Sun in Sagittarius Venus in Libra
I affirm that I am willing to attract someone who is smart, adaptable, sociable, creative, open-minded, and resourceful. My partner will be cooperative, creative, considerate, adaptable, and romantic, someone I can share ideals with. My mate will be the perfect one for me to learn how to become my highest self.

Sun in Sagittarius Venus in Scorpio
I affirm that I am willing to attract someone who is smart, adaptable, sociable, creative, open-minded, and resourceful. My partner will be deep,

intelligent and magnetic, someone I can merge with deeply. My mate will be the perfect one for me to learn how to become my highest self.

Sun in Sagittarius Venus in Sagittarius
I affirm that I am willing to attract someone who is smart, adaptable, sociable, creative, open-minded, and resourceful. My partner will be adventurous, generous, magnanimous, tolerant, and optimistic. My mate will be the perfect one for me to learn how to become my highest self.

Sun in Sagittarius Venus in Capricorn
I affirm that I am willing to attract someone who is smart, adaptable, sociable, creative, open-minded, and resourceful. My partner will be mature, organized, honorable, trustworthy and faithful. My mate will be the perfect one for me to learn how to become my highest self.

Sun in Sagittarius Venus in Aquarius
I affirm that I am willing to attract someone who is smart, adaptable, sociable, creative, open-minded, and resourceful. My partner will be brilliant, unique, an idealist and a true friend. My mate will be the perfect one for me to learn how to become my highest self.

Sun in Capricorn

Sun in Capricorn Venus in Scorpio
I affirm that I am willing to attract someone who is kind, sensitive, caring, reflective, appreciative, expressive, creative, sympathetic and unselfish. My partner will be deep, intelligent and magnetic, someone I can merge with deeply. My mate will be

the perfect one for me to learn how to become my highest self.

Sun in Capricorn Venus in Sagittarius
I affirm that I am willing to attract someone who is kind, sensitive, caring, reflective, appreciative, expressive, creative, sympathetic and unselfish. My partner will be adventurous, generous, magnanimous, tolerant, and optimistic. My mate will be the perfect one for me to learn how to become my highest self.

Sun in Capricorn Venus in Capricorn
I affirm that I am willing to attract someone who is kind, sensitive, caring, reflective, appreciative, expressive, creative, sympathetic and unselfish. My partner will be mature, organized, honorable, trustworthy and faithful. My mate will be the perfect one for me to learn how to become my highest self.

Sun in Capricorn Venus in Aquarius
I affirm that I am willing to attract someone who is kind, sensitive, caring, reflective, appreciative, expressive, creative, sympathetic and unselfish. My partner will be brilliant, unique, an idealist and a true friend. My mate will be the perfect one for me to learn how to become my highest self.

Sun in Capricorn Venus in Pisces
I affirm that I am willing to attract someone who is kind, sensitive, caring, reflective, appreciative, expressive, creative, sympathetic and unselfish.

Sun in Aquarius

Sun in Aquarius Venus in Sagittarius
I affirm that I am willing to attract someone who is dynamic, playful, creative, loving, and loyal. My partner will be adventurous, generous, magnanimous, tolerant, and optimistic. My mate will be the perfect one for me to learn how to become my highest self.

Sun in Aquarius Venus in Capricorn
I affirm that I am willing to attract someone who is dynamic, playful, creative, loving, and loyal. My partner will be mature, organized, honorable, trustworthy and faithful. My mate will be the perfect one for me to learn how to become my highest self.

Sun in Aquarius Venus in Aquarius
I affirm that I am willing to attract someone who is dynamic, playful, creative, loving, and loyal. My partner will be brilliant, unique, an idealist and a true friend. My mate will be the perfect one for me to learn how to become my highest self.

Sun in Aquarius Venus in Pisces
I affirm that I am willing to attract someone who is honorable, courageous, dignified, devoted, magnanimous, and noble. My partner will be compassionate, intuitive, humble, adaptable, patient and unselfish. My mate will be the perfect one for me to learn how to become my highest self.

Sun in Aquarius Venus in Aries
I affirm that I am willing to attract someone who is dynamic, playful, creative, loving, and loyal. My partner will be assertive, demonstrative, energetic,

confident, inspiring, quick-witted, and enthusiastic. My mate will be the perfect one for me to learn how to become my highest self.

Sun in Pisces

Sun in Pisces Venus in Capricorn
I affirm that I am willing to attract someone who is dependable, discerning, practical, and serves a higher cause. My partner will be mature, organized, honorable, trustworthy and faithful. My mate will be the perfect one for me to learn how to become my highest self.

Sun in Pisces Venus in Aquarius
I affirm that I am willing to attract someone who is practical, honest, healthy, discerning and unselfish. My partner will be brilliant, unique, an idealist and a true friend. My mate will be the perfect one for me to learn how to become my highest self.

Sun in Pisces Venus in Pisces
I affirm that I am willing to attract someone who is dependable, discerning, practical, and serves a higher cause. My partner will be compassionate, intuitive, humble, adaptable, patient and unselfish. My mate will be the perfect one for me to learn how to become my highest self.

Sun in Pisces Venus in Aries
I affirm that I am willing to attract someone who is dependable, discerning, practical, and serves a higher cause. My partner will be magnetic, sharp, honest, genuine and true. My mate will be the perfect one for me to learn how to become my highest self.

Sun in Pisces Venus in Taurus
I affirm that I am willing to attract someone who is dependable, discerning, practical, and serves a higher cause. My partner will be dependable, affectionate, creative, durable, patient, devoted, and stable. My mate will be the perfect one for me to learn how to become my highest self.

EPILOG

IMAGINE YOU FOUND HER

Imagine you found the one you've been looking for since the beginning of time. Imagine you somehow got very, very lucky and actually found the one you've loved at the core of your being without knowing what she would look like, sound like, smell like, or be like.

Imagine the woman you have loved for all time. Imagine the woman you would never possibly leave for another. Imagine the woman, who for all her flaws and shortcomings, is the love of your life. This life. Other lives. All lives. She is the one you loved with all your heart for as long as you can remember loving.

You have known her since the beginning of time, and yet she is new each day. You have known her forever, and yet your love is new each day. You have seen her age through the years, and yet she is beautiful each day.

She is the woman of your heart and soul and dreams. She is the one you have longed for since the beginning of your ancient memories at the core of your being.

For all her imperfections, you accept them, because she is the expression of your Soul. And for all your imperfections, she accepts them, because you are the expression of her Soul. There are no major imperfections in either of you or your love for each other.

You knew her when you were both young. You knew her as a young woman, full of hope. You knew each other as long distance friends. You knew her as a young mom and impeccable professional. And you knew her as a woman who hoped to find her beloved. And she did.

You loved her through thick and thin, through everything her past could throw at her. You saw her strength, her determination, her loyalties, and her dedication to being true to herself and all that was good and valuable in her life.

You loved her through her tragedies and triumphs, always giving her the space she needed to be fully there, and also being fully there when she needed to express herself and all she was going through. At times the words disappeared as you were left staring at the most beautiful woman you ever saw.

You have loved her at her best. You have loved her at her worst. You love waking up with her. You love going to sleep with her. You love every wrinkle for the rich history they reveal of the two of you together. You love every smile for its radiance. You love to hear her voice. You love her in her silence.

You are friends. You are lovers. You are companions. You are free to be yourselves. You are free to do what each of you must to be who you must be in your worlds. You are secure as individuals, and secure as a partnership, as nothing could ever shake your love and dedication to each other. You look forward to coming home because you know she will be there to greet you.

You have always liked each other. You can talk with each other. There has always been a deep, loving, genuine friendship, an easy give and take which left you both with a good feeling for the connection. There was never a time when you wondered about each other's loyalties, and each of you across the years rejoiced when you reunited, whether as friends, lovers, or sweethearts.

She has been one of the best friends you ever had across the years. She has always been honest, caring, and genuine. She always brought out the best in you, and no matter what happened, she was open, understanding, and kind. Always genuinely herself, she inspires a new outpouring of love every day. Even at our advanced age, she will forever be my bride, my sweetheart, and my joy.

This is the woman of my heart and soul and dreams.

This is true love.

ABOUT THE AUTHOR

Robert Wilkinson is a practicing professional astrologer with more than 50 years of experience as a counselor, public speaker, author, publisher, and strategic analyst. With an advanced education in social and humanistic psychology, historical cycles, and Eastern philosophies and spiritual practices, he offers the world a holistic view of the many interrelated things that impact personal and global evolution. He has found that by understanding the patterns of our inner and outer reality, we can find ways to live a more Soulful existence in practical ways, and reclaim our power to become the Loving Wise Intelligence which is our true nature.

He also has been a professional political analyst and a multi-media producer and director, giving him a wide variety of worldly experiences which ground the synthesis of philosophical and spiritual approaches he offers in his talks, workshops, classes, and articles. He believes that we all have the power to live our life with intention and purpose, allowing us to become the perfect expression of our Higher Self and the living worldly expression of our heart, Soul, and Spirit.

His website Aquarius Papers – Global Astrology (www.aquariuspapers.com) is one of the longest running websites of its kind, offering thousands of articles on a wide variety of astrological, metaphysical, and cultural subjects to visitors from over 130 countries. He is the author of the pioneering work "A New Look at Mercury Retrograde," the first major work on the subject, "Saturn: Spiritual Master, Spiritual Friend," an operations manual for personal evolution, and "Love Dad," a grief manual for those who have lost a loved one. He also has other books in development, including one exploring the mysterious mind of cats.

Printed in Great Britain
by Amazon